וְהִגַּדְתָּ

Pesaḥ Haggada

Inspirational Reflections for the Seder Night

Rabbanit Yemima Mizrachi

Inspirational Reflections for the Seder Night

Edited by Yikrat Friedman

Translated by Rena Siev

Maggid Books

Parasha Ve'Isha

Rabbanit Yemima Mizrachi
Inspirational Reflections for the Seder Night

First Edition, 2025

Maggid Books
An imprint of Koren Publishers Jerusalem Ltd.

POB 8531, New Milford, CT 06776-8531, USA
& POB 4044, Jerusalem 9104001, Israel
www.korenpub.com

Editor: Yikrat Friedman

Cover and book design: WWW.DOSA.CO.IL / דוסה

Illustrations: Hallel Sharabi

Parasha Ve'Isha Publishing
Tel: 077-8066747
www.parasha.org | info@parasha.org

The publication of this book was made possible
through the generous support of *The Jewish Book Trust.*

We thank all the authors and creators who expressed their consent for the use of their work in this publication. The Maggid team did everything it could to locate the copyright holders of the material taken from external sources. We apologize for any omission or error, and if they are brought to our attention, we will work to correct them in future editions.

ISBN 978-1-59264-694-4, *hardcover*

printed in Israel

This book is lovingly dedicated
to all the women who manage
to balance profound Torah learning
with Pesaḥ preparations and have the
freedom to take deep pride in both of them.

– Yemima

It is a positive
commandment
of the Torah
to relate
the miracles
and the wonders
wrought for our ancestors
in Egypt
on the night
of the fifteenth
of Nisan, as it states,
"Remember
this day on which
you left Egypt,"
just as it states,
"Remember
the Sabbath day."
From where
is it derived
that this mitzva
is fulfilled on
the night of the fifteenth?
The Torah states
"You shall tell
your child
on that day."

– Rambam, *Mishneh Torah*,
Hilkhot Ḥametz UMatza, ch. 7

Table of Contents

Rabbi Kalonymus Kalman Schapira of Piaseczno was someone who believed deeply in the *afikoman*. He composed incredible teachings, and about 70 percent of them discuss Egypt, Egyptian slavery, and the Egyptian redemption. He lived during the terrible days of the Holocaust, and he decided to do something completely illogical: He hid his amazing writings in milk canisters, buried them beneath the ground, and believed that one bright day (which actually happened, in 2022/5782), someone would print the Haggada that he authored, the Piaseczno Haggada (which was edited by his great-nephew Amotz Schapira). He lived by the faith that pain also has its place, that no tear is shed without scarring the world's expanse. We found his *afikoman* and, together with him, we read about the significance of everything we experienced until this point in time:

> It can be compared to one who climbs a high mountain. Would we say that he has ascended the mountain only once he reaches the peak? Every single step that he takes is also an ascent. And even when he stands in place on the middle of the mountain, he has already climbed the mountain, above the rest of the nation, who remain on the ground below.... And all deeds are ascents and preparations until he reaches the mitzva.
>
> What derives from this is that a Jew who prepares something for a mitzva must understand that he is preparing not only the act, but also himself. And part of himself is revealed [through this process]. And when he does the mitzva itself, that entire part will be revealed.[4]

We are on a pilgrimage right now, the Rebbe of Piaseczno says. And all the exhaustion and all the commotion, and the children who have been pulling at our skirts throughout the days that preceded this great night, are part of this pilgrimage. Don't take this exhausting journey away from us.

Rabbi Elhanan Nir asks, "What is it about the frenzy of cleaning that takes hold of us in the early, luscious, green days of spring that is foundational to our awareness of the holiday of freedom? Why is it that only when it comes to this holiday man is instructed to be so attentive to the intricate details, and not depend on the other people in his home?"[5]

And Rabbi

Introduction

For Seven Days Our Hearts Are Open

It's hard to believe in the power of the *afikoman*. When the wise son asks: "What are the testimonies, the statutes, and the laws?"[1] the father responds to him, "After eating the Pesaḥ offering [*afikoman*], one does not eat anything more."[2]

What is the *afikoman*? What are we really searching for?

It's interesting that we focus on the *afikoman*, the end of Seder night, right at the beginning of the Seder. We arrive at Seder night after weeks of intense preparation, after endless cleaning and cooking. This sometimes makes us feel that "the Pesah service is finished" right away. But this isn't the end, it's just the beginning!

This great night arrives and proclaims: the journey is just beginning! We're setting out for seven days of divine light! We're about to find the *afikoman*!

The *afikoman* is the essence of faith. It's the understanding that this holiday is a holiday of renewal in the sense that it completely dismisses the notion of becoming obsolete. Nothing becomes obsolete. Not our tears. Not our sighs of sorrow. Not even the animalistic groan that man may emit from his throat.

"And God heard their groans."[3] A groan never falls on deaf ears. Even if the redemption doesn't come immediately, the groan has been duly noted. It's there, hidden away, and one day it will be revealed.

It's almost against our nature. Rabbi Elhanan Nir notes:

> Modern man identifies life with the intensity of activity and movement. To him, life is an ongoing sequence of opportunities, coupled with the fear of missing out on them (in short, FOMO). Vacant space, blocks of unstructured time, stir his anxiety. These things don't make him feel the winds of freedom. Instead, they cause him to sense the tolling bells of death. That which primitive man considered to be part of the rhythm of life, which is built from activity and passivity (action and inactivity), becoming full and becoming empty, has been transformed by modern man into something inferior and worthy of contempt. Into shame. At any given second, he is convinced that he is missing something, that something important and decisive is taking place at that precise moment. In this way, he is denied the possibility of rest.[11]

This is how man approaches the Seder night and the seven-day holiday (so much stress!). "For seven days the roses bloom…and [for] seven days the tables are set, and [for] seven days the hearts are open."[12]

Such anxiety. The fear of encounter. Will we be able to encounter things face-to-face?

Are You Ready for an Encounter?

The holiday of Pesaḥ is filled with encounters: With tradition, with family, with ourselves.

The Jewish people were able to escape this packed encounter for 210 years. And they allowed themselves to be consumed by this comfortable freedom. They were busy, they were enslaved, they would have loved to be able to dedicate the time, so they thought, to go out and meet someone new, to spend more time at home with someone "old," but what could they do? There simply wasn't any time.

Over the past year, we went all around the town – through the streets, across the squares – imagining to ourselves that we were "searching for the one we love,"[13] but perhaps we simply loved to roam and wander.

When we were at home and had the opportunity to engage with the people around us, with the child who avoids us, and frankly who we also try to avoid, with our husbands, who are so easy to avoid, since after such a long and intense day "I have taken off my dress; how can I put it on again?"[14] And you'll go to sleep once again, very much in love, without encountering one another.

And then

And Rabbi Shagar,[6] his teacher, explains:

The rigidity and neurosis that are part of halakhic existence are full partners of this existence, and one should not rush to allay them with different types of "psychological treatment." The desire to rid oneself of these elements (from the cleaning) in the religious experience is akin to psychiatric treatment that conceals the patient's symptoms. Though this treatment might alleviate the suffering, the patient must pay up front via his personality – the human and halakhic personality are dulled.[7]

Let's try to explain this hidden, concealed, obscured, *afikoman* language. The happiness associated with this holiday is the small pain in our back and the hands that have become somewhat dry. These things are part of our pilgrimage. Don't take them away from us!

Okay, understood. So where are we now?

We've reached the peak. And it shines with the most unusual light, seven days of the most intense light.

On the Seder night, the Divine Presence will enter. It comes into each home on the Seder night with breathtaking awesomeness; "and with an awesome happening – this is the revelation of the Divine Presence."[8]

Now stop. Just breathe in the intense light. Zelda says:[9]

> There is so much light around me
> and the pain is so great –
> one more moment and my soul will leave me.[10]

Will we know how to take a step back and rest?

exquisitely as possible, and you'll see that all the anxiety ahead of the family gathering will melt away and be transformed into incredible happiness.

And then, at the climax of the Seder, God will ask you the toughest question of all: Are you ready to engage with Me? Now. With the love of your life. Are you ready to try again? And this time around, the encounter will be filled with kindness, without judging, without guilt, without searching for the *ḥametz*. It will be only about finding it, the hidden half, the *afikoman*.

The moment that you recite Song of Songs is the moment that you answer: Yes. I'm ready for another encounter.

As Rabbi Nir explains:

> Song of Songs declares that the world isn't only predators and victims, winners and losers, who are engaged in a never-ending power struggle. Rather, it is also an expanse where two people can recognize one another, two people who know that each one's chance is actually found within the other, and, in a deep sense, until he comes in contact with the other, he himself has not yet been formed.
>
> This is how the days of Nisan are transformed into a miracle of contact and intimate introspection. Man leaves the walls that he carefully guarded throughout the entire winter…[for this reason,] Pesaḥ is also the head of the year, but it is not marked by the strict judgment of Tishrei, and instead offers intimacy and kindness. Song of Songs is the *UNetaneh Tokef* of these days.[21]

And when the voice of your beloved doesn't come knocking, "you must open for him."[22] Stand in the doorway, the doorway that God skipped over so many times, the doorway upon which you poured your rage on so many occasions, and wait there again. For your Eliyahu. Tonight, even his soul is stirred ahead of the encounter.[23]

And then the day comes. We are commanded to have a "family offering"[15] and it demands of us the inner strength to go out again, but this time in order to engage with others. "Get up, come out, my sister, my bride."[16]

We have subjugated ourselves to freedom.

The cleaning process ahead of the holiday marks the beginning of our encounter. And suddenly, "the rooms are filled on account of knowledge."[17] Suddenly, we'll understand ourselves and the things that belong to us. We'll understand the inner recesses of our children's hearts, and peek into the dark corners that we preferred to avoid. We'll experience a unique closeness to God, reminiscent of "a king [who] is tangled up among its tresses."[18] The King who wants us to encounter Him and "liberate" Him from the mechanical act of cleaning and engage with Him in the inner recesses of our hearts can be found among the myriad of things that fill the rooms of this home: "The king has brought me into his chambers."[19]

The holiday meal on the Seder night is an intense encounter with our family. Rabbi Shagar qualifies this:

> The act of eating draws us together. The delicious and filling meal is not necessarily the varied menu and the array of food, because the blessing is actually the word of God found within the matza, the way that the family members look kindly toward one another…the year's blessing is entirely dependent on the love, trust, and kindness that exist among the people around the table. Egotistical eating does not indicate bounty. It is always about self-preservation and therefore won't lead to happiness.
>
> In this way, the Seder night serves to rejuvenate the Jewish family. First and foremost, this pact is about a sense of belonging. The positive energy prompted by the meal creates camaraderie among the people gathered around the table. The good feelings brought on by the eating experience are akin to appearing [before God] today, instead of [in] the Temple.[20]

I find these words so inspiring! There is no Temple today – but your home is a place of sanctification! There are no offerings or Paschal lambs, but there is a family offering. Prepare the most delicious food, set your table as

An Encounter with the Empty Chair

On this holiday, there isn't a person in the world without an empty chair at his table. A hole in his heart. For me, it's my father. For others, it's a relative who isn't with them right now. For divorced women, it might be the children who are with the other side of the family. For singles, it's the chair itself, which suddenly feels less stable beneath us.

Yehuda Gizbar notes:

> And she stops saying yes when they offer her a guy ("Ro'i, 29, from a good family") and she stops dealing with the whole saga of being single and says, enough. Now I'm not looking for a husband. Instead, I'm going on a journey to find myself. And she goes to workshops and lectures and takes long trips to India and South America and lives her life the way she wants to live. But when she tries to retrieve the large pot that she put away on top of the cabinet, she finds herself wobbling on a rickety chair and muttering, Where is he, for goodness' sake? When will he come? I can't wait any longer.
>
> And this shows her that she never really stopped. She never really forgot.[24]

The Seder night necessitates having a proper family. And what is someone who hasn't yet "found her place" supposed to do?

Why are you still single? Only God knows. And I know one thing: God wants you. He wants your prayers.

The Zohar explains that on the Seder night God comes down and takes stock of His broken vessels, the people who find themselves disjointed and out of whack on the Seder night.[25] When we recite *Shfokh ḥamatkha*, "Pour out Your rage," God enters our homes and says to us: Enough. "And I passed by you and I saw you wallowing"[26] – in your tears, and I see the stress. The stress brought on by the years that have gone by, the stress brought on by your anxieties, the pressure that you feel from your parents. "I saw that your time for love had arrived."[27] Now we are here. This year you're still stuck. But *next year*, I promise you, you'll be in your own home. With your husband. With your baby. A free woman.

Compassion is stirred specifically by the loneliness felt on this family-oriented night, the Seder night. Just turn to Him. Every Seder night, God passes by and redeems, and rescues, and saves so many lonely men and women. I bless all of us with freedom, happiness, beauty, wealth, majesty, redemption. Not necessarily in this order.

Yemima Mizrachi, Jerusalem

Ahead of *bedikat ḥametz*, the floor is mopped extensively, a sacred mopping. With a ton of water. Ahead of *bedikat ḥametz*, we shut off our cell phones and devices. This is a time to focus – this is the time when we can fix everything.

This process spreads light upon so many things that we suppress.

Why Did You Remain Silent?

What are we doing? Rejuvenating ourselves. Even the concept of rejuvenation and finding ourselves has been transformed in recent years into something super-exciting. Rejuvenation has become the inverse of becoming obsolete.

Rejuvenation is an unequivocal statement that the legal world doesn't recognize, at least not yet. In the legal world, cases are bound by a statute of limitations: Why did you remain silent? Why didn't you expose the truth? Now this incident is bound by a statute of limitations. Why didn't you examine these dark corners by candlelight in time?

And the answer: Because in real time, and for a long time after, her vocal cords were simply blocked.

But God sees those who aren't able to scream, those who cannot express themselves, those who cannot complain. In Egypt, for 210 years, the Israelites didn't sigh or groan or attempt to approach these dark corners with a candle.

The act of rejuvenation remembers. Suddenly, "And God heard their groans." Ahhh… "And He saw, and God knew."[29]

Tears and sighs are never bound by a statute of limitations. Your tears hang in the great expanse of the world, and at the end of the Seder we recite in Song of Songs: "Open for me, my sister, my love…for my head is covered with dew,"[30] the dew of your tears that have welled up. My head is completely drenched in your tears. Open up for Me. I have come to bestow upon you an extraordinary redemption!

And this search (*bedikat ḥametz*) tells you: "As long as the candle burns, there's still time to repair."[31] Don't be scared. Don't be anxious.

Everything becomes clarified.

And clearer.

And the next day, when the *ḥametz* burns, it also goes up in smoke.

The Rebbe

Bedikat Ḥametz and Biur Ḥametz

An Encounter with Things We Preferred to Forget

On the evening of the fourteenth [of the month of Nisan], one searches for ḥametz by candlelight.

– Mishna Pesaḥim 1:1

"In memory of the Exodus from Egypt." These words accompany us all year long, but Pesaḥ brings us back to those days, to this time, in a far more potent way. According to Torah law, it is forbidden to have *ḥametz* in our possession during Pesaḥ, as it states: "Throughout the seven days matzot shall be eaten; no *ḥametz* shall be found with you, and no leaven shall be found in all your territory."[28]

And after we cleaned and searched for crumbs in every nook and cranny, *bedikat ḥametz* arrives. As young children we were taught that this is a ceremonial search for ten small pieces of *ḥametz* that were carefully wrapped ahead of time. In truth, though, these moments are sacred and holy. Rabbi Yeruham Levovitz of Mir explains that one cannot imagine the way that God rehabilitates our souls during *bedikat ḥametz*. By the glow of the candle, even the most severe sins can be rehabilitated at this point in time. *It is impossible to describe the greatness of a Jew as he stands and checks for ḥametz in his home.*

It's an incredible opportunity for prayer. Throughout the duration of *bedikat ḥametz*, pray that the elements of our lives that are *ḥametz* will be cleansed, specifically the emotional wounds: "May we merit to eradicate the imperfections of our souls," as the kabbalists and Hasidim say in their prayers.

The kabbalists have the custom of placing salt on the plate that is used to hold the candle and the ten pieces of bread that are found. Rabbi Mutzafi writes: "There is a correct and ancient custom to put salt in the dish because the 'external things' (negative forces) are envious of this search."[35] They know that this process cleanses you and the air that surrounds you, so they come to cause damage. Salt keeps them away (you can do this even if you don't fully understand it).

Rabbi Mutzafi recalls: "My father, z"l, would spend forty minutes bending over in all the corners of the house, opening closets, checking racks, climbing up on the shelves, opening every drawer and asking: "Did you check here? Did you clean here?" and he would check all the nooks and crannies, and behind all the doors, and on the doorposts, and I would accompany him, with a plate that held a knife, salt, a piece of ḥametz, and matches."[36]

We carefully search the nooks and crannies of our homes, and it's important to me to explain that it is these nooks and crannies themselves that we're looking for. It is through them that we can be reborn, that we can repair what is broken. We're searching for freedom. This is a night of searching, and it precedes the holiday of searching; we search for the crumbs, and later we'll search for the *afikoman*, and eventually we'll sing the song of the great search: "I sought the one I love,"[37] from Song of Songs.

The Rebbe of Ishbitz writes that one who conducts this search carefully and meticulously, and refrains from speaking the entire time aside from things related to the mitzva, will merit a great blessing: *Each man will know the root of his shortcomings*. Everything will become much clearer: "This is what I want to study/this is what I need to do/this is what I must say to my mother/this relationship needs to end." You'll realize incredible things about yourself. "Man's soul is the lamp of the Lord, revealing all his inmost parts"[32] – he promises that this candle will reveal hidden things to you. It will reveal to you the intuition you never even realized you had. (Rabbi Shimshon Pincus would say that all his spiritual achievements, and the fact that he became a rabbi, came from carefully searching for the *ḥametz* in the nooks and crannies.[33])

We scour the entire house for *ḥametz* remnants that may have escaped our cleaning. We hide ten small pieces of bread, all wrapped up, throughout the house, so that our blessing won't be for naught if we don't find anything. The next day, we throw these pieces of bread in the fire with all the other remaining *ḥametz*.

Halakha maintains that *bedikat ḥametz* can be conducted with a flashlight too. Even a cellphone can be used (which is the polar opposite of getting rid of *ḥametz*…it's like lighting a baguette and using it to help you find *ḥametz*). But Rabbi Ben Tzion Mutzafi writes that it should be done with only a candle made from wax. Why specifically wax? The Hebrew word for "wax" (*shaava*) is spelled with the same Hebrew letters as the word "performs" (*oseh*): "to the One who alone works great wonders."[34] During *bedikat ḥametz* we should direct our hearts with the prayer: "Perform miracles for me. And completely destroy all the *ḥametz* and missed opportunities in my body and soul."

Moreover, the Hebrew word for "wax," *shaava*, sounds very similar to the word for "shout," *shava*. Every prayer and every shout during *bedikat ḥametz* is accepted.

So, when you search for *ḥametz* in the bedroom, pray for a strong marriage, for peace in your home, for love.

When you search your kids' rooms, ask for faith, happiness, good friends, and success.

When you look through the pockets of your clothing, ask for livelihood.

Early the next morning, you'll burn all the *ḥametz* that you hid and found. At the same time, you'll also burn all your missed opportunities.

Embrace the incredible good *segula* (*segula*) of the Ḥida, a *segula* that brings about so much salvation each year, salvation that people share with me. During *bedikat ḥametz*, when we hide ten pieces of bread, the Ḥida instructs us to list ten of our life's regrets on small notes of paper: "I feel that I aged/I missed my professional opportunity/I missed finding my direction in life/I passed up on this child's education," and place one of these notes in each bag that has a piece of bread.

In Pesaḥ terminology, a crumb indicates delay. "It is our will to perform Your will, and what prevents us? The yeast in the dough.[40] Make a list of the delays and setbacks that you want to move past (medical results/an unmarried son/an unhappy daughter/an unhappy bank account). Make sure to write down things that trouble you and concern you, and not the names of specific people.

The next day, toss the crumbs of bread into the fire with these notes.[41]

Yemima, what kind of idolatrous practice is this?

You're right. This is a constellation that doesn't exist in Judaism. To pray about something that already happened and say: "I wish this never happened" is called "a prayer for the past." For example, when you see an ambulance race by, you're not supposed to say, "Just don't let it be my grandmother." Is this really possible? Can the ambulance driver really pull your grandmother out of the ambulance now and pick up an innocent passerby instead? You cannot retroactively undo the past. It's acceptable and appropriate to pray for the future: "If it's my grandmother, I hope that she's on her way to have a baby." (In years past, this used to be a funny joke. Nowadays, it's actually realistic.)

Praying for the past is a decisively un-Jewish thing to do. But once a year we have the possibility of praying for the past. As we stand before the burning *ḥametz*, we call out: "God, make it as though what is there, what was, was never ever there."

And then you recite the text of *bitul ḥametz*.

Why is this such a good time to conduct a search? Because the act of searching endows us with so much faith. You know, beyond a shadow of doubt, that the things you're seeking – the *afikoman* and the pieces of bread – are there. Song of Songs comes along and tells you: Your spouse is also there. Even the child who has distanced himself from you is there. There is no such thing as "I sought him, I did not find him."[38] It's not possible. It cannot be. You worked hard and didn't meet success? Don't believe this! There's no such thing as a search that doesn't yield results.

The other half of the *afikoman*, like your other half, is there. Not only that, but he desperately wants you to find him. Far more than you pine to find him, he wants to be found, like "a missing item that is actively pursued" in rabbinic terminology.

Love wants to be found.

The crumbs of *ḥametz* scream from the corners of the house: "We're here! We're here!"

So too, the other half of your soul.

As well as the Creator of the world.

> Being careful with a crumb of *ḥametz* is extremely important and lofty.
> By doing so a person is assured that he will not commit a sin or transgression the entire year.
> And the evil inclination will not have a hold on him.
> And he will not even somewhat be approached by any element of the forces of impurity.
> And he will not be damaged the entire year.
> And he will be preserved and protected,
> and he will be subject to the rule of holiness,
> as stated in the Zohar:
> The days of Pesaḥ are the root and foundation of all the days of the year.
> And the entire year will be peaceful and serene.[39]

Biur Ḥametz

ביעור חמץ

On the night before Pesaḥ (eve of the fourteenth of Nisan , and if falls on Shabbat - eve of the thirteenth of Nisan), search for ḥametz with a candle. Before searching, the following is said:

I am prepared and ready to fulfill the positive and negative commandments of checking for leaven. For the sake for the unification of the Holy One, blessed be He, and His Divine Presence, through He who is hidden and unseen, in the name of all Israel. Establish for us the work of our hands, establish the work of our hands. *Ps. 90*

בָּרוּךְ Blessed are You, Lord our God, King of the Universe, who has made us holy through His commandments, and has commanded us about the removal of leaven.

After the search, say the following:

Any type of leaven that may still be in my possession, that I have not seen or not removed or that I do not know about, let it be nullified and considered ownerless like the dust of the earth.

Shaḥarit of Erev Pesaḥ, the fifth hour of the day, the ḥametz is burned. Before the burning of the ḥametz, the following is said:

I am prepared and ready to fulfill the positive and negative commandments of burning leaven. For the sake for the unification of the Holy One, blessed be He, and His Divine Presence, through He who is hidden and unseen, in the name of all Israel. Establish for us the work of our hands, establish the work of our hands. *Ps. 90*

After burning the ḥametz, it is annulled when the following is said:

Any type of leaven that may still be in my possession, that I have not seen or not removed or that I do not know about,

אור לארבעה־עשר בניסן (ואם חל בשבת – אור לשלושה־עשר) בודקין את החמץ לאור הנר.

לפני הבדיקה מברכים:

הִנְנִי מוּכָן וּמְזֻמָּן לְקַיֵּם מִצְוַת עֲשֵׂה וְלֹא תַעֲשֶׂה שֶׁל בְּדִיקַת חָמֵץ
לְשֵׁם יִחוּד קֻדְשָׁא בְּרִיךְ הוּא וּשְׁכִינְתֵּהּ עַל יְדֵי הַהוּא טָמִיר וְנֶעְלָם בְּשֵׁם כָּל יִשְׂרָאֵל.
וִיהִי נֹעַם אֲדֹנָי אֱלֹהֵינוּ עָלֵינוּ, וּמַעֲשֵׂה יָדֵינוּ כּוֹנְנָה עָלֵינוּ, וּמַעֲשֵׂה יָדֵינוּ כּוֹנְנֵהוּ: תהלים צ

בָּרוּךְ אַתָּה יהוה אֱלֹהֵינוּ מֶלֶךְ הָעוֹלָם
אֲשֶׁר קִדְּשָׁנוּ בְּמִצְוֹתָיו וְצִוָּנוּ
עַל בִּעוּר חָמֵץ.

אחר הבדיקה אומר:

כָּל חֲמִירָא וַחֲמִיעָא דְּאִכָּא בִרְשׁוּתִי
דְּלָא חֲמִתֵּהּ וּדְלָא בִעַרְתֵּהּ
לִבְטִיל וְלֶהֱוֵי הֶפְקֵר כְּעַפְרָא דְאַרְעָא.

ערב פסח שחרית, בשעה החמישית של היום, שורפים את החמץ. לפני שריפת החמץ אומר:

הִנְנִי מוּכָן וּמְזֻמָּן לְקַיֵּם מִצְוַת עֲשֵׂה וְלֹא תַעֲשֶׂה שֶׁל שְׂרֵפַת חָמֵץ
לְשֵׁם יִחוּד קֻדְשָׁא בְּרִיךְ הוּא וּשְׁכִינְתֵּהּ עַל יְדֵי הַהוּא טָמִיר וְנֶעְלָם בְּשֵׁם כָּל יִשְׂרָאֵל.
וִיהִי נֹעַם אֲדֹנָי אֱלֹהֵינוּ עָלֵינוּ, וּמַעֲשֵׂה יָדֵינוּ כּוֹנְנָה עָלֵינוּ, וּמַעֲשֵׂה יָדֵינוּ כּוֹנְנֵהוּ: תהלים צ

אחרי שריפת החמץ מבטלו בלבו ואומר:

כָּל חֲמִירָא וַחֲמִיעָא דְּאִכָּא בִרְשׁוּתִי
דַּחֲמִתֵּהּ וּדְלָא חֲמִתֵּהּ
דְּבִעַרְתֵּהּ וּדְלָא בִעַרְתֵּהּ

Let it be nullified and considered ownerless

Like the Dust of the Earth.

Eiruv Tavshilin

עירוב תבשילין

בחוץ לארץ, אם חל ערב פסח ביום רביעי,
עושים עירוב תבשילין.
נוטלים מצה ותבשיל ומברכים:

Outside of Israel, if Erev Pesaḥ falls out on Wednesday, an Eruv Tavshilin is made. Take a piece of matza and a cooked dish and say:

בָּרוּךְ אַתָּה יהוה
אֱלֹהֵינוּ מֶלֶךְ הָעוֹלָם
אֲשֶׁר קִדְּשָׁנוּ
בְּמִצְוֹתָיו וְצִוָּנוּ עַל מִצְוַת
עֵרוּב.

בָּרוּךְ Blessed are You, Lord
our God,
King of the Universe, who
has made us holy through His
commandments,
and has commanded us about
the mitzva of Eiruv.

ואומר: בְּדֵין עֵרוּבָא יְהֵא שְׁרֵא לָנָא
לְמֵיפֵא וּלְבַשָּׁלָא וּלְאַטְמָנָא
וּלְאַדְלָקָא שְׁרָגָא
וּלְמֶעְבַּד כָּל צָרְכָּנָא
מִיּוֹמָא טָבָא לְשַׁבְּתָא
לָנוּ וּלְכָל יִשְׂרָאֵל הַדָּרִים
בָּעִיר הַזֹּאת.

And say: By this Eiruv may we
be permitted to bake,
cook, insulate food,
light a flame and do
everything necessary
on the festival for
the sake of Shabbat,
for us and for all Jews
living in this city.

Eliyahu's Cup – The Cup That Belongs to Us

After we burn the *ḥametz*, we should set our table for the Seder. "Spread a table for me in full view of my enemies"[43] – setting the table early in the day is a *segula* against anger and petty fights. We should set the table with a sense of awe and reverence. We should start from the middle – Eliyahu's cup should be placed in the center. The Sar Shalom of Belz notes: "They were exiled by goblet, and they'll be redeemed by goblet." The first exile was triggered by the goblet that Yosef hid in Binyamin's sack that caused the brothers to become suspicious of one another: "It's in your sack. No, it's in yours."[44]

And Yosef showed them: "Your suspicions about Binyamin were unfounded. Likewise, your suspicions about me were also baseless. Don't you see? All the civil wars that tear brothers apart are senseless and unfounded."

The Yismaḥ Yisrael of Alexander explains: All the suspicions that we harbor against one another are senseless and unfounded! Empty your sacks! Empty your hearts that are full of spite and wariness toward others. It's not worth it. Pesaḥ is a "family offering." Don't become like the "children who were exiled from their father's table."[45] How can Eliyahu come if we are at odds with one another? If we're fighting with one another? If we're in the midst of investigating one another and cross-examining witnesses and state witnesses and witnesses for the defense? Haven't we been down this road one time too many?

Let's use this day to pick up the phone, make peace, and reconcile. One of my students had not had a baby for years. She reached out to her mother-in-law and reconciled with her after five years of estrangement. "I can't start the holiday like this," she said and picked up the phone and told her mother-in-law that she loved her. And brought a sweet little baby into this world.

We need to clear the air of suspicion.

In the words of Rabbi Elhanan Nir:

On this night we are filled with trust in mankind, in family, in community, and in the nation throughout the generations. In contrast to the great inner anxieties with which we approach the days of Tishrei, the period of the Days of Awe when we strike our chests and declare, "We have become guilty, we have betrayed," in the days of Nisan, we usher in the days of love. The transition from awe to love demands self-forgetfulness, doing away with the old form and assuming a new form. When man is ready to go for seven days without the evil inclination, without hating others, without suspicion, without jealousy, the entire world concedes to him, like a "face answers to face in water." Something about this message causes the worlds to shake and tremble and removes the company of messengers of destruction, to the point that the force of destruction itself passes over the entrance and doesn't cause harm. It's a night of protection, and this isn't just an empty statement. In the geonic period, the custom to leave the door to the home unlocked on this night was established. My father used to tell us that we do not recite the bedtime Shema on this night because we do not need protection, because there are no demons.[52]

Someone who wants peace in her home, someone who wants her family to live in peace with one another, someone who has a complicated family situation, should place Eliyahu's goblet in the center of the table and think to herself: "God, please let us have a family offering. Please, let us live in harmony."

And Eliyahu will respond: "I'm on my way. You put a goblet on the table for me! I'm coming." "Behold, I will send the prophet Eliyahu."[46] This is a special *segula* for peaceful parent-child relationships: "He shall reconcile parents with children and children with their parents."[47]

What is so special about this cup?

The Temple was the most magnificent of buildings, and the beauty of the Temple was reflected by Rabbi Yoḥanan. The Talmud recommends: Anyone who wants to see something resembling the beauty of Rabbi Yoḥanan (in other words, the beauty of the Temple) should take a silver goblet and fill it with pomegranate seeds, surround it with red roses, and position it between the sunlight and the shade, and perhaps he will be fortunate enough to sense "a semblance of Rabbi Yoḥanan's beauty."[48]

What does this description tell us?

The goblet, as noted, is symbolic of redemption.

The pomegranate seeds inside the goblet represent the simple and uneducated Jewish people. "Your forehead (*rakatekh*) like a pomegranate" – even "the emptiest (*reikim*) among you are filled with mitzvot like a pomegranate."[49] On the days before Pesaḥ, we see this all around us. People who do not seem to be particularly attached to holiness stand in line at the hardware store and the kosher shops and invest a lot of money, thought, and passion in the upcoming holiday.

The red roses represent us, the rose among the thorns. We're surrounded by enemies who hate us. We need to remember this when we become isolationist and rigid and argumentative. As far as our enemies are concerned, the different subsectors within the Jewish community and our different agendas are entirely irrelevant.

Place the goblet between the sunlight and the shade – this is a rough description of the Seder night; "Draw near the day that is neither day nor night."[50]

Enough is enough. Let's dissolve the veil of uncertainty. Let's move out of the shade and stand in the light. It's time to let go of the power struggles.[51] Otherwise, how will Eliyahu be able to come?

Our Personal *Avoda*: Arranging the Seder Plate

Arranging the Seder plate echoes God arranging the heavenly constellations in the sky. As we set each symbolic food in its place, we pray that doing so will bring favor and *mazal* down into the world.

Right now, the heavens are open, and the Seder plate symbolizes the heavens above each person's head., showering divine love and blessing into their life..

The Hebrew word for Seder plate (*ke'ara*) is comprised of the same Hebrew letters as the word for heavens (*rakia*). The Ben Ish Ḥai writes that the seven heavens open above the Seder plate. As you arrange the Seder plate, pray with your entire heart. These are special moments, and they are filled with hope and purpose.

Place the *maror* at the center of the Seder plate[54] and think about all the pain in your life. Think to yourself: May it be Your will that all of this will be surrounded by salvation and sweetness.

To the right of the *maror* is the bone: redeem me with an outstretched arm (the Hebrew word for this bone, *zeroa*, recalls God saving us with His *zeroa*, His outstretched arm). The bone on the Seder plate recalls the Paschal lamb. It is roasted rather than cooked. Likewise, it isn't eaten on the Seder night or the next day.

To the left is the egg, which recalls the *ḥagiga* sacrifice: May there be celebrations in this home. Fill this home with happiness and joy throughout the entire year.

Sweet *ḥaroset*: May all my pain be coated in sweetness. (Soon we'll learn that *ḥaroset* sweetens rivalry between sisters. Think about this too.)

Salt water: When will You see all my tears?

Moreover, the Hebrew word for the Seder plate (*ke'ara*) is composed of the same letters as the Hebrew word for barren (*akara*). A woman who feels that nothing is going the way that it should, not in her marriage, not in childbearing, not with her kids, should ask to overcome these feeling of emptiness and disappointment as she arranges her Seder plate, to break the mold and turn over a new leaf.

Rabbi Mutzafi notes that the three matzot under the Seder plate symbolize wisdom, insight, and discernment.

The Seder Plate

A Preliminary Encounter with the Holiday

The Seder plate should be the most beautiful one in the world, Rabbi Mutzafi writes. This is neither a halakhic obligation nor an absolute requirement, but we live in a sovereign world, in a world of desire and love and opening of the heart, and this night actually has the capacity to bring wealth into the world.

If one has the means, he should try to prepare an exquisite Seder plate for the Seder table, because it is the key to livelihood for the year in its entirety, since on Pesaḥ we are judged concerning grain. And if one has the means, it is correct to have a silver Seder plate. And the Seder plate should be arranged while it is still day (meaning in the afternoon, before the Seder night begins).[53]

קערת הסדר
Passover Seder Plate

זרוע
Bone

ביצה
Egg

מרור
Maror

חרוסת
Ḥaroset

כרפס
Karpas

חזרת
Ḥazeret

This is Rabbi Mutzafi! Not Rabbanit Yemima. Rabbi Mutzafi is all about the simplicity of the kabbalists, and he speaks about this beauty and physicality so vividly and expressively. Because it is the Holy of Holies. He writes about his father who used to stand in line to buy things for the holiday. "Abba, why? You're older. You're a well-respected man. Why do you go out and do errands and stand in line?"

"I couldn't believe it," his father, the great Rabbi Salman Mutzafi, said. "I was simply standing in line, and I saw a man who looked completely secular buying a jar of paint and a brush because Pesaḥ is coming. Hashem, what a holy people!"

In days gone by, our mothers used to "really" clean. They would even dismantle the pot handles and pour boiling water throughout the entire house. In days gone by, nullifying the *ḥametz* was extremely important, because people lived in homes with dirt floors, and there were certainly crumbs that remained. Nowadays, nullifying the *ḥametz* is less critical to us. Our Pesaḥ preparations are focused primarily on the element of beauty. We're busy beautifying our homes, getting new linen, installing new light fixtures.

Rabbi Yitzchak Hutner explains that when we are far more fixated on beauty than *ḥametz*, it's a sign that Mashiaḥ is on his way.

There isn't a woman in the community who didn't try to beautify her own little corner of the world the week before the holiday. We're no longer fighting a battle between *ḥametz* and kosher. We're fighting a battle between those things that are imperfect and that which is beautiful. That's why the woman in Song of Songs is told: "My love, you are as beautiful as Tirtza."[56] Tell me, he couldn't find a more spiritual compliment to throw her way? But, this *is* a spiritual compliment. Don't tell me, "You did a great job cleaning." That's the kind of compliment you can give to your cleaning lady. Tell me, "Beautiful. You're beautiful, my beloved." This is the holiest compliment. A compliment that is the Holy of Holies.

The days when Jews needed to celebrate the Seder in hiding, submissively, are long over. Gone. Beautify religion, prepare the most incredible explanations for the Seder, become a retailer of beauty.

And clothing. "Every woman shall ask her neighbor, ask any woman lodging with her, for objects of silver and gold, and clothing."[57] Buy yourself something new. This is freedom!

My father

Setting the Table for the Seder

I want to talk about beauty.

The holy Jewish people have the custom of beautifying and decorating their Seder table with expensive and exquisite dishes, gold, silver, and copper.

And the chairs are decorated in expensive and elaborate silk and tapestries, and even if they have to borrow these items, it is appropriate to do so.

This is all in honor of this great night, which is like the World to Come in the Garden of Eden, in honor of God, the Source of our strength, may He be blessed.

They are joined by heavenly angels who come to our homes to rejoice with us on our Festival of Freedom and hear words of praise and lauding in His honor, may He be blessed.

And as he glorifies and praises, so they will treat him in the World to Come in the Garden of Eden, and he is qualified for wealth and for his prayer to be answered.

(To the best of your ability, set your table as you imagine the Garden of Eden to be!)

And it is good to add an exquisite (new) dish each year and in this way remember and recognize the kindnesses that God, may He be blessed, performed for us throughout this year too. Likewise, the table should be adorned and decorated with spices, flowers, and roses, especially those that smell good.[55]

The Rebbe of Piaseczno also writes about the Seder plate:

And he needs to remember that everything comes full circle, and the fact that he entertains the poor at his table is only because God endowed him with great abundance. And when he comes to the Seder night, he needs to know that he is in the Garden of Eden now, and he should envision the Garden of Eden and that the meal he eats is redolent [with the scent] of the World to Come, and the heavenly angels are crowded around his table to listen to his joyful singing and our Father and King stands and rejoices and delights in our singing and praise.[61]

According to the Shelah HaKadosh, after the table is set, one should bathe "as if he were just released from captivity and is bathing for the first time in a long time in hot water."[62] Yes, a shower! These are the little things, the small acts of freedom that prepare you for the big night that is just around the corner.

Helpful tip: Take an afternoon nap. You need to save your strength for the great night that lies ahead. You need strength to speak nicely, to say the right thing about belief and faith to your children, because every word of faith that a mother shares with her children on the Seder night leaves a deep mark on their souls. And if you don't have children, you need strength to tell yourself the right things about faith, about all the good things that will come to be on account of this Seder night, with God's help.

My father, my teacher, z"l, told me that this night is redolent with the scent of the Garden of Eden, and every Pesaḥ night, the aroma of the Garden of Eden is aroused because of the special capacity of this night, ever since Yaakov approached his father to receive the blessings, and he smelled the scent of his clothes.[58] And every Seder night this scent is aroused again and perfumes each and every individual according to his level.[59]

There is a custom to use round plates at the Seder. (If someone already has a set of hexagon-shaped, triangular, or rectangular plates – no worries. You can use them.) Rabbi Mutzafi explains the significance of this shape:

> The plates that are placed on his table should ideally be circular. Daat Zekeinim, one of the Tosafists, tells us that Avraham hosted the angels on Pesaḥ. And he gave them, the angels, round matzot, and the reason is that everything comes full circle. And the dishes for the meal are round, to remind us that everything comes full circle.[60]

The Seder night is so beautiful, and the host can easily become overly proud and think to himself, "My power and the might of my hand have won this wealth for me." The round plate keeps his arrogance in check.

The Prayer of Rabbi Shimshon of Ostropoli

The holiday has not yet begun. There is an incredible *segula* known as "The Prayer of Rabbi Shimshon of Ostropoli."

Rabbi Shimshon of Ostropoli was a rabbi and a kabbalist, a genius who was a noted Torah scholar and expert in Kabbala. He lived in the Jewish community of Polonoyye, and he was killed as a martyr in the Khmelnytsky uprising in 1648. He left behind many kabbalistic writings. It is said that one who recites the prayer he composed before the Seder will be saved from all misfortune.

> This letter was composed by Rabbi Shimshon of Ostropoli to explain the words of the Arizal in the book *Pelaot Rabbot* about the names of the angels through which Pharaoh was struck, and the holy names associated with this matter. After copying the words of the Arizal, Rabbi Shimshon explains at length what this means. At the end of the letter, the magnitude of the *segula* of studying it is discussed: "One who studies this incredible and awesome secret properly, even just once a year, and especially on the eve of Pesaḥ, is guaranteed that he will be saved throughout that year from any obstacle and strange death and any mishap. And his enemies will not dominate him, and his foes will fall before him, and wherever he turns he will be successful and prosper. Amen, Selah.'[63]

The full text of this prayer can be found at the end of the Haggada on page 444. It's a text that's difficult to understand. Just say the words.

Candle Lighting
הַדְלָקַת
נֵרוֹת

[Who has] brought us to this time – Do you still have elderly parents whom you can interact with? This also shouldn't be taken for granted. Not everyone is so lucky. And if you still have a grandmother and grandfather that you can reach out to and hug and kiss – wow.

"Who has given us life! Sustained us! And brought us to this time!" May it always be like this! And when the Seder night falls on Friday night, as we light the candles we will pray "and cause our light to illuminate, that it not be extinguished forever."[64] May all this goodness remain with us forever. It is so important to ask for this.

And now, Rabbi Mutzafi adds, "We should pour out our hearts for the Jewish people."[65]

The holiday candles have so much power. They radiate such lofty light.

Life, sustenance, the ability to interact. This blessing endows us with so much. After everything that we went through in recent days, we finally have a feeling of home. A feeling that we have arrived at our place.

Thoughts About Candle Lighting

Candle lighting is a "wow" moment. With tears in our eyes, we recite the *Sheheḥeyanu* blessing that can never be taken for granted: Blessed…who has given us life, sustained us, and brought us to this time.

Who has given us life – Because there are several empty spots at the table this year, and no, they aren't all for Eliyahu the prophet. So, thank You for endowing us with life, because not everyone was blessed with life.

And we cannot recite this blessing if we didn't revitalize someone this year, even just a little. Otherwise, the blessing would be recited in the singular: "Who has given me life." We need to reach out to the downtrodden and revitalize them, to the best of our ability, because when something is really not okay, the deep pain at the Seder table is just awful. We should recite the blessing of "Who has given us life" in tears. Because this is hardly a trivial matter.

[Who has] sustained us – This sustenance refers to both vitality itself as well as financial matters, physical sustenance. We have food, we have clothing – these things shouldn't be taken for granted. Not everyone had enough sustenance this year. "Would you believe that I dream of schnitzel on my kids' plates?" a student once said to me, as she was going through a very difficult time. "But I won't stand in line for food packages before Pesaḥ, because nobody would ever believe that 'the wife of so-and-so' is in such a desperate situation."

(On Shabbat, add the words in parentheses):

בָּרוּךְ Blessed are You, Lord our God, King of the Universe,
who has made us holy through His commandments,
and has commanded us to light (the Shabbat light and)
the festival light.

בָּרוּךְ Blessed are You, Lord our God, King of the Universe,
who has given us life, sustained us,
and brought us to this time.

Prayer for a woman to say after lighting the candles:

May it be Your will, Lord my God and God of my forebears, that You give me grace – me (and my husband/and my father/and my mother/and my sons and my daughters) and all those close to me, and give us and all Israel good and long lives. And remember us with a memory that brings goodness and blessing; come to us with compassion and bless us with great blessings. Build our homes until they are complete, and allow Your Presence to live among us. And may I merit to raise children and grandchildren, each one wise and understanding, loving the Lord and in awe of God, people of truth, holy children, who will cling on to the Lord and light up the world with Torah and with good actions, and with all the kinds of work that serve the Creator. Please, hear my pleading at this time, by the merit of Sara and Rivka, Raḥel and Leah our mothers, and light our candle that it should never go out, and light up Your face, so that we shall be saved, Amen.

כאשר יום החג הוא בשבת מדליקים נרות לפני כניסת השבת ומברכים:

בָּרוּךְ אַתָּה יהוה אֱלֹהֵינוּ מֶלֶךְ הָעוֹלָם
אֲשֶׁר קִדְּשָׁנוּ בְּמִצְוֹתָיו
וְצִוָּנוּ לְהַדְלִיק נֵר (שֶׁל שַׁבָּת וְ) שֶׁל יוֹם טוֹב.

בָּרוּךְ אַתָּה יהוה אֱלֹהֵינוּ מֶלֶךְ הָעוֹלָם
שֶׁהֶחֱיָנוּ וְקִיְּמָנוּ, וְהִגִּיעָנוּ לַזְּמַן הַזֶּה.

תפילה אחרי הדלקת הנרות:

יְהִי רָצוֹן מִלְּפָנֶיךָ יהוה אֱלֹהַי וֵאלֹהֵי אֲבוֹתַי, שֶׁתְּחוֹנֵן אוֹתִי (מוסיפה: וְאֶת אִישִׁי / אם הוריה חיים: וְאֶת אָבִי / וְאֶת אִמִּי / אם יש לה ילדים: וְאֶת בָּנַי וְאֶת בְּנוֹתַי) וְאֶת כָּל קְרוֹבַי, וְתִתֶּן לָנוּ וּלְכָל יִשְׂרָאֵל חַיִּים טוֹבִים וַאֲרֻכִּים, וְתִזְכְּרֵנוּ בְּזִכְרוֹן טוֹבָה וּבְרָכָה, וְתִפְקְדֵנוּ בִּפְקֻדַּת יְשׁוּעָה וְרַחֲמִים, וּתְבָרְכֵנוּ בְּרָכוֹת גְּדוֹלוֹת, וְתַשְׁלִים בָּתֵּינוּ וְתַשְׁכֵּן שְׁכִינָתְךָ בֵּינֵינוּ. וְזַכֵּנִי לְגַדֵּל בָּנִים וּבְנֵי בָנִים חֲכָמִים וּנְבוֹנִים, אוֹהֲבֵי יהוה יִרְאֵי אֱלֹהִים, אַנְשֵׁי אֱמֶת זֶרַע קֹדֶשׁ, בַּיהוה דְּבֵקִים וּמְאִירִים אֶת הָעוֹלָם בַּתּוֹרָה וּבְמַעֲשִׂים טוֹבִים וּבְכָל מְלֶאכֶת עֲבוֹדַת הַבּוֹרֵא. אָנָּא שְׁמַע אֶת תְּחִנָּתִי בָּעֵת הַזֹּאת בִּזְכוּת שָׂרָה וְרִבְקָה וְרָחֵל וְלֵאָה אִמּוֹתֵינוּ, וְהָאֵר נֵרֵנוּ שֶׁלֹּא יִכְבֶּה לְעוֹלָם וָעֶד, וְהָאֵר פָּנֶיךָ וְנִוָּשֵׁעָה. אָמֵן.

> When the Seder night falls on Shabbat we add the formulation "with love" to the text of Kiddush…and tremendous love comes down to the world. The attribute of love on Shabbat is expressed through the sacrifices offered when Pesaḥ falls on Shabbat. Because on all holidays, the sacrificial offerings include a sin-offering. We bring a sin-offering on the holidays because I have sinned.[67] Also on an ordinary Pesaḥ that does not fall on Shabbat we offer a sin-offering. But in the Musaf service on Shabbat when the Seder night falls on that [Shabbat], we do not bring a sin-offering. And God shows His love for His people when Pesaḥ falls on Shabbat, as He removes before Him every semblance of sin, and says, "Love covers over all wrongs" (Prov. 10:12).[68]

When the Seder night falls on Shabbat, you're sin free. You didn't fall prey to sin, or missed opportunities, or *ḥametz*. You're spotless, and you can't even imagine to what extent.

And the Woman Asked, "So, Where Are You for the Seder?"

Rabbi Elimelekh Biderman writes:

> Every Jew who comes to the Seder night should know that he's starting from scratch now.
>
> It is as if his entire past never happened. And he should ask the Master of the world to forgive him for his entire past.
>
> On the Seder night incredible things can be achieved with each appeal and each request, before Maariv, during Maariv, during Hallel [recited] at Maariv.
>
> After that, as he walks toward the Seder. During the Seder, during the meal, during the Hallel after the Seder.[69]

The entire time, these questions should be running through our minds: "Master of the world, what will be? What will happen? What great news do You have in store for me?"

On this

Hallel at Night

The Maariv service before the start of the Seder has an unusual twist: We recite Hallel in its entirety. Usually, Hallel is recited only by day. The Seder night, though, is a night that is also day, "a night that is as light as day."[66]

It's the only night when Hallel is recited – twice actually: before the Seder and during the Seder.

According to Rabbi Ovadia Yosef, a woman must recite Hallel before the Seder, either in the synagogue or at home.

The Gematria (numerical value) of the Hebrew term for the entire Hallel (*Hallel gamur*) is equivalent to the value of God's name Shaddai, the name associated with incredible miracles that defy the nature of the world. Fasten your seatbelts. Miracles are about to happen. The incredible night has arrived.

This day is all about love.

And when the first night of Pesaḥ falls on Shabbat? Wow. The word "love" appears incessantly in our prayers. Rabbi Joseph B. Soloveitchik writes:

This is *the* question: "Where will you be for the Seder this year?" And, one way or another, the answer always needs to be: "With my Dad. I'm going to my Father for the Seder."

And we need to ask God, like in Song of Songs, "Where will You pasture?"[70] Where do You pasture (eat) tonight? Where will You be for the Seder? Come to me. We have lots of room. Look, "I rose to open the door for my beloved!"[71]

Don't stop asking questions. Questions are indicative of redemption. All our preparations, all the cleaning, are all part of a tremendous question. And the Seder night is all about questions and answers, and you must not stop asking. "And here the son asks: What makes this night unlike [the others]?"[72] Ask, because this is the way to refresh old beliefs and air out preconceived notions. Ask, and you will experience complete renewal.

> God, may He be blessed, wants us to approach the Seder night with the feeling that we will be hearing the words of the living God from the Holy One, blessed be He, Himself. And every single thing said on the Seder night brings us tremendous closeness, as we say at the beginning of the Seder: "I shall prepare the feast of the Holy One, blessed be He, and His Divine Presence."
>
> And on this day, that is as light as day, God gives everyone the power to be "the son [who] asks." And every Jew is like the high priest who serves in his white priestly garments and has the most incredible capacity for prayer.[73]

On this night,

every request has the capacity to accomplish incredible things, because on this night all the gates above are open.

God, may He be blessed, wants us to come to the Seder night with the feeling that we are about to hear incredible new tidings. Therefore,

the biggest question of the year –

when one asks his friend: "Where will you be for the Seder, with God's help? Who will you be sitting with on the Seder night?"

And even if the answer is: "In this place, or that place, with this person, or that person," the inner truth is that when this question is asked, the answer resounds throughout the expanse of the world: "We will all be having the Seder with our Father in heaven." Because on the Seder night we will all be by [our] Father for the Seder. We are all ushered into the Holy of Holies and conduct our Seder with our Father, may He be blessed.

And on this night, which is as light as day, God, may He be blessed, gives everyone the power to be "the son [who] asks." And when he asks, he is like the high priest who serves in his white priestly garments who had the most incredible capacity for prayer.

Wow wow wow!

קַדֵּשׁ • וּרְחַץ • כַּרְפַּס • יַחַץ

Kadesh · *Urḥatz* · *Karpas* · *Yaḥatz*

מַגִּיד • רַחְצָה • מוֹצִיא מַצָּה

Maggid · *Raḥtza* · *Motzi Matza*

מָרוֹר • כּוֹרֵךְ • שֻׁלְחָן עוֹרֵךְ

Maror · *Korekh* · *Shulḥan Orekh*

צָפוּן • בָּרֵךְ • הַלֵּל • נִרְצָה

Tzafun · *Barekh* · *Hallel* · *Nirtza*

psalms. In a similar sense, we yearn for an uplifting night that will take us higher and higher and carry us away in song. We want to go higher, step by glorious step, and eventually reach the throne of glory.

Rabbi Elimelekh Biderman writes that on the Seder night we are like someone who has lost something. Others ask the hopeful seeker: Are there any identifiable markings (*simanim*)? These identifiable markings will help him locate what has gone missing – and what is it? The holy Divine Presence.

So she was holy (*Kadesh*). And she was scrubbed clean (*Urḥatz*). And then everything was undermined and became unstable: She suffered through misfortune (*Karpas* is comprised of two different words: *mekher*, "sale," and *passim*, "stripes," which is a reference to the sale of Yosef, the biblical character who was given a striped coat). She was split in half (*Yaḥatz*) but never stopped praying and pleading (*Maggid*) and trying to cleanse herself from her sins and the dust of the road (*Raḥtza*). She ate poor man's bread (*Motzi Matza*) and swallowed bitterness (*Maror-Korekh*) and set her table for redemption (*Shulḥan Orekh*), and she anxiously awaits the day when she will recite the blessing on that which is hidden, namely Mashiaḥ (*Tzafun-Barekh*), and praise You, God (Hallel), and be cherished and desired (*Nirtza*)! Master of the world, do You know someone like this? Because we are searching for her. And these are her identifiable markings (*simanim*).[76]

It's a Long Story and We Can Make Peace with It

Things happen in order, but sometimes this order is destabilized. Why does this happen? There are so many people who go through life feeling like a giant question mark.

On the Seder night, when you conduct everything in proper order, God will help you understand. Beginning with *Kadesh, Urḥatz* (things are finally getting started), until *Shulḥan Orekh* (When are we finally going to eat? I haven't had a bite all day and I'm starving), you'll feel somewhat at peace with the difficult things that have happened to you. This sense of peace is known as redemption. You'll get an answer to the questions that trouble you most of all: Why? How can it be?

I need to share with you Rabbi Shlomo Wolbe's astonishing words:

> The Seder night is a cure for jealousy, and no one can escape the thicket of jealousy and make peace with himself until he understands and comprehends the matter of "For this purpose you have been chosen."[77] Because the secret of his life, of his attributes and his essence, is nothing other than divine providence.

And the

The Simanim
Kadesh Urḥatz
An Encounter with the Seder

Our Personal *Avoda: Kadesh Urḥatz*

Kadesh, Urḥatz...think about the kids who have a hard time staying focused, the ones who struggle to remember things. Pray that they should be able to organize the things they find confusing into rhyme, change assignments into songs, until everything becomes methodical and clear. Until they feel cherished, once and for all.

The Hidden Symbols (*Simanim*) of Love

Kadesh Urḥatz Karpas Yaḥatz...the fifteen-word summary of the Seder service. There are some that say that Rashi, Rabbi Shlomo Yitzḥaki, was the one who composed this. Ideally, one should recite these words, the *simanim*, three times in a row. Rabbi Alexander Ziskind explains that reciting the parts of the Seder in order is *one of the greatest tikkunim* because it is simply an incredible prayer. These words imply *great and incredible secrets*.[74]

Fifteen words, the Gematria value of the name of God (*Yah*), the name of God that enabled us to be liberated from Egypt; "From the straits did I call upon God (*Yah*), God (*Yah*) answered me with expansiveness."[75]

It's the fifteenth day of the month, the fifteenth of Nisan.

Dayeinu, the liturgical poem that is so central to the Haggada, is composed of fifteen statements. In the Temple there were fifteen steps, and in the book of Psalms there are fifteen psalms that begin with the words *shir lamaalot*. The Levites would stand on the Temple steps and sing these

What Comes First – Getting Married or Accepting Things the Way They Are?

The order of the Haggada is rather interesting. First comes *Kadesh*, and then *Urḥatz*. First comes marriage (*kiddushin*) and then the process of cleansing and purification. We're used to thinking the opposite: I'm not ready to get married yet. First, I need to work on my anger and stinginess. First, I need to pray three times a day and lose forty pounds.

Alternatively: First, I need to cleanse him of all his faults, and then we'll talk.

But the Haggada comes along and tells you: No. You have it all wrong. Tonight, the logical order is completely inverted. *Kadesh, Urḥatz*: Take us with all our faults and shortcomings. Don't wait until we're perfect. Like a mother who can smell her baby's diaper as he crawls toward her, and nonetheless scoops him up and kisses him before she changes him. This is Pesaḥ, *an expression of jumping and leaping.*[81] The "logical" order is irrelevant on the Seder night.

In this way, the Seder night allows us to encounter a doctrine of redemption that defies logical order.

And, in a more general sense, when do we most need structure and order? When things are so lofty and sublime that we are likely to get lost:

For example, when the high priest encounters the Holy One, blessed be He, "upon a high and exalted throne"[82] on Yom Kippur, we need the structure of the Temple service (*seder haavoda*).

And in prayer, when we encounter the Divine Presence, we need the structure of a prayerbook (*siddur*).

And when we blow the shofar, when we encounter Avraham at the binding of Yitzḥak, we need "the order of our shofar verses" (*seder shofrateinu*).[83]

When everything that surrounds us is chaotic, the Seder arrives.

> And the Seder night and the story of the Haggada endow us with belief in divine providence. This [divine providence] is what created him; this [divine providence] is what assigned him his role in life.
>
> There's no place to compete or compare oneself to others. "One reign does not overlap with another."[78] We received everything through divine providence, and he leaves the Seder night without bitterness and without competition.[79]

Wow. Don't you see? If you proceed according to the correct order (*seder*), you'll walk away with an answer to the ultimate question: What is my purpose in this world? For this purpose, I have been chosen! This is why I went through what I went through. Including the bitterness (*maror*). Including the subjugation. This is my *seder*, the carefully arranged order of my life.

Understanding this, in and of itself, cleanses our souls.

The Rebbe of Modzitz detects a powerful allusion in the words *Kadesh Urḥatz*, whose Gematria value is equivalent to the Gematria value of the words *Im Elokim, im anashim*, "With God, with man."[80] This is the grand finale to all the Pesaḥ cleaning, cleansing the relationship between man and God and cleansing the relationships between man and his fellow. Yes, the Seder night marks our liberation from bitterness, our liberation from competition. Focus on this; think about it carefully. For, if things haven't been properly cleansed, how can we approach the Seder?

Understanding that the story is long and drawn out, and that things are carefully arranged in order (*seder*), *is* the Seder night! And this is what I want, this passionate embrace at the end, with God, with man.

Kadesh / Kiddush

קַדֵּשׁ

Kiddush

An Encounter with All the Souls, the Ones That Are Present and the Ones That Aren't

Let's begin with Rabbi Joseph B. Soloveitchik's inspiring words about Kiddush:

> At Kiddush on the Seder night one should ask for *kiddushin* with the One whom his soul loves, *kiddushin* with *Knesset Yisrael*. Kiddush reminds anyone who hears it that he was chosen by the Master of the world, "You have chosen us from all the peoples; You loved us and found favor in us."[84] Kiddush on the Seder night is pure love.[85]

To feel that you are chosen and desired, You have chosen us, is just incredible. The knowledge that you are chosen, that someone chose you – is unparalleled. Kiddush is essentially *kiddushin* (marriage), a moment of connection between lovers. "For us did You choose, and us did You sanctify from all the peoples." You have been sanctified. Your Father is here, and He loves you so much.

The kabbalists add that during Kiddush on the Seder night, the congregation of Israel is lovingly secluded with their beloved. You'll suddenly feel that your Seder table has become crowded, because the souls of the fathers and mothers of this household are present during the recitation of Kiddush.

The Chafetz Chaim would cry uncontrollably. "Don't you see?" he told his students. At Kiddush at the Seder, all the family members who passed away appear: The grandfather, the grandmother, the father. The brother who died young. All these deceased family members come to Kiddush.

Such beautiful words. It's not like some group gift with the same uniform message for everyone ("Children, I bless you with health, a great year for all of us, marriage, and livelihood"). Every person receives a personal blessing, in sync with his needs and abilities. It's powerful.

Why Do We Recline While We Drink?

We recline when we drink the four cups of wine.[88] In a general sense, "tonight we are all reclining" – what does this mean?

We lean to the left. According to the kabbalists, if, God forbid, there is a decree hanging over your head, you escape it by leaning to the left. "God turned (*vayasev)* the people toward the way of the wilderness";[89] God turns the nation around, so they won't see the Philistines preparing to fight against them. Turning around, leaning, enables one to bypass difficult decrees.

The Shelah HaKadosh adds that this detour made the nation's journey longer. Rather than traveling directly from Egypt to the land of Israel, an eleven-day journey, God extended their trip by taking them around through the wilderness. Everyone knows the end of the story: They remained in the wilderness for forty years.

This begs the question: Why? Why should it take forty years if it could have been done in eleven days?

Perhaps God is saying: You're a woman who's all about deadlines. Fit-it-all-in-get-it-all-done-get married-have-kids-why-aren't-things-going-the-way-I-planned? But if He would have brought you there immediately, you would have encountered a war and been terrified ("Perhaps the people will reconsider when they see a war"[90]), and you would have wanted to return to Egypt. You would have been willing to forgo the entire redemption.

So I'm taking you on the circuitous route. Because speed is not the most important factor here. The most important thing is that you shouldn't be afraid. Don't you understand that your Father is protecting you from so much fear? True, you're going to need to hang around a little longer, but you need to understand that I'm making it better for you, more comfortable, more satisfying, more pleasant. Efficiency is not the most supreme value. Neither is output. Not even "likes."

Serenity, living your life without fear, that's the most important thing. "The main thing is to have no fear at all."[91] The main thing is not to frighten yourself into thinking that this principle doesn't apply to you. Not to deny this principle.

Your Father is protecting you from fear. You're well protected, and preserved; "this night is kept as one of watchfulness for the Lord."[92]

One of the saddest lectures I ever gave was delivered to a group of thirty-six widows whose husbands had died in the Mount Carmel forest fire. At the end of the talk, a Druze widow shared that she dreamed that her husband came home.

After she spoke everyone jumped in: Me too! Me too! They all dreamed that their husbands walked through the door of their homes one more time. One dreamed that he was wearing his uniform, another dreamed that he was wearing Shabbat clothing. Just let him walk through the door one more time, they said. Just one more time – that would have been enough.

It will happen on the Seder night. For them, and for all of us. All the people whom you long for – the one that you wish will come one more time and recite Kiddush for you, the one that you pine to see just once more – will come. The Chafetz Chaim explains that at Kiddush it feels crowded, and immediately afterward it feels spacious again. What happened? All the deceased members of the family came for Kiddush, and then left.

After Kiddush, bless one another. Bless each person with the blessing he needs most: This year you'll recover. This year you'll get married. This year you'll excel at school like you always dreamed you would. This year you'll overcome your debt. On this night, "the treasuries of dew are opened."[86] A new reality is born; people are born again.

> There is great value to the blessing [bestowed] from one man to his fellow on this night after Kiddush, for the gates of heaven are open, the angels utter a song, and the Holy One, blessed be He, judges the world regarding the grain in the fields, and the treasuries of dew are opened. And on this night Yitzḥak blessed Yaakov with blessings, and my father, my teacher of blessed memory, with great light upon his face, would bless all the people at the table, man and woman, old and young, even a baby in a crib, he would bless each one according to his blessing, in accordance with his concerns and character.
>
> And at this moment, the heavens rumble. And in the lower [world] it is announced: "The voice – is the voice of Yaakov!" And when he blesses, his portion is with the voice, the voice of Yaakov.
>
> And after the blessing he is like Yaakov who left his father Yitzḥak's presence, adorned like a bridegroom and like a bride with her adornments, and dew from the heavens would fall on him and beneath him and his bones were invigorated and he became a mighty-one, the knight of Yaakov.[87]

Are You Important?

Must women recline at the Seder? With time, halakha determined that women are not obligated to recline, based on the opinion that nowadays the obligation to recline is not absolute.[94]

According to the Talmud, only important people are obligated to recline. "A woman [who is] with her husband is not required to recline, but if she is an important woman (and not subordinate to her husband), she is required to recline."[95]

Later halakhic authorities ruled that while it's true that women who aren't important are not obligated to recline, in our generation, there are important women, and they should recline.

Rabbi Moshe Feinstein rendered a halakhic decision that resonates strongly with me: "With time, they recognized that men did not have reason to hold themselves above their wives, and the women recognized the great need their husbands had for them. And the minority of important women in all time periods were women like this who recognized that their husbands needed them, just like they needed their husbands, and they recognized that their husbands knew this."[96] Correct, he says (and apparently concurs with the halakhic position of his predecessors). Only an important woman should recline. But who is deemed to be an "important woman"? It's not just a woman who is held in high esteem (by her husband and children). It's someone who understands that she is inherently valuable, since she is the daughter of God.

The Hebrew word for important, *ḥashuv*, is actually a passive participle (as opposed to an adjective). Rabbi Moshe Feinstein says: Just like it's possible to nullify *ḥametz* in our hearts, importance is also an internal feeling, a matter of the heart. Do you feel important? If yes, you should certainly recline. Because you understand how important you are. And if you don't feel that inner sense of importance, and you don't sense that you're the daughter of a king, don't recline.

Importance is dependent on self-awareness. It's like matza that doesn't need someone to come along and make it rise from the outside. In a word, you're a matza. The fact that you pushed yourself to do so much (like the Hebrew word *mitzui* which is related to the word *matza*) should make you feel important, terribly important and incredibly special.

When a woman recognizes her own self-worth, she is important.

Turning Toward Our Roots

Rabbi Samson Raphael Hirsch makes a sweet comment: Why do we lean to the left? To show that the elderly are more important on the Seder night. They sit at the head of the table, and we lean toward them to demonstrate that they are the reason we are here, and we're here on account of them. And this is cause for celebration. A generation is upheld by a generation that is upheld by the previous generation.

Don't forget the elderly! What makes this night unlike all the others? The elderly!

Rabbi Hayim Navon writes:

> The internal process that we go through on the Seder night is not guided by celebrities with an extreme life story, the kind of people that we love to invite as lecturers and guests, but rather by our grandfathers. My most beautiful memories from the Seder night are specifically from my elderly grandfathers and grandmothers and the Seder nights that they led, which weren't focused on me, and not everything there was age appropriate for me. Our preschool-aged children have more than enough educational activities geared toward young kids. The breathtaking impression of the Seder night is generated specifically through the understanding that on this night they take part in the real adult activities. Children love the Seder night specifically because they aren't the stars of the night, but equal participants. And since nobody lives forever, there's only a limited number of Seder nights that they will be able to experience alongside their grandparents.
>
> Today, I would give anything to spend another Seder night in the company of my grandfather and father, of blessed memory, but this won't happen in this lifetime. Every Seder night that I spent with them as a child was a precious experience that left a lasting impression on me.[93]

the chief cupbearer's dream, and hoped to go free. Yet when the chief cupbearer was released from prison, "the chief cupbearer did not remember Yosef; he forgot him.[99]

Who remembers him? The four matriarchs. The four of them stand before God, and his mother, Raḥel, leads the pack. They say: We have suffered too much. Enough, God, please. How much can this boy suffer? How much can this girl endure?

They stand by him, feeling meager and poor, until the turning point arrives: "He was rushed from the dungeon."[100]

When you feel like the entire world has forgotten you, when you're stuck behind bars, your four matriarchs will come and stand by you. They'll rush you out of the dungeon with each cup that you drink. They'll stand by your side and stretch out their arms and tell you: Get up. You're not allowed to fall into despair. You're a free woman (*bat ḥorin*)![101]

Do you know what the Hebrew word *bat* indicates? It means to be deserving of something (for example, a *bat mitzva* is deserving of mitzvot). The distinction of being a free woman (*bat ḥorin*) means that you're deserving of freedom. On this night, you sit and find yourself in the world of freedom. It is as if you're in the middle of something wondrous and incredible, a place that is entirely good. Everything you dream about on the Seder night will hopefully be transformed into reality in the coming year.

On this night you're a *bat ḥorin*, and every single cup of wine that you drink at the Seder is as nurturing as mother's milk.

The Four Cups

An Encounter with the Matriarchs

Rescued from the Dungeon

The four cups are analogous to the four matriarchs.

On Seder night, the three patriarchs are symbolized by the three matzot. It is insightful to note that after we eat the matza, we're basically done with it, while the four cups of wine accompany us throughout the night. The four matriarchs, Sara, Rivka, Raḥel, and Leah, hold our hands throughout the long process of redemption and encourage us: Don't give up. Don't despair. No matter what.[97]

What is the intrinsic connection between the matriarchs and the cups of wine? Rabbi Moshe Shapira explains beautifully: The Hebrew letter that symbolizes "four" (*dalet*) derives from the same etymological root as the word "meagerness" (*dalut*). Our matriarchs were so meager. They beseeched God for strength, and redemption, and children. They begged Him to remember them, and completely change their lot in life, and enable them to overcome their infertility.

He explains that when the chief cupbearer dreamed his dream in jail, and Yosef interpreted his dream for him, the word "cup" appears four times. "Pharaoh's cup was in my hand…into Pharaoh's cup…I placed the cup…. and you will place Pharaoh's cup in his hand."[98]

This was one of Yosef's most difficult moments. Yosef was imprisoned, overlooked, and forgotten. He interpreted

The First Cup
Is Symbolic of Sara, Our Matriarch

The first cup of wine is poured, lift the cup with the right hand and say (on Shabbat add the words in parentheses):

I am prepared and ready to fulfill the commandment of the first of the four cups. For the sake for the unification of the Holy One, blessed be He, and His Divine Presence, through He who is hidden and unseen, in the name of all Israel.

Kiddush for Seder Night – Nusaḥ Ashkenaz

On Shabbat say:

Gen. 1 *quietly:* And it was evening, and it was morning –

Gen. 2 יוֹם הַשִּׁשִּׁי the sixth day.
Then the heavens and the earth were completed,
and all their array.
With the seventh day, God completed the work He had done.
He ceased on the seventh day from all the work He had done.
God blessed the seventh day and declared it holy,
because on it He ceased from all His work He had created to do.

כוס ראשונה
כנגד שרה אימנו

מוזגים כוס ראשון, נוטלו ביד ימינו ומקדש (בשבת מוסיפים את המילים בסוגריים):

הִנְנִי מוּכָן וּמְזֻמָּן לְקַיֵּם מִצְוַת כּוֹס רִאשׁוֹן מֵאַרְבַּע כּוֹסוֹת
לְשֵׁם יִחוּד קֻדְשָׁא בְּרִיךְ הוּא וּשְׁכִינְתֵּהּ עַל יְדֵי הַהוּא טָמִיר וְנֶעְלָם בְּשֵׁם כָּל יִשְׂרָאֵל.

קידוש לליל הסדר בנוסח אשכנז

בשבת אומרים:

בראשית א בלחש: **וַיְהִי־עֶרֶב וַיְהִי־בֹקֶר**

בראשית ב **יוֹם הַשִּׁשִּׁי: וַיְכֻלּוּ הַשָּׁמַיִם וְהָאָרֶץ וְכָל־צְבָאָם: וַיְכַל אֱלֹהִים בַּיּוֹם הַשְּׁבִיעִי**
מְלַאכְתּוֹ אֲשֶׁר עָשָׂה, וַיִּשְׁבֹּת בַּיּוֹם הַשְּׁבִיעִי מִכָּל־מְלַאכְתּוֹ אֲשֶׁר עָשָׂה:
וַיְבָרֶךְ אֱלֹהִים אֶת־יוֹם הַשְּׁבִיעִי, וַיְקַדֵּשׁ אֹתוֹ, כִּי בוֹ שָׁבַת מִכָּל־מְלַאכְתּוֹ,
אֲשֶׁר־בָּרָא אֱלֹהִים, לַעֲשׂוֹת.

Please pay attention, my masters.

בָּרוּךְ Blessed are You, LORD our God, King of the Universe,
who creates the fruit of the vine.

בָּרוּךְ Blessed are You, LORD our God, King of the Universe,
who has chosen us from among all peoples, raised us above
all tongues, and made us holy through His commandments.
You have given us, LORD our God, in love (Shabbat
for rest), festivals for rejoicing, holy days and
seasons for joy, (this Shabbat day and)
this day of the festival of Matzot, the
time of our freedom (with love),
a holy assembly in memory
of the Exodus from Egypt.
For You have chosen us
and sanctified us
above all peoples,
and given us as our heritage
(Your holy Shabbat in love and favor and)
Your holy festivals for joy and gladness.
Blessed are you, Lord, who sanctifies (the Shabbat,)
Israel and the festivals.

סַבְרִי מָרָנָן

בָּרוּךְ אַתָּה יהוה אֱלֹהֵינוּ מֶלֶךְ הָעוֹלָם, בּוֹרֵא פְּרִי הַגָּפֶן.

בָּרוּךְ אַתָּה יהוה אֱלֹהֵינוּ מֶלֶךְ הָעוֹלָם, אֲשֶׁר בָּחַר
בָּנוּ מִכָּל עָם, וְרוֹמְמָנוּ מִכָּל לָשׁוֹן, וְקִדְּשָׁנוּ בְּמִצְוֹתָיו
וַתִּתֶּן לָנוּ יהוה אֱלֹהֵינוּ בְּאַהֲבָה (שַׁבָּתוֹת לִמְנוּחָה
וּ) מוֹעֲדִים לְשִׂמְחָה, חַגִּים וּזְמַנִּים לְשָׂשׂוֹן, אֶת
יוֹם (הַשַּׁבָּת הַזֶּה וְאֶת יוֹם) חַג הַמַּצּוֹת הַזֶּה
זְמַן חֵרוּתֵנוּ (בְּאַהֲבָה) מִקְרָא קֹדֶשׁ
זֵכֶר לִיצִיאַת מִצְרָיִם, כִּי בָנוּ
בָחַרְתָּ וְאוֹתָנוּ קִדַּשְׁתָּ
מִכָּל הָעַמִּים, (וְשַׁבָּת)
וּמוֹעֲדֵי קָדְשְׁךָ
(בְּאַהֲבָה וּבְרָצוֹן)
בְּשִׂמְחָה וּבְשָׂשׂוֹן הִנְחַלְתָּנוּ.
בָּרוּךְ אַתָּה יהוה, מְקַדֵּשׁ (הַשַּׁבָּת וְ) יִשְׂרָאֵל וְהַזְּמַנִּים.

On Motza'ei Shabbat, add:

בָּרוּךְ Blessed are You, LORD our God,
King of the Universe,
who creates the lights of fire.

בָּרוּךְ Blessed are You, Lord our God,
King of the Universe,
who distinguishes between sacred and secular,
between light and darkness, between Israel and the nations,
between the seventh day and the six days of work.
You have made a distinction
between the holiness of the Sabbath
and the holiness of festivals, and have sanctified
the seventh day above the six days of work.
You have distinguished and sanctified
Your people Israel with Your holiness.
Blessed are You, Lord,
who distinguishes between sacred and sacred.

Continue on page 86 for Sheheḥeyanu.

במוצאי שבת מוסיפים:

בָּרוּךְ אַתָּה יהוה
אֱלֹהֵינוּ מֶלֶךְ הָעוֹלָם
בּוֹרֵא מְאוֹרֵי הָאֵשׁ.

בָּרוּךְ אַתָּה יהוה אֱלֹהֵינוּ מֶלֶךְ הָעוֹלָם
הַמַּבְדִּיל בֵּין קֹדֶשׁ לְחֹל
בֵּין אוֹר לְחֹשֶׁךְ
בֵּין יִשְׂרָאֵל לָעַמִּים
בֵּין יוֹם הַשְּׁבִיעִי לְשֵׁשֶׁת יְמֵי הַמַּעֲשֶׂה
בֵּין קְדֻשַּׁת שַׁבָּת לִקְדֻשַּׁת יוֹם טוֹב הִבְדַּלְתָּ
וְאֶת יוֹם הַשְּׁבִיעִי מִשֵּׁשֶׁת יְמֵי הַמַּעֲשֶׂה קִדַּשְׁתָּ
הִבְדַּלְתָּ וְקִדַּשְׁתָּ אֶת עַמְּךָ יִשְׂרָאֵל בִּקְדֻשָּׁתֶךָ.
בָּרוּךְ אַתָּה יהוה הַמַּבְדִּיל בֵּין קֹדֶשׁ לְקֹדֶשׁ.

שהחינו בהמשך בעמוד 87.

Kiddush for Seder Night – Nusaḥ Edot Hamizraḥ

On Shabbat say:

Gen. 1 *quietly:* And it was evening, and it was morning –

Gen. 2 יוֹם הַשִּׁשִּׁי the sixth day.
Then the heavens and the earth were completed,
and all their array.
With the seventh day, God completed the work He had done.
He ceased on the seventh day from all the work He had done.
God blessed the seventh day and declared it holy,
because on it He ceased from all His work He had created to do.

קידוש לליל הסדר בנוסח עדות המזרח

בזמן הקידוש עומדים.

כשיום טוב חל בשבת, קודם שאומרים 'אֵ֣לֶּה מוֹעֲדֵ֣י', מוסיפים:

יֽוֹם הַשִּׁשִּֽׁי׃ וַיְכֻלּ֛וּ הַשָּׁמַ֥יִם וְהָאָ֖רֶץ וְכָל־צְבָאָֽם׃ בראשית א
וַיְכַ֤ל אֱלֹהִים֙ בַּיּ֣וֹם הַשְּׁבִיעִ֔י מְלַאכְתּ֖וֹ אֲשֶׁ֣ר עָשָׂ֑ה בראשית ב
וַיִּשְׁבֹּת֙ בַּיּ֣וֹם הַשְּׁבִיעִ֔י מִכָּל־מְלַאכְתּ֖וֹ אֲשֶׁ֥ר עָשָֽׂה׃
וַיְבָ֤רֶךְ אֱלֹהִים֙ אֶת־י֣וֹם הַשְּׁבִיעִ֔י וַיְקַדֵּ֖שׁ אֹת֑וֹ
כִּ֣י ב֤וֹ שָׁבַת֙ מִכָּל־מְלַאכְתּ֔וֹ אֲשֶׁר־בָּרָ֥א אֱלֹהִ֖ים לַעֲשֽׂוֹת׃

אֵ֚לֶּה מוֹעֲדֵ֣י יְהֹוָ֔ה מִקְרָאֵ֖י קֹ֑דֶשׁ אֲשֶׁר־תִּקְרְא֥וּ אֹתָ֖ם בְּמוֹעֲדָֽם׃ ויקרא כג
וַיְדַבֵּ֣ר מֹשֶׁ֔ה אֶת־מֹעֲדֵ֖י יְהֹוָ֑ה אֶל־בְּנֵ֖י יִשְׂרָאֵֽל׃

Please pay attention, my masters.

בָּרוּךְ Blessed are You, LORD our God, King of the Universe,
who creates the fruit of the vine.

בָּרוּךְ Blessed are You, LORD our God, King of the Universe,
who has chosen us from among all peoples, raised us above
all tongues, and made us holy through His commandments.
You have given us, LORD our God, in love (Shabbat
for rest), festivals for rejoicing, holy days and
seasons for joy, (this Shabbat day and)
this day of the festival of Matzot, the
time of our freedom (with love),
a holy assembly in memory
of the Exodus from Egypt.
For You have chosen us
and sanctified us
above all peoples,
and given us as our heritage
(Your holy Shabbat in love and favor and)
Your holy festivals for joy and gladness.
Blessed are you, Lord, who sanctifies (the Shabbat,)
Israel and the festivals.

המקדש להוציא אחרים ידי חובתם, מוסיף:

סַבְרִי מָרָנָן (עונים: לְחַיִּים)

בָּרוּךְ אַתָּה יְהֹוָה, אֱלֹהֵינוּ מֶלֶךְ הָעוֹלָם, בּוֹרֵא פְּרִי הַגָּפֶן.

כשליל הסדר חל בשבת, מוסיף את המילים המופיעות בסוגריים.

בָּרוּךְ אַתָּה יְהֹוָה, אֱלֹהֵינוּ מֶלֶךְ הָעוֹלָם אֲשֶׁר בָּחַר
בָּנוּ מִכָּל עָם וְרוֹמְמָנוּ מִכָּל לָשׁוֹן, וְקִדְּשָׁנוּ בְּמִצְוֹתָיו
וַתִּתֶּן לָנוּ יְהֹוָה אֱלֹהֵינוּ בְּאַהֲבָה (שַׁבָּתוֹת לִמְנוּחָה
וּ) מוֹעֲדִים לְשִׂמְחָה חַגִּים וּזְמַנִּים לְשָׂשׂוֹן, אֶת
יוֹם (הַשַּׁבָּת הַזֶּה וְאֶת יוֹם) חַג הַמַּצּוֹת הַזֶּה
אֶת יוֹם טוֹב מִקְרָא קֹדֶשׁ הַזֶּה,
זְמַן חֵרוּתֵנוּ בְּאַהֲבָה מִקְרָא קֹדֶשׁ,
זֵכֶר לִיצִיאַת מִצְרָיִם. כִּי בָנוּ
בָחַרְתָּ וְאוֹתָנוּ קִדַּשְׁתָּ
מִכָּל הָעַמִּים. (וְשַׁבָּתוֹת
וּמוֹעֲדֵי קָדְשֶׁךָ (בְּאַהֲבָה וּבְרָצוֹן)
בְּשִׂמְחָה וּבְשָׂשׂוֹן הִנְחַלְתָּנוּ.
בָּרוּךְ אַתָּה יְהֹוָה מְקַדֵּשׁ (הַשַּׁבָּת וְ) יִשְׂרָאֵל וְהַזְּמַנִּים.

On Motza'ei Shabbat, add:

בָּרוּךְ Blessed are You, LORD our God,
King of the Universe,
who creates the lights of fire.

בָּרוּךְ Blessed are You, Lord our God,
King of the Universe,
who distinguishes between sacred and secular,
between light and darkness,
between Israel and the nations,
between the seventh day and the six days of work.
You have made a distinction
between the holiness of the Sabbath
and the holiness of festivals,
and have sanctified
the seventh day above the six days of work.
You have distinguished and sanctified
Your people Israel with Your holiness.
Blessed are You, Lord,
who distinguishes between sacred and sacred.

Continue on page 86 for Sheheḥeyanu

במוצאי שבת, מברך על הנר וחותם בברכת 'הַמַּבְדִּיל בֵּין קֹדֶשׁ לְקֹדֶשׁ':

בָּרוּךְ אַתָּה יְהֹוָה,
אֱלֹהֵינוּ מֶלֶךְ הָעוֹלָם,
בּוֹרֵא מְאוֹרֵי הָאֵשׁ.

בָּרוּךְ אַתָּה יְהֹוָה, אֱלֹהֵינוּ מֶלֶךְ הָעוֹלָם,
הַמַּבְדִּיל בֵּין קֹדֶשׁ לְחֹל
וּבֵין אוֹר לְחֹשֶׁךְ,
בֵּין יִשְׂרָאֵל לָעַמִּים
וּבֵין יוֹם הַשְּׁבִיעִי לְשֵׁשֶׁת יְמֵי הַמַּעֲשֶׂה.
בֵּין קְדֻשַּׁת שַׁבָּת לִקְדֻשַּׁת יוֹם טוֹב הִבְדַּלְתָּ,
וְאֶת יוֹם הַשְּׁבִיעִי מִשֵּׁשֶׁת יְמֵי הַמַּעֲשֶׂה הִקְדַּשְׁתָּ
וְהִבְדַּלְתָּ, וְהִקְדַּשְׁתָּ אֶת עַמְּךָ יִשְׂרָאֵל בִּקְדֻשָּׁתֶךָ.
בָּרוּךְ אַתָּה יְהֹוָה, הַמַּבְדִּיל בֵּין קֹדֶשׁ לְקֹדֶשׁ.

שהחינו בהמשך בעמוד 87

Blessed are You,
Lord our God,
King of the Universe,

who has given
us life,
sustained us,
and brought us

to this time.

Drink while reclining to the left.

בָּרוּךְ אַתָּה יהוה
אֱלֹהֵינוּ מֶלֶךְ הָעוֹלָם

שֶׁהֶחֱיָנוּ
וְקִיְּמָנוּ
וְהִגִּיעָנוּ

לַזְּמַן הַזֶּה.

שותים בהסבת שמאל.

Washing

וּרְחַץ

בעל הבית והמשתתפים נוטלים ידיהם ללא ברכה לאכילת הכרפס.

The leader and participants wash their hands without a berakha prior to eating the Karpas.

Karpas

כַּרְפַּס

נוטל מן הכרפס פחות מכזית, טובלו במי מלח או בחומץ ומברך (מכוון לפטור בברכה זו גם את המרור):

Take less than a kezayit, dip it in salt water or vinegar and (keeping in mind that this brakha will also include the maror), say:

**בָּרוּךְ אַתָּה יהוה
אֱלֹהֵינוּ מֶלֶךְ הָעוֹלָם
בּוֹרֵא פְּרִי הָאֲדָמָה.**

בָּרוּךְ Blessed are You,
Lord our God,
King of the Universe,
who creates
the fruit of the ground.

אוכלים בלי הסבה.

Eat without reclining.

But these women were focused on the beautiful future of their unborn babies who, in all likelihood, wouldn't even live. They fought for aesthetics.

Rabbi Yitzchak Hutner suggests that we should transform the battle of good versus evil into a battle between things that are pure and things that are less pure. Let's ask beauty to prevail over ugliness. This is what war will look like at the end of days. As you prepared for Pesaḥ, you were certainly more caught up in the aesthetics of your home than in obliterating *ḥametz*. This is what things will look like in the era of Mashiaḥ. Religiosity will be more focused on beautification than on rigid boundaries. We've come of age.

More than anything else, the Seder night brings to light the daughter of Israel within me, the one that I believe in. She calls on us to conduct a Seder that is beautified, to conduct ourselves in consonance with a different world order.

Karpas

An Encounter with Hate and Love

Karpas. We dip a vegetable in salt water, reminiscent of Yosef's tears as he was sold into slavery.

The first syllable of *karpas, kar*, derives from the second half of the Hebrew word for sale (*mekher*). The second half of the word *karpas*, *pas,* derives from the first half of the Hebrew word for stripes (*passim*), which invokes Yosef's special coat of many colors. The Ben Ish Ḥai explains that this is symbolic of the sale of the stripes. The Egyptian exile was triggered by the animosity between the brothers. How many salty tears will yet be spilled by this animosity? God, please save us from hatred and rivalry.

Karpas also attests to something else, an act that seems excessive and pointless and overly focused on aesthetics. Our Sages note that in Egypt the Jewish women would eat *karpas* so their unborn children would have green eyes.… Why did they bother themselves with this nonsense? Why did they care? Their unborn children would drown in the Nile! Who cares what color their eyes are? Focus on survival!

Yaḥatz / Splitting

יַחַץ

מחלק את המצה האמצעית לשני חלקים.
מצפין את החלק הגדול לאפיקומן,
ומחזיר את החלק הקטן לבין שתי המצות השלמות.

Break the middle matza into two pieces.
The bigger portion is hidden away to serve as the afikoman, and the smaller portion is placed between the two whole matzot.

Afikoman!

This Is Where Things Begin

The middle matza is split in two. The bigger portion is hidden away to serve as the *afikoman*. *Yaḥatz* – split. Man feels split, deficient, lacking in three primary areas of life: "It is as difficult to match a couple as the splitting of the sea;[102] the task of providing a person's food [livelihood] is as difficult as the splitting of the Reed Sea; a person's orifices [health] is as difficult as the splitting of the Reed Sea."[103]

At *Yaḥatz*, we should think in our hearts: Grant me the things that I am missing that make me feel so deficient, so incomplete: marriage, health, livelihood. Send me my other half.

God answers us with the *afikoman*. He has already hidden your salvation for you. All you need to do is find it.

I heard in the name of Rabbi Mordekhai Eliyahu that one should not allow the children to look for the *afikoman* until *Shulḥan Orekh* (the meal) so they won't miss the most important part of the Seder.

What should we do if we can't find the *afikoman*? This can also happen…The good news – you can use a different matza as the *afikoman* and eat it instead. It's not the end of the world. Take this idea with you: Don't eat yourself up about those things that slipped through your fingers, even though you were certain they were meant to be. "He [my beloved] had slipped away, gone,"[104] and also the *afikoman* was lost, and…they'll be another. A different wonderful guy, a different wonderful home. You will yet receive the entire blessing that God has put away for you.

We'll encounter the *afikoman* again at *Tzafun* and divide it up among those present with all the proper intentions and blessings.

Maggid / Telling

מַגִּיד

Maggid

An Encounter with Those Who Have Recited the Haggada Throughout the Generations

How will you say it? In a roundabout way. Indirectly.

We have reached the story of the Haggada. *Maggid* is an encounter with ancient words that have been recited long before our time. During the Holocaust. During the Inquisition. Through these words we connect to generations past, both recent and centuries ago, to souls that are quite ancient.

The Haggada bids you to declare (*taggidi*). But, in general, women don't make declarations. They talk. What's the difference between these two things? The Torah states: "So shall you say to the house of Yaakov [these are the women] and declare to the children of Israel [these are the men]."[105] The Hebrew word "Haggada" indicates "things as hard as wormwood,"[106] speaking directly. "Declare to me, you whom I have loved,"[107] because I myself cannot declare. I cannot speak directly. I say things (*omeret*) in the way in which the hem (*imra*) encircles the bottom of a dress, circuitously, indirectly.

Rabbi Hutner explains that women are bound by a decree, a barrier known as: "your urge shall be for your husband."[108] The Hebrew word for "urge" (*teshuka*) is similar to the Hebrew word for "silenced" (*shetuka*). You cannot express the things that sit in the deepest part of your soul, the things that trouble you most in your relationship with your husband. The most personal questions: "Do you still love me? Am I beautiful to you? Do you care about me? When will you say something kind to me? Am I number one in your eyes? Would you choose me again?" You would die of pride before you said these things out loud. For this reason, "women

On this night, the smallest anecdotes do the trick. They imbue us with faith, without coming on too strong. For this reason, we say: "One might have thought this meant from the beginning of the month." Is it possible to tell our children the story of the Egyptian Exodus from Rosh Ḥodesh Nisan? The answer: You can talk to your kids about the Egyptian Exodus whenever you like, obviously, but "and so it says 'on that day.'" The Seder night is a special time and, on this night, the simplest story can penetrate one's heart and fill it with deep faith. The Ḥatam Sofer writes: "On this night, a father's words will permeate his son's ears."

Which simple stories are we referring to? There are many sweet midrashim about the ten plagues, for example. During the plague of blood, a thirsty Egyptian saw a Jewish man drinking a cup of water. He forced the Jew to share the cup with him, and an incredible thing happened: The Jew drank water while the Egyptian man drank blood. In stories like this, the bad guys suffer the consequences. The good guys see the light and are compensated for all their suffering. It's so straightforward. Rabbi Shimshon Pincus quipped to *Daf Yomi* learners: Seder night is a *seder bekiut*, not a *seder iyun*!

You don't need to deliberate and make things complex. "And even were we all wise…still the command would be upon us." Forget about all your cleverness. Now's the time to tell the story. The Rebbe of Slonim explains that on the Seder night, stories radiate a special light, the light of sapphires.

Rabbi Hayim Navon writes:

> I have seen an upside-down world: In many schools, they are convinced that education should happen via attractions rather than through books. I meet more and more educators who have been influenced by this prevailing anti-intellectual propaganda, as if learning and knowledge are dry and suffocating. And on the Seder night we realize that you don't need to aim low to succeed. Specifically at home, on the Seder night, the entire family sits together and reads a book. In order to stir strong emotions we don't need dramatic effects, we don't need rappelling and fireworks. Small acts can have a big impact, if they are done with purpose and dedication, in a loving environment.
>
> This is the time to find the light within the home, not beyond it. In a world that is so competitive, our Seder night does not need to be the most profound, the most innovative, or the most attractive. The food does not need to be the most gourmet, and the words of Torah do not need to be the most sophisticated. It's sufficient for this night to be the most us.[111]

How Should

took nine *kav* of conversation,"[109] because we want to say things that are as hard as wormwood, and we can't. Instead, it comes out as a lot of chatter.

When you struggle to speak directly, you end up telling some kind of story. This is the Pesaḥ Haggada, Rabbi Hutner explains. For this reason, the conversation skirts through the sidelines, and this is the abundance of words in the Haggada. In essence, the Jewish people ask God: Am I still beloved and connected to You?[110] All the stories and rituals described in the Haggada are designed to help you say what's in your heart: You have chosen us from all the peoples – God, do You love me? Would You choose me again? What makes this night different from all other nights? Am I different and special to You, God? Have you seen all I've been through this past year? I feel like *Ḥad Gadya*, one little kid, devoured and attacked. Yet I still want to sing to You, even before You bring salvation. But I want to sing to You. Even before You bring salvation. Let's say Hallel.

Rabbi Wolbe explains that when we open our mouths on the Seder night (homiletically, the word "Pesaḥ" can be broken down into the two Hebrew words *peh saḥ,* or a mouth that converses), it is the opening of the mouth of the Jewish people. The entire text should be read like a love letter. It's not a story that happened thirty-three hundred years ago, blood-frogs-lice-wild animals. Say to Him: Are You here? You won't skip over me this year? You really care about me? Will I be married by next Seder night? After all, many years ago the Jewish people were in terrible pain. And You saved them. You split the sea for them. And what about me?

When will God answer us? By the matza. We'll get there soon.

Maggid rectifies the power of our mouths. The Rebbe of Izbiz writes that one who recites the Haggada aloud purifies all the powers of his mouth – speaking and eating – for the entire year.

The Simple Path to Faith

A word of advice about the simplicity of the Seder: Embrace the simplicity.

All year long, we feel compelled to share new and complicated ideas. Our hearts refuse to embrace simple faith, because we live in sophisticated times. But on the Seder night, the simplest story is the one that penetrates our hearts.

Stories That Endow Us with Strength for the Entire Year

And once we're talking about stories, share one midrash about Pesaḥ, one about matza, and one about *maror*. These are the three words that one is obligated to say on the Seder night.[116] We'll discuss them briefly here and expound upon them in depth later.

Pesaḥ – this is redemption. For example, there are dozens of sweet midrashim about how the frogs jumped into the dough. Pharaoh's wife was baking cookies and suddenly, a frog jumped out. There are detailed midrashim about the miracles that happened when God split the Reed Sea. The good guys are saved, and the bad guys are punished.

Matza – this represents the struggle against evil. Tell a story about a struggle. My child, we need to fight against evil. We need to protest it and battle it. Don't think that evil is inevitable.

So, how do we do this? First of all, we reach out to someone who is big and great. The Jewish people constantly cried out to Moshe.

Secondly, we pray to God. "And the children of Israel groaned under the burden of work and they cried out, and their plea rose to God."[117] You must make yourself heard.

And most importantly: You need to talk about the good things that lie in store! One of my most favorite midrashim discusses how the Jewish people would rest from their work on Shabbat, "and they had in their hands scrolls and they would delight in them each Shabbat."[118] The Jewish people had scrolls that discussed the redemption. They would read to one another about what would be when they left Egypt: "We're going to live in spacious homes, and we're going to celebrate the holidays in freedom and abundance, and one day Pharaoh will come in his pajamas and tell us 'Get up and go out from among my people.'"[119]

What's the point? Fight it. Don't drown in the evil that surrounds you!

And *maror* – this is the time to talk about the great suffering endured by the Jewish people. In the midrashim, this suffering is primarily expressed through family-oriented difficulties: Why did the Nile River turn to blood during the first plague? Because the Egyptians didn't allow the Jewish women to immerse for their husbands. The pain of Jewish babies drowning in the Nile, as their parents helplessly looked on from so far away. The pain of the heads of the families, who needed to perform forced labor in the fields, so far from their families.

A simple story about Pesaḥ (the redemption). One about matza (the struggle). And one about *maror* (the terrible difficulties). These are stories that imbue us with strength for the entire year.

A happy

How Should We Read the Haggada?

Rabbi Soloveitchik says:

> The Haggada is a dialogue. One man asks, and another one responds, because God appears to man only when he seeks Him. A man who doesn't seek, a man who expects God to reveal Himself to him without making an attempt to find Him, will never encounter God.
>
> The Ramban says in his commentary on the verse "Shall you seek out His presence and come there,"[112] that you should go from a distant land and ask: "Where is the House of God?"[113] This question in and of itself has the power to redeem and sanctify. And someone who does not constantly ask, "Where is the path that leads to the Temple?" [or to borrow Rebbe Nahman's terminology, "Where am I in the world?"[114]] will never find the Temple.
>
> On the first night of Pesaḥ we tell the story of a man who sought out God for a very long time [Avraham] until God finally responded to his curiosity.
>
> On the Seder night we try to stir the curiosity of the children, and in this way to make them into people who seek out God their entire lives. Children have their own honest and innocent questions. You can never anticipate what a child will ask. Children think differently than we do.[115]

One Miracle Triggers Another

Sharing a miracle at the Seder table is a powerful *segula*.

This is written in the Zohar HaKadosh and it's really incredible: One who joyfully tells the story of the Egyptian Exodus will rejoice with the Divine Presence in the World to Come, and this is the greatest of all joys. And God is so pleased with the story that man retells at the Seder, that He calls the entire heavenly entourage and tells them: "Come, listen to My children, who joyfully tell the story of My redemption."

And everyone gathers, and God becomes filled with compassion for us and says: "They are so worthy of additional miracles. I performed miracles for them years ago [during the Egyptian Exodus, and it was a long time ago] and they still talk about them and are not ungrateful!" And what happens – the attribute of compassion becomes stronger and brings about additional miracles.

When you retell simple stories, God sends more and more miracles in your direction.

Our Personal *Avoda*: This is the Bread of Oppression

"This is the bread of oppression" –
this is the bread of hardship and poverty.

Come for dinner!

But what exactly are we meant to eat
if we're impoverished?

When hardship is shared with another,
it's transformed into wealth.

Here, at this point,
pray for the children who have strayed
far from their parents' Seder tables,
for the doctors and nurses who have to work,
away from their families,
for the divorced parents who are alone,
missing their children,
for the single people whose time has not yet come.

Pray that by next year,
they'll no longer be free and all alone,
but gathered the Seder table
with their families, sharing this bread of hardship
and oppression, which is more valuable than gold.

A happy and kosher Pesaḥ to the entire beloved people of Israel,
who, year after year, whether stringently or randomly,
whether with deep intent, or because that's how it is,
read the Haggada with varying degrees of
textual understanding, and not always in its entirety,
and not always knowing the tune for "When Israel came out of Egypt,"
and struggling through the words "Had he drowned our enemies in it
without providing for our needs for forty years in the desert,"
and not understanding "After eating the Pesaḥ offering
one does not eat anything more,"
even though it was explained to them several times before,
but understanding that this is our story, and therefore it's okay
if not everything is understood. Since when does man completely
understand himself,
and his nation? Most importantly, we must continue to try to understand,
and most importantly we must continue to tell the story."[120]

– Irit Linor

The seder plate is held up and the middle matza is displayed while reciting:

I am prepared and ready to fulfill the commandment of telling the story of the Exodus from Egypt. For the sake for the unification of the Holy One, blessed be He, and His Divine Presence, through He who is hidden and unseen, in the name of all Israel.

מגביה את הקערה, מראה המצה הפרוסה שבין שתי השלמות ואומר:

הִנְנִי מוּכָן וּמְזֻמָּן לְקַיֵּם מִצְוַת לְסַפֵּר בִּיצִיאַת מִצְרַיִם
לְשֵׁם יִחוּד קֻדְשָׁא בְּרִיךְ הוּא וּשְׁכִינְתֵּהּ עַל יְדֵי הַהוּא טָמִיר וְנֶעְלָם בְּשֵׁם כָּל יִשְׂרָאֵל.

לַחְמָא עַנְיָא

דִּי אֲכַלוּ אֲבָהָתַנָא בְּאַרְעָא דְמִצְרָיִם
כָּל דִּכְפִין יֵיתֵי וְיֵיכֻל, כָּל דִּצְרִיךְ יֵיתֵי וְיִפְסַח
הָשַׁתָּא הָכָא לְשָׁנָה הַבָּאָה בְּאַרְעָא דְיִשְׂרָאֵל
הָשַׁתָּא עַבְדֵי לְשָׁנָה הַבָּאָה בְּנֵי חוֹרִין.

THIS
IS THE BREAD OF OPPRESSION

our fathers ate in the land of Egypt.
Let all who are hungry come in and eat;
let all who are in need come and join us for the Pesaḥ.
Now we are here; next year in the land of Israel.
Now – slaves; next year we shall be free.

This Is Where Freedom Lies

"This is the bread of oppression," we joyfully sing and announce: "Let all who are hungry come in and eat! Let all who are in need come and join us for the Pesaḥ!" Anyone who wants to come in is invited. Anyone who wants to eat – make yourselves at home and join us!

But isn't this hypocritical? How exactly do we intend to host all the needy people? Anyhow, if we really wanted to have them, we would have invited them ages ago, not at the very last second! Moreover, if you're all about hospitality, why are you inviting them in Aramaic?

Rabbi Wolbe explains so beautifully: "'This is the bread of oppression' is actually an invitation extended by God – to you. *And every man needs to know that on the Seder night he is not eating at the [Seder] table that he chose to eat at, but rather at God's table.* The table belongs to God and He invites you here, and invites you with these other people."[122]

Yemima, why am I stuck with this family? I didn't want to spend the Seder night with them.

Because God saw, Rabbi Wolbe says, that at this table and with this group of people you will receive everything that you *need*, all the things you need for the coming year. In this environment, you will overcome all your hunger, all your subordinance and subjugation, and stand tall. This year, God decided to endow you with abundance at this table, in this setting. Your freedom lies at this Seder table, with this family.

It's a profound statement. So many women feel distressed by the family complexity that surrounds them on the Seder night and the fact that they aren't where they wanted to be. And the words "this is the bread of oppression" tell you that this bread, this Seder table, was specifically designed for you. Everything has been planned ahead of time. Perhaps this year you feel a sense of exile, like you don't belong at this table, but *next year* – you'll be free.

And what should you do? Come to the Seder table as beautiful as possible. As magnificent as possible. Come forth in all your glory, as if you are already there.

This Is the Bread of Oppression

An Encounter with One Who Is Lacking

If the Household Is Too Small

The Paschal lamb is eaten in a group. The group needs to finish eating by morning, and there cannot be any leftovers. If there aren't enough people to finish an entire lamb, they need to join others and create a group.

The Torah states this in a rather unusual fashion: "If the household is too small for a lamb."[121] This formulation is incorrect. Really, it should say: "If the lamb is too big for this small household." Effectively the Torah is telling us: You think that you have so much and therefore your home is full of joy. But if you don't share what you have with the poor and destitute, with those who are hungry and those in need, then your house lacks happiness and joy, no matter how much you have. It lacks potential. "If the household is too small" – when your wealth is scattered in every corner of your home and your children don't appreciate anything, your household has become small. What a sad place to live.

Therefore, on this magnificent night, a night that is beautiful and exquisite, we begin with a reminder: "Children, remember. Joy isn't about how much you have. Abundance does not equal blessing. Did you reach out to someone in need? *This* is the sign of a home that has a lot."

מוזגים כוס שני ומסלקים את הקערה, והבן שואל:

The second cup of wine is poured and the Seder plate is covered.
The youngest child asks the following questions:

WHAT MAKES

THIS NIGHT UNLIKE ALL OTHER NIGHTS,

שֶׁבְּכָל הַלֵּילוֹת אָנוּ אוֹכְלִין חָמֵץ וּמַצָּה
הַלַּיְלָה הַזֶּה כֻּלּוֹ מַצָּה

שֶׁבְּכָל הַלֵּילוֹת אָנוּ אוֹכְלִין שְׁאָר יְרָקוֹת
הַלַּיְלָה הַזֶּה מָרוֹר

שֶׁבְּכָל הַלֵּילוֹת אֵין אָנוּ מַטְבִּילִין אֲפִלּוּ פַּעַם אֶחָת
הַלַּיְלָה הַזֶּה שְׁתֵּי פְעָמִים

שֶׁבְּכָל הַלֵּילוֹת אָנוּ אוֹכְלִין בֵּין יוֹשְׁבִין וּבֵין מְסֻבִּין
הַלַּיְלָה הַזֶּה כֻּלָּנוּ מְסֻבִּין

Our Personal *Avoda*: What Makes This Night Unlike All Other Nights?

Now, as the youngest child (or an older one) sings this song, take a moment and make a request. Ask for something. Ask to find favor. Ask to want to find favor. Ask for it to happen already, *tonight, tonight.*

so that every other night we eat either bread or matza,
but tonight there is only matza?

And that every other night we eat many different greens,
but tonight we will eat bitter herbs?

And that every other night we do not dip [our food] at all,
but tonight we will dip it twice?

And that every other night some sit to eat and some recline,
but tonight we are all reclining?

a Rebbe who would come knocking at the family's front door and say: "I heard your daughter's getting married; please don't attend the wedding." The moment you ask the question you open up the possibility for this to happen.

And this is what the Seder night is all about.

The question is the range of possibilities that are transformed into reality the moment the question is asked. Will we know to ask why we recline? Will we know to ask why we eat matza? Once we ask the question, the world will provide us with an answer. I told my students that they need to ask God, the Great Rebbe in the heavens above, a question like: I feel like I can't not be at my wedding this year. What do You say?

And He will nod His head toward you, because the question has been asked. It has created the possibility. The world will answer your question, because your question is symbolic of what will happen in the future. It's a "question mark" that marks the path of what will come.

And a child who has left the fold doesn't want to be asked questions that push him further away. You can simply ask, "When are you coming back?" and the potential has been created. It has been transformed into a realistic possibility.

If I Could Only Ask My Father, or: What Do You Ask When You Are Far Away?

Rabbi Shagar writes with pain that the greatest type of freedom is the ability to ask something of a father or a mother.

He subtly expresses:[123] "It isn't only the characteristics of modern times that spoil parent-child relationships. Many parents, and grandparents nowadays, lived through the horrors of the Holocaust, and this brought on their fear and lack of trust in the world. And these lead to a barrier and the inability to talk and communicate."

It is obvious that he is writing with infinite pain about the thundering silence in his childhood home.

If so, we must strive to find freedom within our home. Enough running away from our mother or father; enough avoiding the son or daughter who is stuck or struggling. Freedom can be found within your home.

Rabbi Shagar goes on to say: "What is the nature of conversation between fathers and sons? What is the nature of familyhood when innocence has been lost? It's a deep conflict, and it shapes the way culture is transmitted." And in our context, it also shapes the transmission of Torah.

He notes that "freedom is the ability to talk [and I emphasize: In the home! In the home!] with your children, with your parents. An ability that we generally aren't capable of," he writes in pain.

How can

What Makes This Night Unlike All Other Nights

An Encounter with Life's Questions and Challenges

Three small Hebrew words (five in English) precede the four famous questions: "And here the son asks." Many are inclined to skip these words, which seem largely technical. But in truth, they are so important. Don't skip them. They contain an important message, and these words are filled with deep joy.

Here – at this exact moment.

The son – this refers to you and every person gathered around the Seder table.

Asks – prays and makes a request of God.

Tonight, unlike all the other nights, is an opportune time for prayer. It is a time of heavenly compassion, when hearts are more easily opened, and prayers accepted.

Question Mark

"And here the son asks." This night is predicated on questions. Answers not included, by the way.

I was once involved in an attempt to reconcile a girl who had left the fold with her mother, who awaited her return. The mother said that she hadn't attended her daughter's wedding, which was conducted in a way that she found objectionable. When asked why, she responded: "The Rebbe said."

You need to understand something important: The Rebbe said, because he was asked. There's no such thing as that you can also make the heavens laugh? My little girl, do you want to make the heavens laugh? So listen. Difficult things will happen that will make people want to kick and rebel, because they can't go on anymore. But if you don't kick, you'll bring immense joy to the heavens.

This is the internal freedom within the family unit. Search for it. Ask about it. This is the tenth crumb of bread. In our homes, there are people who not only haven't yet been found, but nobody has ever bothered to search for them. Here, now you have the opportunity to encounter them.

What's the Answer?

The Maharal insists that the four questions don't have an answer.[125] You might think that the question is: "What makes this night unlike all other nights?" And the answer is: "That every other night...but tonight we are all reclining." Or, "tonight we will dip it twice."

No, the Maharal says. Not at all. These are questions that go unanswered.

And this is the most important part. Hold onto this big question. What's going on over here? I feel that something is different, I don't know what changed, but I feel so overwhelmed and unsettled.

This is the only way that you'll end the Seder night differently than you started it. At the end of the night, you'll be a different woman. Yesterday, you were a tired and stressed Cinderella, and suddenly, wow. What changed? What's all this royalty? Suddenly, you'll experience a moment of exhilaration.

An Incredible *Segula* for Children

Rabbi Pincus used to say that childless couples arouse compassion because they need to ask the four questions to one another. And with these three Hebrew words, "and here the son asks," they stir up an incredible amount of compassion. Shouldn't there be a little child here to ask these questions?

And God will say, just like Ḥana was told in the Tabernacle in Shilo: "May the God of Israel grant you what you have asked Him."[126] Hopefully, from now on, you'll never again need to ask these questions.

Ma Nishtana – What makes this night unlike all other nights? It's hardly incidental that we ask a young child to sing this song out loud, to stir mighty divine compassion.

How can we do this?

"The question should be raised," he says. "Who is this person, who is so close to me, and so far from me?"

Wow. Every single woman in the world has someone in her life to whom she ought to be asking this question.

"This question is asked from a detached place, but it can function as a springboard for profound and close familiarity," he concludes.

In these words, I detect an actual sense of mourning. Why didn't I ask my father and mother why they were distant? Meaning, we didn't raise other questions, so why didn't I ask this question that's almost external, almost detached, almost unrelated, but really expresses deep longing for connection?

"How can it be that the people who are closest to me are the ones who are the most distant?" We must ask ourselves this question.

I know young people who suddenly burst out and say: "There's no communication in this house! Why don't we communicate? Why don't we speak?" Yes, this should be asked.

For me, every Seder night fills me with deep longing for my father, *z"l*. If only I could ask my father questions today. I would ask him so many things. In truth, I said goodbye to him with a big question. My last conversation with him, shortly before the holiday of Sukkot (and I can feel the tears welling up in my eyes again), was the last time we spoke to one another.

He asked: What are you learning now?

And I told him that I was learning that when God brings Mashiaḥ, He will give the non-Jews the mitzva of sukka and then He will bring out the sun and warm up the world, and they'll suffer from the heat and kick the sukka and leave. And God – will laugh at them, "and only on this day alone will God laugh."[124]

My father, his face contorted in pain, hardly able to fill his lungs with air, asked me perhaps four times: Why did He laugh? Why did He laugh?

These were the final words we exchanged with one another. And this question remains suspended in midair. And I have no one to ask, so I make up all kinds of answers. I can't just sit tight and hold onto the question that my father asked me.

It seems to me that my father was saying: Listen, Yemima. You love making people laugh, right? Do you know

I'm (Not) Just Asking (Anymore)

Rebbe Nahman notes that reciting these four questions is a *segula* to eradicate all the questions that one may have about the way God runs His world. With these four questions, God extricates you from all the questions in the world. All the questions, all the things you struggle to understand about the things God does – the four questions are a song that resolves your difficulties and soothes your mind.

Arousing Compassion

It's an incredibly opportune time for prayer. Rebbe Nahman explains that this is one gigantic prayer. On many occasions, you made a request, and God didn't give you what you wanted – why? Perhaps because you were undeserving. Each time that you said "I want this," the prosecuting angel stood up and said: "Objection! She doesn't deserve it based on the way she conducts herself."

The prosecuting angel just waits for you to open your mouth so he can jump. And everything remains stuck, locked. There's some kind of a decree.

The remedy is: "They can pray and superimpose their prayers on a *maamar*."[127] Everything depends on how it's said. Instead of saying "God, please, I want," you need to bypass the prosecuting angel. Meaning, tell a story. Speak! This is the Haggada – it's a story: "We were slaves to Pharaoh." God, I was certain that this year things were going to go well for me, that I would get married, that I would overcome my debt. You know how hard it is for me (use other words, too; it never hurts to make yourself a little pathetic).

Tell Him how much you're suffering. "What makes this night unlike all the other nights?" Tonight, show me a change. Make tonight different than all the other nights! Because I feel like nothing has changed, nothing. Every time that I sense salvation, it slips through my fingers. I have pined so deeply for an enriched life, for a life that isn't boring, but ultimately my life is like *maror* that I "do not dip at all." I have lost my vitality…show me a change for the better!

So here and now the son – that's you – asks, makes a request without making a formal request. If there is one moment that a father's compassion spills over toward his son, it's right now. God's compassion overflows toward His daughter as she pours out her heart! It's a powerful prayer, unlike all the others.

מחזירים את הקערה למקומה.
עורך הסדר מגלה את המצות ואומר:

עֲבָדִים הָיִינוּ

לְפַרְעֹה בְּמִצְרָיִם
וַיּוֹצִיאֵנוּ יהוה אֱלֹהֵינוּ מִשָּׁם
בְּיָד חֲזָקָה וּבִזְרוֹעַ נְטוּיָה.
וְאִלּוּ לֹא הוֹצִיא הַקָּדוֹשׁ בָּרוּךְ הוּא
אֶת אֲבוֹתֵינוּ מִמִּצְרַיִם
הֲרֵי אָנוּ וּבָנֵינוּ וּבְנֵי בָנֵינוּ
מְשֻׁעְבָּדִים הָיִינוּ לְפַרְעֹה בְּמִצְרָיִם.
וַאֲפִלּוּ כֻּלָּנוּ חֲכָמִים, כֻּלָּנוּ נְבוֹנִים,
כֻּלָּנוּ זְקֵנִים
כֻּלָּנוּ יוֹדְעִים אֶת הַתּוֹרָה
מִצְוָה עָלֵינוּ לְסַפֵּר בִּיצִיאַת מִצְרָיִם
וְכָל הַמַּרְבֶּה לְסַפֵּר בִּיצִיאַת מִצְרַיִם
הֲרֵי זֶה מְשֻׁבָּח.

The seder plate is returned to its place.
The seder leader uncovers the matzot and recites:

WE WERE SLAVES

to Pharaoh in Egypt,
and the Lord our God
brought us out of there
with a strong hand and
an outstretched arm.
And if the Holy One, blessed be He,
had not brought our fathers
out of Egypt –
then we, and our children,
and the children of our children,
would still be enslaved to
Pharaoh in Egypt.
And even were we all wise,
all intelligent, all aged and
all knowledgeable in the Torah,
still the command would be upon
us to tell of the coming out of Egypt;
and the more one tells
of the coming out of Egypt,
the more admirable it is.

ONCE,

Rabbi Eliezer
and Rabbi Yehoshua
and Rabbi Elazar ben Azaria
and Rabbi Akiva and Rabbi Tarfon
reclined [for the seder] in Benei Brak.
And they told of the Exodus from Egypt
all that night;
until their students came in and said,
"Teachers – the time for saying the
Shema of the morning has come."

Our Personal *Avoda*: An Encounter Between Teachers and Students

It's incredible to read about the *Tanna'im* who sat together in Benei Brak.

Pray that our generation will also be blessed with great leaders whom we can learn from, not just formal halakhot, but also a way of life.

After a great rabbi passes away, this is what we remember about him. After the great leaders of the generation pass away, it's the little stories that remain behind.

מַעֲשֶׂה

בְּרַבִּי אֱלִיעֶזֶר
וְרַבִּי יְהוֹשֻׁעַ
וְרַבִּי אֶלְעָזָר בֶּן עֲזַרְיָה
וְרַבִּי עֲקִיבָא וְרַבִּי טַרְפוֹן
שֶׁהָיוּ מְסֻבִּין בִּבְנֵי בְרַק
וְהָיוּ מְסַפְּרִים בִּיצִיאַת מִצְרַיִם
כָּל אוֹתוֹ הַלַּיְלָה
עַד שֶׁבָּאוּ תַלְמִידֵיהֶם וְאָמְרוּ לָהֶם
רַבּוֹתֵינוּ הִגִּיעַ זְמַן קְרִיאַת שְׁמַע שֶׁל שַׁחֲרִית.

Rabbi Elazar ben Azaria said: *Berakhot 12b*
I am almost seventy years old,
and never have I merited to find the command
to speak of the Exodus from Egypt at night –
until Ben Zoma interpreted:
It is written,
"So that you remember *Deut. 16*
the day of your Exodus from Egypt
all the days of your life."

"The days of your life" would mean in the days;
"all the days of your life" includes the nights.

But the sages say,
"The days of your life" would mean only in this world;
"all the days of your life" brings in the time of the Messiah.

אָמַר (לָהֶם) רַבִּי אֶלְעָזָר בֶּן עֲזַרְיָה ברכות יב:
הֲרֵי אֲנִי כְּבֶן שִׁבְעִים שָׁנָה
וְלֹא זָכִיתִי שֶׁתֵּאָמֵר יְצִיאַת מִצְרַיִם בַּלֵּילוֹת
עַד שֶׁדְּרָשָׁהּ בֶּן זוֹמָא
שֶׁנֶּאֱמַר
לְמַעַן תִּזְכֹּר אֶת־יוֹם צֵאתְךָ מֵאֶרֶץ מִצְרַיִם דברים טז
כֹּל יְמֵי חַיֶּיךָ:

יְמֵי חַיֶּיךָ הַיָּמִים
כֹּל יְמֵי חַיֶּיךָ הַלֵּילוֹת.

וַחֲכָמִים אוֹמְרִים
יְמֵי חַיֶּיךָ הָעוֹלָם הַזֶּה
כֹּל יְמֵי חַיֶּיךָ לְהָבִיא לִימוֹת הַמָּשִׁיחַ.

controversy, halakhic disputes fuel the fire; and worse yet, they inflame ignorance and the truth is lost.

And do you know what? Rabbi Elazar ben Azaria said: Tonight we're not going to talk about halakha. It's a tense time. Instead, let's tell our shared story. Let's remind ourselves that "we are all sons of the same man,"[129] and all of us, all the children, share the same narrative – "one who is wise, one who is wicked, one with a simple nature, and one who does not know how to ask."[130]

Let's sit together at the Seder, traditional Jews and secular Jews and learned Jews and those who are distanced and those who are close, and simply tell this incredible story. The story that connects us to one Father.[131]

Why did Yaakov's children descend to Egypt in the first place? Because, Rabbi Hayim Ephraim Zeitchik explains, some members of the nation felt they were more important, more righteous as it were, than the others. The children of Raḥel and Leah felt they were more worthy than the children of Bilha and Zilpa, the maidservants. On the Seder night, God places us all on equal footing. We're all His children now. Choose: How do you want Him to place us on equal footing? With a steamroller, God forbid? Like they did in Egypt when they made all the Jewish babies into bricks?[132] With horrifying car ramming attacks, when suddenly we're all the same? Or by appreciating one another and what each one brings to the table?[133]

We share the same story. Let's move forward toward the place that is greater than the sum of its parts, and greater than the sum of its controversies.

Men of Freedom, Men of Wealth

Meet the five freest men in the Haggada: "Rabbi Eliezer and Rabbi Yehoshua and Rabbi Elazar ben Azaria and Rabbi Akiva and Rabbi Tarfon reclined [for the Seder] in Benei Brak." Where were they? In hiding. In those days, the Romans ruled the country and decreed decrees against the Jews. Learning Torah was forbidden by the regime. Rabbi Akiva was the best-known member of the group. Soon, he would die a harsh and cruel death.

Their descriptions were posted everywhere: "Wanted Men." And they sat together at the Seder, "and they told of the Exodus from Egypt all that night." Where did this freedom come from? How did they find the strength?

This is

A Post-Controversy Encounter

Teachers and Students

Five *Tanna'im* gather around the Seder table in Benei Brak.

Not too far away, in a nearby city, another story unfolds: "Once, Rabban Gamliel and the elders reclined [for the Seder] in Lod and engaged in [the study of] the halakhot of Pesaḥ."[128]

Take note: One Seder was conducted in Benei Brak with Rabbi Tarfon, Rabbi Akiva, Rabbi Elazar, Rabbi Eliezer, and Rabbi Yehoshua, and a parallel Seder was conducted in the city of Lod, a conflict-laden city often rife with fear. Rabban Gamliel was in Lod, at the alternative Seder.

They (the five *Tanna'im*) told of the Exodus from Egypt, while he (Rabban Gamliel) was engaged in the study of the halakhot of Pesaḥ.

Rabbi Sacks brilliantly explains: Rabban Gamliel was the *nasi*, the head of the Sanhedrin! And he had a long-standing argument with Rabbi Yehoshua and Rabbi Elazar ben Azaria. They divided up to make two different Seders. He sat in Lod and learned halakha, while they sat in Benei Brak and told a story. Why?

Rabbi Sacks knew that this Seder night was beset by controversy and the *Tanna'im* remembered that the Temple was destroyed on account of baseless hatred and controversy. They saw the terrible pain that can be wrought by halakhic disputes when the nation is divided. Arguments and disputes are blessed when the nation lives in peace with one another. But when there's

We cannot allow ourselves to be women of missed opportunities. It's prohibited.

Rabbi Avraham Stav tells us:

> We live in a world that always demands authenticity, that tries to fight against the deceptive elements of reality. But on the Seder night, we are called upon to devote ourselves to a show that's entirely aware that it's a show. To recline on our left like royalty, completely aware that royals have been sitting like regular people for hundreds of years. This show began in Egypt, when the children of Israel were commanded to eat the Paschal lamb with their loins girded and sandals on their feet[137] as if they were about to leave, even though they knew they would only leave in the morning.
>
> The novelty of the Seder night is that authenticity is overrated. In make-believe there is greater potential for depth and imagination. The show that we put on is no less significant than what we do in real life each day. The ability to act things out, to detach from the here and now, actually reflects a deeper understanding of existence.
>
> Nowadays, people like to say that absolute freedom is the ability to be who I really am. But perhaps freedom is actually being the people that we haven't yet become, the people that we want to be. Perhaps real freedom means to dream.[138]

They Suddenly Became Students

The Esh Kodesh notes that the words "their students" ("until their students came in and said") refer to all the dropouts, the ones who were distanced and estranged. On that day, Rabbi Elazar ben Azaria added seven hundred benches to the study hall. On that day, Rabban Gamliel was ousted from his position as *nasi*, because he allowed only the students whose "inside was like their outside," the students who looked and acted like Torah scholars, into the study hall. He had strict standards and elitist entrance exams. And then Rabbi Elazar ben Azaria was appointed, and he let everyone in. These students arrived in the morning and announced: "Teachers – the time for saying the *Shema* of the morning has come!"

This is who they were. They were men of freedom.

When everyone else cried, Rabbi Akiva laughed.[134]

Rabbi Tarfon's elderly mother couldn't walk. He suggested to her: Mom, come. Let's make it as if you're walking. Put your right foot on my left foot, and your left foot on my right foot, and we'll walk. Do you see? You're walking, you're free![135]

Rabbi Yehoshua was an ugly man, and the Caesar's daughter struggled to understand. "Woe to glorious wisdom in an ugly vessel,"[136] she said. But Rabbi Yehoshua was undeterred. He wasn't bound by external looks.

Rabbi Eliezer and Rabbi Yehoshua argued with one another: When will Mashiaḥ come? In the month of Tishrei? In the month of Nisan? Does it really matter, one may ask. After all, they were about to die! But Rabbi Eliezer and Rabbi Yehoshua are men of incredible freedom.

This is known as *alma deḥiro*, the world of freedom.

It doesn't require much. We just need to act as if it's true. These are the keywords to the entire Seder, the greatest expression of the freedom that awaits us later on: "Generation by generation, each person must see himself – as if." Every Seder night, we perform the small motions of freedom, as if we have experienced redemption ourselves. We recline, like princes on royal thrones. We drink the four cups of wine, in affluence. We invest in aesthetics. We pretend that we are princes and princesses and choose to ignore the trivial annoyances and depressing frustrations. Imagine a different world, a world of freedom.

What's the opposite of the "as if" attitude? I always say that the most *ḥametz*-filled words are the words "if only" (*ilu*). These words are an expression of missed opportunities. "If only I would have done that instead.... If only I would have chosen a different career.... If only I would have married that guy." The "if only" attitude is decisively *ḥametz*. Like we tell the wicked son: "Had he been there (*ilu*) he would not have been redeemed." Stop being fixated on what could have been, "if only"; stop running the mistakes you've made through your mind.

Tonight, your mindset cannot be "if only." It needs to be "as if." Come to the Seder as if you have already been redeemed. Filled with joy. And recline – let go once and for all. As if everything is fine. Even if nothing is fine. You're a royal princess in a world of freedom. I already said this. And I'll say it again, and again.

Where Was God During the Disengagement from Gaza?

There is a custom to take the Seder plate from the center of the table and lift it up, and then return it to its proper place. Rabbi Mutzafi notes that his father, the great Rabbi Salman Mutzafi, would "stand up from his place like a lion, raise the Seder plate high and say: 'We must take away the Seder plate after the Seder begins, so the children will ask.'"[140]

The Hebrew word for "Seder plate" (*ke'ara*) and the Hebrew verb "to remove" (*laakor*) share a similar root. Rabbi Mutzafi explains: "This is an allusion, because the key to livelihood is in the hands of the Holy One, blessed be He. And on the Seder night, livelihood comes down to the world, because on this night the treasuries of dew will be opened (the next day, we will begin to recite 'He who causes dew to descend'[141])." And we want to "illustrate that, God forbid, He could remove from man his food source in an instant, and therefore we remove the Seder plate and put it down [immediately], because on this night man's livelihood is decreed, and God can change everything in an instant."[142]

The Hebrew word for Seder plate derives from the same letters as the Hebrew word for removing and uprooting; in an instant God can uproot man's livelihood. And we have been uprooted from so many things this past year. People were uprooted from their jobs, from their relationships, from their sense of security, from the health they used to enjoy.

Removing the Seder plate from the table marks the first stage of the story.

The next stage is bringing it back. Reinstating it in all its former glory.

This is the story of faith on the Seder night.

"Where

Such light. How did they become so righteous overnight?

"Their students came" – the Esh Kodesh explains that they achieved their stature overnight. These students achieved the same stature as their teachers. They were even able to teach them halakhot. This is the power of this night, a night of growing by leaps and bounds with great love.

Yemima, my family is the antithesis of spiritual. It's hard for me.

Don't lose patience with relatives who aren't on your level. Tonight, people skip to higher levels. It's a night that's all about skipping.

On the Seder night we're all together. Because this night is all about love. You should know that tonight we're traveling toward love. Take everything you have and go toward the One who loves you. We're traveling now to see love with our own eyes. And, at the end of the Seder night, anyone who doesn't feel "Wow. God loves me so much," has not fulfilled his obligation.[139]

They say something incredible. Where should we place the emphasis – on "the days of your life" – in the days? Or on "all the days of your life" – the nights? No. The story encompasses far more than this. "All the days of your life" – look at the bigger picture – brings in the time of the Mashiaḥ.

It's not incidental that we are told that "they told of the Exodus from Egypt." What is storytelling? It's the ability to move beyond the pain, suffering, and danger that surrounds you and go to a completely different place. In essence, the ability to tell yourself a story is redemption. It's curative. A person who constantly bemoans his pain won't get better. You need to step out into a different story, liberate yourself from the illness that causes pain and hurt, because the story is so much greater. So, so much greater.

You might think that a story is just a fantasy, an irrelevant parable, a myth. But a story is something that's active, it's an act taking place in the world. When we tell the story of the Exodus from Egypt on the Seder night, something happens. You might not think it's connected to anything else, but it's an action that actively redeems you. And on this night of redemption our souls are sick, very sick. There isn't a person in the world who comes to the Seder night without emotional pain. What's the cure? Tell a story: Once there were plagues. "And this is what has stood by our ancestors and us." And this and this happened. And once Rabbi Eliezer and Rabbi Yehoshua and Rabbi Elazar ben Azaria and Rabbi Akiva and Rabbi Tarfon reclined [for the Seder].

Dad, are you also stuck in place? Stuck in the moment that your child uprooted himself? Enough, He shall reconcile parents with children. Continue to answer their questions, as best as you can. And the end of the verse is especially precious: "and children with their parents."

We have stopped believing that we have the ability to educate our children. We have begun to believe that everything that happens around us – the cell phones, the devices, the content – is stronger than what a parent has to say. But this isn't true. It's simply incorrect.

Sometimes I feel jealous of the women in Egypt. They completely trusted their motherhood! And don't think for a moment that it was easy for them. After all, in Egypt the father would ask, rather appropriately: "How do you intend to educate him here, in this shameful land?" And the mother would answer: "I'll know what to do. I'll know how to endow this little boy or girl with trust and faith in their ability to uproot themselves and return home."

So...*tell them*. Tell them this story and the story of their own lives.

Don't deny the very core of belief.

"And the principle and the main point is that he should not become frightened at all."[144]

And the main point is that "there is no despair in the world at all."[145]

The main point is to wait for the end of the story. Because just like things can suddenly take a turn for the worse, God can restore everything. Don't you see, children? The Seder plate has also returned to its proper place.

This is one of the core principles of faith.

And we must believe in our capacity to function as mothers and fathers. It's so important.

"We were slaves to Pharaoh in Egypt." It's true, we were! For a really long time! It seemed completely hopeless, because no slave had ever gone free from Egypt. A slave would remain a slave forever.

And what happened? "The Lord our God brought us out of there." It turns out that it's possible to go free. It's feasible.

This line

"Where was God during the disengagement?" the children ask. With their own eyes they watched the destruction of the settlements of Gush Katif. Does their question express denial of the very core of our beliefs? Certainly not. To the contrary, we lift the Seder plate *so the children will ask*. These questions are warranted and wanted.

But we want to tell the children: Don't get stuck there. Don't get stuck early on in the Seder, when the Seder plate is removed from the table. There is no hope for redemption *there*. To stay *there* is to miss the most important part; to stay *there* is to set yourself apart from "the main thing," and "the main thing is to have no fear at all" – because the Seder plate will soon return to its proper place.

I receive countless emails, more than ever before, from parents who tell me, "My teenagers. The ones who are coming of age in such difficult years. They're not interested anymore. They've become so distant. Covid robbed them of their place and the official rites of passage, synagogue, day school, high school. It uprooted them from their place. What should I do? I desperately want them to be believing Jews." This is the desperate cry of fathers and mothers.

The Seder night comes precisely at this point. The Ḥatam Sofer writes in his sermon for the Shabbat preceding Pesaḥ: "And even though during the entire year, the father's words will not permeate the son's ears, there's a special *segula* for this night, and the words will penetrate the son's heart."

Faith in the Seder night is not demanded of the son. He himself has been uprooted from the core of what once filled his life. The faith needs to be *yours,* the mother's and the father's. Believe in the faith inside him. *We believe only if we are the children of believers,* the children of parents who believe that we're okay. And asking questions does not *deny* the very core of our beliefs, it *is* the core of our belief! We remove the Seder plate so the children will ask.

We need trust and faith in our capacity to speak with them on this night and say to them: "Extricate yourself from there. Had he been there, he would not have been redeemed. And it's true. Terrible things happened and I cannot understand why they happened or explain them to you. But I ask of you, extricate yourself from there. Come with me tonight to a different place, to *alma deḥiro,* the world of freedom. Believe that the Seder plate can reassume its proper place. Why allow yourself to get stuck in the moment that it's removed from the table? Let's talk about it."

It's terrible. We don't trust our capacity to restore their faith! For this reason, the *haftara* that we read on the Shabbat preceding Pesaḥ tells us something incredible: "He shall reconcile parents with children."[143] Mom and

This line takes us back to the beginning of the Haggada: "In the beginning our ancestors were idol worshippers." It's true; they were. But now? "But now the Omnipresent has drawn us close to His service." Why do we use the words "but now" to refer to an event that took place three thousand years ago?

Rabbi Wolbe explains: "Each person needs to understand that now, at midnight on the Seder night, the Holy One, blessed be He, actually takes each of us by the hand and draws us close to our redemption."[146]

Each person needs to think that he will be redeemed on *this* Seder night. You need to think to yourself: "There's not a chance that I'll end this night the way I started it." And it's happening now. Right now! How? In a way that defies logic, by leaps and bounds. God draws us close to our redemption; your Father will come to your home. Not over the phone. Not via email. Your Father Himself, He and no other.

Rabbi Wolbe brilliantly explains that the day will come when the media will have extraordinary powers. Everyone will believe what's said in the news, even when it's highly inconceivable and incorrect (and he wrote this back in the day when people still played records on gramophones).

And what happens on the Seder night? "The more one tells of the coming out of Egypt, the more admirable it is." On the Seder night, millions of people all over the world tell the same version of the same story. It's true that the media influences people's choices and constantly redefines and engineers the way people think. But on the Seder night, the entire nation tells the exact same story, and this night is infinitely more powerful.[147]

We say: Things were really bad, we were in trouble, enslaved, and You loved us even though we weren't worthy. You punished all our enemies and took us out and gifted us great treasures. "Pesaḥ, matza, *maror*!"

These words are viral. And when they're said by millions of mouths, they have a profound impact on the world, far more than any algorithm.

Our Personal *Avoda*: We Were Slaves

As we recite "We were slaves," pray that we should know how to tell this shared story to all parts of our nation. That we should know how to bequeath it to our children. That this story should be greater than the sum of all our controversies.

הַמָּקוֹם

BLESSED
is the Omnipresent –

הוּא

BLESSED
is He.

שֶׁנָּתַן תּוֹרָה
לְעַמּוֹ יִשְׂרָאֵל

BLESSED
is the One
who gave His people
Israel the Torah –

הוּא

BLESSED
is He.

Our Personal *Avoda*: Blessed Is the Omnipresent, Blessed Is He

God gave us an incredible gift: "Blessed is the One Who gave His people Israel the Torah."

But He also gave us another incredible gift, a gift that the Haggada immediately proceeds to discuss:

The gift of bringing children into the world.

Pray that each gift should be graciously accepted by the other.

That the two gifts will be each other's blessing.

That the two gifts will embrace each other, and never reject each other.

That each gift will be the other's gift.

The Torah relates
to four types of sons

one
who is wise,

one
who is wicked,

one
with a simple nature,

and one

who does not know how to ask.

כְּנֶגֶד
אַרְבָּעָה בָנִים דִּבְּרָה תוֹרָה

אֶחָד
חָכָם
וְאֶחָד
רָשָׁע
וְאֶחָד
תָּם

וְאֶחָד
שֶׁאֵינוֹ יוֹדֵעַ לִשְׁאֹל

The WISE SON

מַה הוּא אוֹמֵר

דברים ו מָה הָעֵדֹת וְהַחֻקִּים וְהַמִּשְׁפָּטִים

אֲשֶׁר צִוָּה יהוה אֱלֹהֵינוּ אֶתְכֶם:

וְאַף אַתָּה אֱמָר לוֹ

כְּהִלְכוֹת הַפֶּסַח

פסחים קיט: אֵין מַפְטִירִין אַחַר הַפֶּסַח

אֲפִיקוֹמָן.

what does he say?

"What are the testimonies, *Deut. 6*

the statutes and laws,

that the LORD our God commanded you?"

And you must tell him the *Pesaḥim 119b*

laws of Pesaḥ:

"After eating the Pesaḥ offering

one does not eat anything more."

רָשָׁע

מַה הוּא אוֹמֵר
שמות יב מָה הָעֲבֹדָה הַזֹּאת לָכֶם:

לָכֶם וְלֹא לוֹ
וּלְפִי שֶׁהוֹצִיא אֶת עַצְמוֹ
מִן הַכְּלָל
כָּפַר בָּעִקָּר
וְאַף אַתָּה הַקְהֵה אֶת שִׁנָּיו,
וֶאֱמָר לוֹ
שמות יג בַּעֲבוּר זֶה עָשָׂה יהוה
לִי בְּצֵאתִי מִמִּצְרָיִם:
לִי וְלֹא לוֹ
אִלּוּ הָיָה שָׁם, לֹא הָיָה נִגְאָל.

The WICKED SON

what does he say?
"What is this service to you?" *Ex. 12*

"To you," he says, not to him.
When he sets himself apart
from the community,
he denies the very core
of our beliefs.
And you must set his teeth
on edge and tell him,
"Because of this *Ex. 13*
the Lord acted for me
when I came out of Egypt."
"For me," and not for him;
had he been there he would not
have been redeemed.

מַה הוּא אוֹמֵר
מַה־זֹּאת
וְאָמַרְתָּ אֵלָיו
בְּחֹזֶק יָד הוֹצִיאָנוּ יהוה שמות יג
מִמִּצְרַיִם מִבֵּית עֲבָדִים:

The SIMPLE-NATURED SON

what does he say?
"What is this?" Ex. 13
And you must tell him,
"With a strong hand the Lord Ibid.
brought us out of Egypt,
from the grip of slavery."

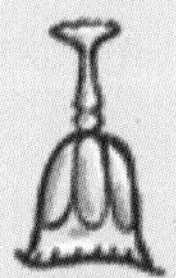

וְשֶׁאֵינוֹ יוֹדֵעַ לִשְׁאֹל

אַתְּ פְּתַח לוֹ
שֶׁנֶּאֱמַר
שמות יג וְהִגַּדְתָּ לְבִנְךָ בַּיּוֹם הַהוּא לֵאמֹר
בַּעֲבוּר זֶה עָשָׂה יהוה לִי
בְּצֵאתִי מִמִּצְרָיִם:

And the ONE WHO DOES NOT KNOW HOW TO ASK

you must open [the story] for him, as it is said:
"And you shall tell your child on that day, Ex. 13
'Because of this the LORD acted for me
when I came out of Egypt.'"

continued in this manner until he stopped [his son] from going. The son returned to his studies, but he felt this lack again. This time too he sought advice from the same friends, and again they advised him to visit the *tzaddik*. Again, he went to his father, and his father dissuaded him and prevented him from going. This happened a number of times. The son continued to feel this lack, and desperately wanted to fill it, and he didn't know what it was. Again, he went to his father, and kept urging him until his father was forced to go with him, because he didn't want him to travel alone, since he was an only son.

"See!" his father said to him. "I'm even going with you, and I'll show you that there is nothing to this man." They harnessed [the horses to] the carriage and set off. His father said to him: "I will make a test: If everything goes smoothly, then it's from Heaven. If not – it's not from Heaven, and we'll return home."

They began to travel until the father and son came to a small bridge. One of the horses fell, the carriage overturned, and they almost drowned. The father said to him, "You see. It's not going smoothly for us. This journey is not approved by Heaven." With that, they returned home.

The son returned to his studies, but the feeling that he was missing something, even though he couldn't pinpoint what it was, returned. He urged his father, and his father was forced to go with him a second time.... While they were traveling, both of the carriage's axles broke. The father said to his son, "You see, we're being directed not to continue. Is it natural for both axles to break at the same time? We've traveled in this carriage many times, and nothing like this has ever happened." And so, they returned home.

And again, the son felt a terrible sense of lack. And he went to his father and urged him again, and again they set out to go to the *tzaddik*, and again there were obstacles and challenges along the way.

And the son died, and he came to his father, the rabbi, in a dream, and he [the father] saw that he [the son] was very angry. He [the father] asked him: "Why are you so angry?" And he [the son] replied: "Go to the *tzaddik* [that he wanted to visit with his son], and he will tell you why I'm so angry."

The dream repeated itself three times until the father understood that it was significant and set out [toward the *tzaddik*]. On the way, he met the merchant he had encountered on one of his previous trips with his son. He recognized him and said: "Aren't you the one that

I met

The Four Sons

An Encounter Between Parents and Children

We can't talk about an encounter between parents and children without Rebbe Nahman.

The Tales of Rebbe Nahman:

The Rabbi's Son

Once there was a rabbi who didn't have any children. Finally, he had an only son and he raised him and married him off, and he [the son] would sit in an upstairs room and learn, as was customary among the wealthy. He would constantly study and pray. However, he felt that something was lacking, though he didn't know what. Somehow, he didn't feel any inspiration in his learning and his prayer. When he confided this to two of his friends, they advised him to go and see a certain *tzaddik*. And this young man did a mitzva that caused him to become an aspect of Lesser Light.

The only son went and told his father that he didn't feel any inspiration in his religious devotion, and since he felt a lack and didn't know what it was, he wanted to visit this *tzaddik*. "Why should you go to him?" replied the father. "You're a more accomplished scholar than him. Your family background is better than his. It isn't fitting that you go to him. Give up this idea!" He [the father]

And the commandment: "Anyone who does not say *these* three things on Pesaḥ…"

This matza!

This maror!

This night. This night!

We run circles around this identity, this enigmatic identity.

And this is *the* encounter of the night. We encounter this wife and this husband and this child and this nation and this faith. On the Seder night, we slowly compose our identity.

The Peri Tzedek notes: When parents give up on their child, they bring him to the elders of the city and say, "*This* son of ours is disloyal and defiant." How did this come to be? The answer: Because he does not heed his father and mother"[149] on the Seder night, when they say "this *maror*, this matza."

This son of ours does not heed; we never sat down with him one-on-one and carefully discussed his identity with him, where he was at, and what he struggled with, and what he could accomplish. Nobody sat with him and showed him: Pesaḥ, matza, *maror*.

A wayward son – What does the Hebrew word for "wayward" (*moreh*) mean? Rebbe Nahman explains: He is in a place of flux. He exchanges good for bad. His identity is ambiguous.

And what happens to him – "He sets himself apart from the community." His personal hurt causes him so much pain.

Kids Equal Pain

Let's try and understand "this."

First and foremost, it's a statement: Parents must make themselves relevant! It's not "that *maror*," "that matza," "that Pesaḥ." No. It's "this *maror*," "this matza." It's here and now. It's real. Through which experiences did you encounter *maror* this past year? When did you encounter the matza (the struggle against bitterness and difficulty)? When things were tough and you were all alone, or when you were sick? And, to your mind, what type of "Pesaḥ," redemption, did this year give you?

Defining

I met in the inn?"

"You certainly did see me," the other replied. Then he opened his mouth and said to him: "If you want, I'll swallow you."

"What are you saying?" he [the father] asked.

"Do you remember," replied the merchant, "when you traveled with your son, and at first the horses slipped on the bridge, and you returned home, and then the axles broke, and then you met me, and I told you that he [the *tzaddik*] was worthless? Since I caused him, your son, to die, you may now make the trip. [This is] because he was an aspect of the Lesser Light, and the *tzaddik* was an aspect of the Great Light, and if the two had come together, Mashiaḥ would have come; but now that I caused him to die, you may make the trip."

As he spoke, he vanished, and he [the father] did not have anyone with whom to speak. And the rabbi traveled to the *tzaddik* and cried out: "Woe! Woe! Woe is to those who are lost and can no longer be found!"

May God return our lost ones. Amen.[148]

The title of this story in and of itself begs an important question: Why is this story called "The Rabbi's Son"? It's a story about a father and his son! De facto, this is a very common parenting mistake. There needs to be a father and a son. One must never be a rabbi to his child, before he is a father to him.

As for the son – why can't your father be your Great Light, even just a little? When will you encounter him for real? Will you wait, God forbid, for one of you to die, to really encounter one another?

This Identity, This Encounter, This Night

I'm not familiar with another text that uses the word "this" and approaches the question of identity as frequently as the Haggada:

"What is *this* service to you?" the wicked son asks.

"Because of *this*," we answer him.

The simple-natured son asks: "What is *this*?"

It hurts! Kids equal pain.

And once we have recognized the pain of the parents, we can tell them: Embrace them. Tolerate them now.

This is so important to me. And with extraordinary caution and care, accept them.

Why? Because he's in pain. And she's in pain. So let's talk to one another, let's encounter one another.

And we need to understand that "he wasn't born like this, so take responsibility." It's not the mother who's at fault; it's the midwife.

Let's discuss one of Rebbe Nahman's most potent stories, "The Story of the Son of the King and the Son of the Maidservant Who Switched Places." This is actually a reference to us.

The Tales of Rebbe Nahman:

The Exchanged Children

What's the hot-button topic that challenges this generation? Questions of identity: Who am I? What am I? Why did I come here and where am I going? Where am I in the world? Because maps and Waze are useless if you don't know where you are.

> Once there was a king who had a maidservant to serve the queen in the palace. The time came for the queen to give birth. The maidservant also gave birth at the same time.
>
> And the midwife switched the babies.

This has happened to all of us. In this generation, everyone has replacement parts. And you can't even remember if you're the daughter of a king or the daughter of a maidservant.

The king's son grew up and people would always whisper around him: You were switched. You were exchanged. He's no longer certain if he's the son of the king or a servant. He gets into drinking and starts visiting brothels, God forbid. He starts running after animals. And he's not even sure if he's chasing someone, or running away from someone.

This is

Defining these three things define our Jewish identity. **Anyone who does not say these three things on Pesaḥ has not fulfilled his obligation.**

Maror refers to a directive that a person cannot uphold. – something that defies the Torah or basic morality and is beyond our physical strength and emotional wherewithal. This is the definition of *maror*.

As a case in point, our Sages explain that in Egypt tasks usually performed by men were assigned to the women, and tasks usually performed by women were assigned to the men. There was a deliberate blurring of identity.

Matza is man's ability to struggle against evil. It's an intermediate stage. It won't be perfect, we'll always miss something, but we'll demonstrate some capacity to fight against evil. And the matza is expressed by an act that is distinctly mine. So, it won't be an incredible bread, and it won't be as extravagant as I may have liked, but it's mine. It marks the very best that I can do right now, this matza. And I love it. At this point in time, this is what I can do in order to escape this great suffering. And it's a lot, because it's mine. The very things that they sought to take away from me – my body is not my own. My soul is ruled by a foreign power. That's it, no more. Perhaps it's thin and crumbly and brittle, but it belongs to me.

Pesaḥ – the significance of the redemption is closeness, "He has neither relative nor redeemer."[150] "Come near to me and redeem me."[151] Pesaḥ is an encounter. On Pesaḥ we will be a "group," as per the Torah's requirement for the Paschal lamb to be eaten in a group setting. Again, the question that hovers over the entire night is: Will we have an encounter? Will we be brave enough to facilitate this encounter?

Will we really encounter our children?

Nobody said it would be easy. The Haggada says something very important here: **The Torah relates to four types of sons. One who is wicked.** There is such a thing. And please, there is something almost violent in always saying: "Accept. Embrace. Tolerate. Hold on tight." Sometimes, it's hard. Sometimes, kids cause us pain, a lot of pain. And if we are told that "the existence of wayward children in a person's home is more troublesome than the war of Gog and Magog,"[152] let's not be demagogues right now. Don't fly the flag that is sometimes so harsh, that insists, "It's your son, it's your daughter" (and I admit that I'm the first one to fly this flag). Don't fly it only when you speak about the child's pain. The parents are also hurting. A lot!

And for this reason, it's heroic to sit with him, and talk to him, and answer him, and attempt to set his teeth on edge, to dull the sting somewhat – not in order to take revenge, but in order to protect ourselves from pain, because sometimes we have been stung. And it hurts. And you can say this, because the Haggada itself bravely says it. So please say it too: It hurts! Children cause pain.

One day, after going down such a dreadful path, this child will discover that he knows how to lift roses from the floor. He'll realize that he knows how to conduct a Seder himself, when he's on a trek in the middle of India with a bunch of new friends. Wait a second, how do you know how to do this? You planted this song within me, Mom and Dad. I know how to conduct this holiday, more or less. I'm connected. I'm beloved. It seems that this guy, my father, loves me. Apparently, this woman, my mother, knows what she's doing.

When the king's son realizes his true identity at the end of the story, he doesn't say, "Finally, I know who I am." He says: "Now I understand whose son I am." It's a powerful tribute to the empty chair in his life, his father's chair, his mother's chair.

Speak to your children. *You must open the story for him*. Get them to talk. The Seder table is the place for this to happen. Their hearts are open, and you can do it. Most importantly, teach them that things happen one stage at a time. There's *maror*, children. And after the *maror* comes the struggle, which is symbolized by the matza. And eventually Pesaḥ, the redemption, will come. It always does.

It's a brilliant move by the Sages. The entire digital world of gaming is based on "I finished level X! Yes! I made it to the next level!" Apparently, it's not that this generation is impatient and doesn't have it in them to wait. The point is that the next stage needs to be beautiful and interesting enough. Speak to your kids. They understand that things progress stage by stage.

When the Suffering Reaches a Crescendo

This boy "sets himself apart from the community." And this girl too. They can't take it anymore. No one is immune to this.

And the Haggada asks of us: Remember that your story isn't the be-all and end-all. Remember that you're part of a much bigger story. Don't set yourself apart from the community. "When he sets himself apart from the community, he denies the very core of our beliefs." Which "core" does this refer to? The core belief that *the main thing is to have no fear at all*. If your vantage point is limited to your own life, how can you *not* be afraid?

Escape your own story. Connect to the community, forcefully. On the Seder night, pray for big things: Redemption! Mashiaḥ! When you're part of the greater story, then "in your blood, live."

Big prayers are so important on this night. We need you.

A Prayer

This is the enigma of the story of the king's son and the maidservant's son who were switched. Our identities have become blurred. Kids grow up without a clear religious identity, and even without a clear gender identity. The terrible distress in Rebbe Nahman's story revolves around the eternal question that I carry inside: Am I living a double life? Is my religiosity authentic? Is my femininity authentic? Is my Judaism authentic? Is my motherhood authentic? Or am I just a stranger?

At the end of this twisted and winding and incredible story, there's a test. Because everyone keeps saying that he's really a prince. And here's the test:

> They took him to the house and showed him the throne. And he saw that it was extremely tall. As he contemplated the throne, he realized it was made of the same type of wood as the box. He gazed further and he saw that a rose was missing from the top of the throne. If the rose was on the throne, then the throne, would have the same power as the box [which could produce music whenever it was placed on any kind of beast or animal or bird]. Then he gazed even more and noticed that the rose missing from the top of the throne was lying at the bottom of the throne, and it had to be taken and placed on the top and then the throne would have the same power as the box. [He then saw that] the same was true of the bed. It had to be moved somewhat from the place where it stood. The table also had to be moved somewhat, and the lamp likewise had to have its position adjusted. The birds and the beasts also had to be moved to different places. For the king had very cleverly disguised everything so that only a very wise person would be able to contemplate it and then rearrange it correctly.

The importance of arranging things in proper order (*seder*) appears again! This is something that we discussed at the beginning of the Haggada, and we again encounter this structure, which is so necessary. The holiday of Pesaḥ will slowly sharpen our identity.

> The king's real son gave instructions for everything to be rearranged properly, to take the rose from the bottom and insert it on top, and everything else was also rearranged in proper order, and then everything began to sing a very wonderful melody, and he was then given the kingdom. The king's real son, who had now been crowned king, then said to the maidservant's son: Now I understand that I am really the son of the king, and you are really the son of the maidservant![153]

One

Every word in the Haggada has the power to purge. Each word restores the world to its primal state, to a state of neat alignment.

It is instructive to note that the word "one" plays a central role on the Seder night. "The Torah relates to four types of sons: *One* who is wise, *one* who is wicked, *one* with a simple nature, and *one* who does not know how to ask."

The Rebbe of Rozhin explains that if there is a wicked son (there isn't; but the kid who's giving you the most heartache), you should think about him when you say the word "one." When he asks in his brilliance: "What are the testimonies? The statutes? And the laws?" It all seems like a muddle. Can you explain what's going on?[155] You should offer him some relief: One. One. The entire story is one story. And you know what? You're also one child, with many different facets. It's not that you're wicked, or simple-natured. At times you are wise, and at times you don't even know how to ask...and it's all one. It's all part of the same big story. Just wait; we'll make it through, and it's good that you're asking, because questions bespeak freedom.

The strongest one doesn't always survive. It's "one little goat, one little goat," the very same goat from beginning to end. Don't let the cat and the dog and the water and the fire and even the slaughterer confuse you. And when it seems like so many things are happening, each one progressively worse, each one increasingly frightening, remember that it's one story; "Who knows one? I know one: Hear O Israel, the Lord our God is *One*."

A Prayer for the Children

Everything that you do tonight is part of "and you shall tell your child." It's for your children, even the children who are yet unborn, and also for yourself.

Rabbi Elimelekh Biderman shares with us a prayer for the children:

> Now is the time to ask on behalf of the children. It is possible to accomplish and draw forth wonderful things for them: that the children should have aid and assistance to be preserved in holiness and purity. That they merit to fight, struggle, and overcome all the difficulties and tests of the fiftieth gate of the period before the arrival of Mashiaḥ. That the [blessing] "You, O Lord, protect them" will be fulfilled for them, that they should be preserved in spirituality and physicality, the sons and the daughters, and they should succeed in total perfection in all matters.

The homes we grew up in didn't equip us with the tools we need to understand the challenges that confront the generation we're raising. For me, the significance of *leil shimurim*, "a night of protection," is: "You, O Lord, protect those from this generation forever."[154] On this night of protection, I beseech the ultimate Guard to protect our children from the things we don't even know about, those things that our children don't know you need to avoid.

Mekhilta, Masekhet Pesaḥ, parasha 17

And you shall tell your child
One might have thought
this meant from the beginning of the month.
And so it says, "on that day."
Had it said only "on that day,"
one might have thought [the obligation] applied during the day.
And so it also says, "Because of this" –
"because of this" can only be said
when matza and bitter herbs are there before you.

IN THE BEGINNING,
our ancestors were idol worshippers.

BUT NOW
the Omnipresent has drawn us close
in His service;

מכילתא
מסכתא דפסחא
פרשה יז

וְהִגַּדְתָּ לְבִנְךָ יָכוֹל מֵרֹאשׁ חֹדֶשׁ
תַּלְמוּד לוֹמַר: בַּיּוֹם הַהוּא
אִי בַּיּוֹם הַהוּא יָכוֹל מִבְּעוֹד יוֹם
תַּלְמוּד לוֹמַר: בַּעֲבוּר זֶה
בַּעֲבוּר זֶה לֹא אָמַרְתִּי
אֶלָּא בְּשָׁעָה שֶׁיֵּשׁ מַצָּה וּמָרוֹר מֻנָּחִים לְפָנֶיךָ.

מִתְּחִלָּה

עוֹבְדֵי עֲבוֹדָה זָרָה הָיוּ אֲבוֹתֵינוּ

וְעַכְשָׁו

קֵרְבָנוּ הַמָּקוֹם לַעֲבוֹדָתוֹ

as it is said:

"Yehoshua said to all the people, *Josh. 24*
'This is what the Lord God of Israel has said:
Beyond the river your ancestors always dwelled –
Teraḥ the father of Avraham, the father of Naḥor –
and they served other gods.
But I took your father Avraham from beyond the river,
and I led him all the way across the land of Canaan,
and I multiplied his offspring and gave him Yitzḥak.
And to Yitzḥak I gave Yaakov and Esav,
and I gave Esav Mount Seir as an inheritance,
**WHILE YAAKOV AND HIS CHILDREN
WENT DOWN TO EGYPT.'"**

Our Personal *Avoda*: From Disgrace to Glory

The Mishna teaches us: "He begins with [the Jewish people's] disgrace and ends with [their] glory."[156] Ask for the disgraceful things in your life to be transformed into incredible glory. That the "night [shall be] as light as day.[157]"

שֶׁנֶּאֱמַר

יהושע כד

וַיֹּאמֶר יְהוֹשֻׁעַ אֶל־כָּל־הָעָם
כֹּה־אָמַר יהוה אֱלֹהֵי יִשְׂרָאֵל
בְּעֵבֶר הַנָּהָר יָשְׁבוּ אֲבוֹתֵיכֶם מֵעוֹלָם
תֶּרַח אֲבִי אַבְרָהָם וַאֲבִי נָחוֹר
וַיַּעַבְדוּ אֱלֹהִים אֲחֵרִים:
וָאֶקַּח אֶת־אֲבִיכֶם אֶת־אַבְרָהָם מֵעֵבֶר הַנָּהָר
וָאוֹלֵךְ אוֹתוֹ בְּכָל־אֶרֶץ כְּנָעַן
וָאַרְבֶּ אֶת־זַרְעוֹ, וָאֶתֶּן־לוֹ אֶת־יִצְחָק:
וָאֶתֵּן לְיִצְחָק אֶת־יַעֲקֹב וְאֶת־עֵשָׂו
וָאֶתֵּן לְעֵשָׂו אֶת־הַר שֵׂעִיר לָרֶשֶׁת אוֹתוֹ

וְיַעֲקֹב וּבָנָיו יָרְדוּ מִצְרָיִם:

BLESSED IS THE ONE WHO HAS KEPT HIS PROMISE TO ISRAEL

blessed is He.
For the Holy One calculated the end
and fulfilled what He had spoken
to our father Avraham
in the Covenant between the Pieces.
As it is said:
"He said to Avram, Gen. 15
'Know that your descendants
will be strangers in a land not their own,
and they will be enslaved
and oppressed for four hundred years;
but know that I shall judge the nation that enslaves them,

AND THEN THEY WILL LEAVE
WITH GREAT WEALTH.'"

Our Personal *Avoda*: Blessed Is the One Who Has Kept His Promise

"Blessed is the One Who has kept His promise to Israel, blessed is He" – on occasion, our belief in God's capacity to keep promises is undermined.

Ask to remember that God will yet endow us with incredible goodness.

"God is not human to be capricious."[158]

בָּרוּךְ שׁוֹמֵר הַבְטָחָתוֹ לְיִשְׂרָאֵל

בָּרוּךְ הוּא.

שֶׁהַקָּדוֹשׁ בָּרוּךְ הוּא חִשַּׁב אֶת הַקֵּץ

לַעֲשׂוֹת כְּמָה שֶׁאָמַר לְאַבְרָהָם אָבִינוּ

בִּבְרִית בֵּין הַבְּתָרִים

שֶׁנֶּאֱמַר

בראשית טו

וַיֹּאמֶר לְאַבְרָם יָדֹעַ תֵּדַע

כִּי־גֵר יִהְיֶה זַרְעֲךָ בְּאֶרֶץ לֹא לָהֶם

וַעֲבָדוּם וְעִנּוּ אֹתָם אַרְבַּע מֵאוֹת שָׁנָה:

וְגַם אֶת־הַגּוֹי אֲשֶׁר יַעֲבֹדוּ דָּן אָנֹכִי

וְאַחֲרֵי־כֵן יֵצְאוּ בִּרְכֻשׁ גָּדוֹל:

The matzot are covered, the wine cup is raised, and the following is said:

AND THIS

[promise] is what has stood
by our ancestors and us;
for it was not only one man
who rose up to destroy us:
in every single generation
people rise up to destroy us

BUT THE HOLY ONE, BLESSED BE HE, SAVES US FROM THEIR HANDS.

The wine cup is put down and the matzot are uncovered.

Our Personal *Avoda*: And This Is What Has Stood

Ask to be granted our forefather's ability to remain standing. "Standing means nothing other than praying."[159] "The hands are the hands of Esav"[160] but the voice, the voice of prayer, is everything. Ask now for the power to pray.

מכסה את המצות, אוחז את הכוס ואומר:

שֶׁעָמְדָה לַאֲבוֹתֵינוּ וְלָנוּ
שֶׁלֹּא אֶחָד בִּלְבָד עָמַד עָלֵינוּ לְכַלּוֹתֵנוּ
אֶלָּא שֶׁבְּכָל דּוֹר וָדוֹר
עוֹמְדִים עָלֵינוּ לְכַלּוֹתֵנוּ

וְהַקָּדוֹשׁ בָּרוּךְ הוּא
מַצִּילֵנוּ מִיָּדָם

מניח את הכוס ומגלה את המצות.

The next day, the king declared that it was against the law to employ someone to clean your stable. But that same night, the scene repeated itself, and the meal was a meal, and it was especially joyous. "I joined the army. I use my daily wages to buy meat and wine," explained the the hero of the story.

The king went and summoned the recruiting officer and instructed him not to dare pay wages to anyone that day.

The king could not understand how the table was filled with food and the house was joyous that evening. "Okay, what now?"

"I sold the blade from the army sword and used the money to buy food."

"But you're a soldier – you need a sword!"

"I'm a wood craftsman. And afterward, when I receive my daily wages, I'll redeem the blade and repair the sword. Nobody will be able to see a thing because I can repair anything that is broken, so there will be no loss to the king."

But the next day, the man's commander came forth and said, "Someone has been condemned to death. You! Come forward and chop his head off with your sword!" he said to our hero.

What could he do? His blade was made of wood! He answered,

"'Sir, I cannot bear the sight of blood, please..."

"'Come here or I'll chop your head off!"

The man saw that he could not prevail over the king, so he turned to all and proclaimed out loud: "Eternal God! Never in my life have I shed blood. If this man is not guilty, let the blade of my sword turn into wood!" He took hold of the sword and drew it from the sheath, and everyone saw that it was made of wood. Everybody laughed heartily.

And the king laughed: "Crazy guy. From now on, meat and wine every day, on the house."[161]

Faith is the challenge of our lives. "For it was not only one man who rose up to destroy us." The Jewish man in the story was also subject to a new decree each day. Like him, we need to remember that in the end, ultimately, "the Holy One saves us from their hands." This is true regarding our most formidable enemies, as well as our day-to-day challenges.

This is a tale of faith. He answered and said, I told another tale about trust and this is it:

There was once a king who thought to himself: Are there happy people in my kingdom? Who in the world has fewer worries than me? I have everything good: I am the king and the ruler.

He traveled around his kingdom and peeked into the homes. Here people were fighting, there people were yelling, here people worried.... Each and every one had his own worries.

Only in one broken-down cottage did he find an extraordinary couple. The man played the fiddle, his table was filled with wine and food, and happiness abounded in their home.

From where did you get all this? the king asked.

I fix broken things, the man answered. Then, when I've earned five or six shillings, I purchase all this food and drink for myself, and we rejoice and dance.

When the king heard this, he said to himself: I'm going to spoil this for him. The next day, there was an announcement in the land: "It is forbidden to fix broken things in our kingdom."

That night, the king once again went to the broken-down cottage and saw the table filled with fine things and a man and a woman who were very happy.

From where did you get these things? You need money to buy all of this!

He answered him, I used to repair things that were broken, but the king passed a decree prohibiting giving anything to someone else for repair. So, I chopped wood until I gathered enough money for all of this.

The king left him and decreed that nobody may give their wood to anyone else to chop.

That evening, he went again, and the man and the woman were again happy.

"Just a minute," the king asked. "What did you do now?"

"I cleaned a stable," the man answered. "That was the job I found for myself today and I purchased all of this with the money that I earned."

GO [to the verse] AND LEARN

מַה בִּקֵּשׁ לָבָן הָאֲרַמִּי
לַעֲשׂוֹת לְיַעֲקֹב אָבִינוּ
שֶׁפַּרְעֹה לֹא גָזַר
אֶלָּא עַל הַזְּכָרִים
וְלָבָן בִּקֵּשׁ לַעֲקֹר אֶת הַכֹּל

what Lavan the Aramean
sought to do
to our father Yaakov:
Pharaoh condemned only
the boys to death,
but Lavan sought
to uproot everything,
as it is written:

Our Personal *Avoda*: Go and Learn

"Go and learn!" Pray that we do not make the mistake of relating to the Torah and its stories superficially. For this reason, every single detail of the story told by the ensuing verses is immediately backed up with a proof text.

Though we love to draw practical wisdom from the Torah, it's extremely important to be sure to stay close to what is actually stated by the text.

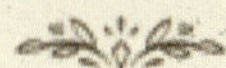

"An Aramean Sought My Father's Death, *Deut. 26*
And he went down to Egypt
and resided there,
just a handful of souls;
and there he became a nation –
large, mighty, and great."

"AND HE WENT DOWN TO EGYPT" –
Compelled by what had been spoken.

"AND RESIDED THERE" –
From this, learn that our father Yaakov went down
not to be absorbed into Egypt,
but only to reside there for a time.
As it is said:
"They said to Pharaoh, *Gen. 47*
'We have come to reside in this land,
for there is no pasture for your servants' flocks,
for the famine is heavy in the land of Canaan;
and now, if you please,
let your servants dwell in the land of Goshen.'"

שֶׁנֶּאֱמַר

אֲרַמִּי אֹבֵד אָבִי וַיֵּרֶד מִצְרַיְמָה דברים כו
וַיָּגָר שָׁם בִּמְתֵי מְעָט
וַיְהִי־שָׁם לְגוֹי גָּדוֹל עָצוּם וָרָב׃

וַיֵּרֶד מִצְרַיְמָה

אָנוּס עַל פִּי הַדִּבּוּר

וַיָּגָר שָׁם ספרי דברים פיסקא שא

מְלַמֵּד שֶׁלֹּא יָרַד יַעֲקֹב אָבִינוּ
לְהִשְׁתַּקֵּעַ בְּמִצְרַיִם, אֶלָּא לָגוּר שָׁם

שֶׁנֶּאֱמַר

וַיֹּאמְרוּ אֶל־פַּרְעֹה לָגוּר בָּאָרֶץ בָּאנוּ בראשית מז
כִּי־אֵין מִרְעֶה לַצֹּאן אֲשֶׁר לַעֲבָדֶיךָ
כִּי־כָבֵד הָרָעָב בְּאֶרֶץ כְּנָעַן
וְעַתָּה יֵשְׁבוּ־נָא עֲבָדֶיךָ בְּאֶרֶץ גֹּשֶׁן׃

"JUST A HANDFUL OF SOULS" –

As it is said:
"Your ancestors were but seventy souls *Deut. 10*
when they went down to Egypt –
and now the LORD has made you as many as the sky has stars."

"AND THERE HE BECAME A NATION" –

From this, learn that Israel was distinct there.

"LARGE, MIGHTY" –

As it is said:
"And the children of Israel were fertile, *Ex. 1*
and they swarmed,
and grew *more and more numerous*
and strong, and the land was filled with them."

בִּמְתֵי מְעָט

כְּמָה שֶׁנֶּאֱמַר

דברים י
בְּשִׁבְעִים נֶפֶשׁ יָרְדוּ אֲבֹתֶיךָ מִצְרָיְמָה

וְעַתָּה שָׂמְךָ יהוה אֱלֹהֶיךָ כְּכוֹכְבֵי הַשָּׁמַיִם לָרֹב:

וַיְהִי־שָׁם לְגוֹי

מְלַמֵּד שֶׁהָיוּ יִשְׂרָאֵל מְצֻיָּנִים שָׁם

גָּדוֹל עָצוּם

כְּמָה שֶׁנֶּאֱמַר

שמות א
וּבְנֵי יִשְׂרָאֵל פָּרוּ וַיִּשְׁרְצוּ

וַיִּרְבּוּ וַיַּעַצְמוּ בִּמְאֹד מְאֹד

וַתִּמָּלֵא הָאָרֶץ אֹתָם:

"AND GREAT" –

As it is said:
"I let you *grow wild* like meadow plants, *Ezek. 16*
and you grew and matured and came forth in all your glory,
your breasts full and your hair grown,
and you were naked and exposed."

Some add:
"And I passed by you *Ibid.*
and saw you wallowing in your own blood –
and I said to you, 'In your blood, live!'
and I said to you, 'In your blood, live!'"

"AND THE EGYPTIANS DEALT CRUELLY WITH US AND OPPRESSED US, AND IMPOSED HARD LABOR ON US." *Deut. 26*

וָרָב

כְּמָה שֶׁנֶּאֱמַר

רְבָבָה כְּצֶמַח הַשָּׂדֶה נְתַתִּיךְ יחזקאל טז

וַתִּרְבִּי וַתִּגְדְּלִי, וַתָּבֹאִי בַּעֲדִי עֲדָיִים

שָׁדַיִם נָכֹנוּ וּשְׂעָרֵךְ צִמֵּחַ, וְאַתְּ עֵרֹם וְעֶרְיָה:

יש מוסיפים:

וָאֶעֱבֹר עָלַיִךְ וָאֶרְאֵךְ מִתְבּוֹסֶסֶת בְּדָמָיִךְ.

וָאֹמַר לָךְ בְּדָמַיִךְ חֲיִי וָאֹמַר לָךְ בְּדָמַיִךְ חֲיִי:

וַיָּרֵעוּ אֹתָנוּ הַמִּצְרִים וַיְעַנּוּנוּ דברים כו

וַיִּתְּנוּ עָלֵינוּ עֲבֹדָה קָשָׁה:

The Haggada states: "And you grew and matured and came forth in all your glory, and I passed by you and I saw you wallowing in your own blood."

The actual text in the book of Ezekiel reads differently: "And I passed by you and I saw you wallowing in your own blood, and you grew and matured."[163]

Why does the Haggada invert the words? The Ari HaKadosh explains: On this night nothing is in order, because *maturity precedes childhood.*

Rabbi Soloveitchik points out: The prophet Yeḥezkel tells us about a girl who sees herself as a young child who doesn't bear any responsibility. One day, a passerby tells her that she's already a mature adult who has the potential to build a community and give of herself to others. He tells her that she is a "large and mighty nation."[164]

This description is breathtaking. In Egypt, the Jewish people suffered from low self-esteem. They didn't believe that they were worthy of freedom, that they were worthy of establishing a covenant of love. They weren't certain that a group of slaves could really earn God's love. They were ignorant and undeveloped.

This is how they came to the Seder night. And God tells them: Conduct yourselves as if you're already there. "This is how you shall eat it," the Paschal sacrifice. "Your loins girded."[165] Get dressed as if you're about to head out on a long trek. You need to pretend that redemption is already here.

"I have marked well (*rao ra'iti*) the plight of My people."[166] The double language used in this verse indicates that God sees two different pictures, one of a neglected young girl, and one of a mature woman who is extraordinarily capable.[167]

Are you willing to don the garb of a capable woman, a woman who knows that her Father favors her? Will you conduct yourself "as if" and pretend to play this role?

Rashi explains that the root word *ad* in the phrase "And came forth in all your glory" (*adi adayim*) shares the same etymological root as the phrase "Trust in the Lord forever" (*adei ad*).[168] Perhaps you don't feel like you have much reason to come forth in all your glory right now, perhaps you don't have a reason to get all dressed up, perhaps you have nothing to wait for. But conduct yourself as if you do, with the full confidence of a mature woman who is so capable.

"He Sought to Uproot Everything"

An Encounter with Those Who Rise Up to Destroy Us

Ordinarily, the phrase "those who rise up to destroy us" is explained as a reference to our physical enemies, those who hate us and want to obliterate us. In contrast to this traditional approach, some suggest that we should move away from this Diaspora mindset. We're a strong nation. We have an army!

But no, this phrase refers to the internal enemies who arise alongside us, each and every morning, to destroy us; "You can't do it," they whisper in our ears. "You won't make it. Women don't really have freedom in this world."

How can we defeat these internal enemies? "I will run from You toward You."[162] When we have doubts about faith, we turn to God. "The Holy One saves us from their hands."

Mature Woman. Capable and Talented. Can You Do it?

On the Seder night, nothing seems to go in logical order. We already spoke about *Kadesh, Urḥatz, Karpas, Yaḥatz*, but the order should really be reversed. First we wash, then we make Kiddush. *Raḥatz, UKadesh, Karpas, Yaḥatz*. Or, Pesaḥ, matza, *maror*. It shouldn't be like this. The order should be inverted! *Maror,* matza, Pesaḥ. Pesaḥ is redemption, matza is the intermediate stage, and *maror* is the great pervasive bitterness in Egypt.

Here too, the Haggada is formulated in inverse order.

"THE EGYPTIANS DEALT CRUELLY WITH US" –

As it is said:
"We must act wisely against [this people], *Ex. 1*
in case it grows great,
and when we are called to war
they may join our enemies,
fight against us,
and rise up to leave the land."

"AND OPPRESSED US" –

As it is said:
"They placed taskmasters *Ibid.*
over [the people]
to *oppress* them under their burdens;
they built store cities
for Pharaoh:
Pitom and Raamses."

וַיָּרֵעוּ אֹתָנוּ הַמִּצְרִים

כְּמָה שֶׁנֶּאֱמַר

שמות א הָבָה נִתְחַכְּמָה לוֹ, פֶּן־יִרְבֶּה
וְהָיָה כִּי־תִקְרֶאנָה מִלְחָמָה
וְנוֹסַף גַּם־הוּא עַל־שֹׂנְאֵינוּ
וְנִלְחַם־בָּנוּ וְעָלָה מִן־הָאָרֶץ:

וַיְעַנּוּנוּ

כְּמָה שֶׁנֶּאֱמַר

שמות א וַיָּשִׂימוּ עָלָיו שָׂרֵי מִסִּים
לְמַעַן עַנֹּתוֹ בְּסִבְלֹתָם
וַיִּבֶן עָרֵי מִסְכְּנוֹת לְפַרְעֹה
אֶת־פִּתֹם וְאֶת־רַעַמְסֵס:

"AND IMPOSED HARD LABOR ON US" –

As it is said:
"The Egyptians enslaved the children of Israel with *heavy labor.*" *Ex. 1*

Deut. 26

"AND WE CRIED OUT

TO THE LORD,
GOD OF OUR ANCESTORS,
AND THE LORD HEARD OUR VOICE,
AND HE SAW OUR OPPRESSION
AND OUR LABOR AND SLAVERY."

וַיִּתְּנוּ עָלֵינוּ עֲבֹדָה קָשָׁה

כְּמָה שֶׁנֶּאֱמַר

שמות א וַיַּעֲבִדוּ מִצְרַיִם אֶת־בְּנֵי יִשְׂרָאֵל בְּפָרֶךְ׃

דברים כו

אֶל־יהוה אֱלֹהֵי אֲבֹתֵינוּ

וַיִּשְׁמַע יהוה אֶת־קֹלֵנוּ

וַיַּרְא אֶת־עָנְיֵנוּ

וְאֶת־עֲמָלֵנוּ וְאֶת־לַחֲצֵנוּ׃

Our Personal *Avoda*: And We Cried Out

Try to be Breslov, just for tonight. Allow your animalistic soul to dominate for a moment. It's okay. Really soon we'll allow ourselves to be intellectual again.

In Egypt, the Jewish people worked in silence, with class. But what seemed like incredible self-control was actually an embodiment of complete subjugation.

When you cry out, your voice is heard. "And they cried out, and their plea rose to God from amid the work."[169]

Rabbi Elimelekh Biderman says that as we recite the words "and we cried out to the Lord" we should simply cry out at the top of our lungs. And think about all the pain that we're going through. He says that this practice has brought about open miracles in the form of marriages/jobs/babies who were suddenly born.

And who will yell loudest "God! Redemption! Mashiaḥ! Salvation!"? Only someone who is in great pain, someone who is empty-handed, someone who has an empty chair at her Seder table. She will remember to pray for everything.

The Rebbe of Piaseczno explains that "the one who cries out reveals a greater part of Mashiaḥ."

When you hear a woman crying out it's because she's giving birth right now, and tonight – we are giving birth to Mashiaḥ. Cry out so that it won't be a stillbirth, God forbid.

There is no greater sorrow. In Hebrew, Mashiaḥ can also be read as meisiaḥ, which literally refers to one who elicits conversation and dialogue. Stillbirth is the obstruction of speech. There's no response at all. There's no baby. Now we cry out with the cries of a woman who has just experienced a stillbirth. We pray that she will have a baby who cries.

"AND WE CRIED OUT TO THE LORD,
GOD OF OUR ANCESTORS" –

As it is said:
"It came to be, as a long time passed, *Ex. 2*
that the king of Egypt died,
and the children of Israel
groaned under the burden of work,
and they *cried out,*
and their plea rose to God from amid the work."

"AND THE LORD HEARD OUR VOICE" –

As it is said:
"And God *heard* their groans, *Ibid.*
and God remembered His covenant
with Avraham, Yitzḥak, and Yaakov."

וַנִּצְעַק אֶל־יהוה אֱלֹהֵי אֲבֹתֵינוּ

כְּמָה שֶׁנֶּאֱמַר

וַיְהִי בַיָּמִים הָרַבִּים הָהֵם שמות ב

וַיָּמָת מֶלֶךְ מִצְרַיִם

וַיֵּאָנְחוּ בְנֵי־יִשְׂרָאֵל מִן־הָעֲבֹדָה

וַיִּזְעָקוּ

וַתַּעַל שַׁוְעָתָם אֶל־הָאֱלֹהִים מִן־הָעֲבֹדָה:

וַיִּשְׁמַע יהוה אֶת־קֹלֵנוּ

כְּמָה שֶׁנֶּאֱמַר

וַיִּשְׁמַע אֱלֹהִים אֶת־נַאֲקָתָם שמות ב

וַיִּזְכֹּר אֱלֹהִים אֶת־בְּרִיתוֹ

אֶת־אַבְרָהָם אֶת־יִצְחָק וְאֶת־יַעֲקֹב:

"AND HE SAW OUR OPPRESSION" –

The separation of husband from wife,
as it is said:
"And God saw the children of Israel, *Ex. 2*
and God knew."

"AND OUR LABOR" –

[The killing of] the sons,
as it is said:
"Throw every boy who *Ex. 1*
is born into the river,
and the girls let live."

וַיַּרְא אֶת־עָנְיֵנוּ

זוֹ פְּרִישׁוּת דֶּרֶךְ אֶרֶץ

כְּמָה שֶׁנֶּאֱמַר

שמות ב וַיַּרְא אֱלֹהִים אֶת־בְּנֵי יִשְׂרָאֵל

וַיֵּדַע אֱלֹהִים:

וְאֶת־עֲמָלֵנוּ

אֵלּוּ הַבָּנִים

כְּמָה שֶׁנֶּאֱמַר

שמות א כָּל־הַבֵּן הַיִּלּוֹד,

הַיְאֹרָה תַּשְׁלִיכֻהוּ

וְכָל־הַבַּת תְּחַיּוּן:

"AND SLAVERY" –

The forced labor that was
pressed down on them,
as it is said:
"I have seen the *slavery* *Ex. 3*
that Egypt forced upon you."

"AND THE LORD BROUGHT US OUT OF EGYPT *Deut. 26*
WITH A STRONG HAND AND AN OUTSTRETCHED ARM,
IN AN AWESOME HAPPENING,
WITH SIGNS AND WITH WONDERS."

"AND THE LORD BROUGHT US OUT OF EGYPT" –

Not through an angel,
not through a seraph,
not through any emissary.
No, it was the Holy One,
His glory, His own presence.

וְאֶת־לַחֲצֵנוּ
זֶה הַדְּחַק
כְּמָה שֶׁנֶּאֱמַר
שמות ג וְגַם־רָאִיתִי אֶת־הַלַּחַץ
אֲשֶׁר מִצְרַיִם לֹחֲצִים אֹתָם:

דברים כו וַיּוֹצִאֵנוּ יהוה מִמִּצְרַיִם
בְּיָד חֲזָקָה וּבִזְרֹעַ נְטוּיָה וּבְמֹרָא גָּדֹל
וּבְאֹתוֹת וּבְמֹפְתִים:

וַיּוֹצִאֵנוּ יהוה מִמִּצְרַיִם
לֹא עַל יְדֵי מַלְאָךְ
וְלֹא עַל יְדֵי שָׂרָף
וְלֹא עַל יְדֵי שָׁלִיחַ
אֶלָּא הַקָּדוֹשׁ בָּרוּךְ הוּא בִּכְבוֹדוֹ וּבְעַצְמוֹ

As it is said:

"I shall pass through the land of Egypt *Ex. 12*
on that night;
I shall kill every firstborn son
in the land of Egypt,
man and beast,
and I shall pass judgment on all the gods of Egypt:
I am the LORD."

"I shall pass through the land of Egypt on that night"	I and no angel.
"I shall kill every firstborn son in the land of Egypt"	I and no seraph.
"And I shall pass judgment on all the gods of Egypt"	I and no emissary.
"I am the LORD"	It is I and no other.

שֶׁנֶּאֱמַר
וְעָבַרְתִּי בְאֶרֶץ־מִצְרַיִם שמות יב
בַּלַּיְלָה הַזֶּה
וְהִכֵּיתִי כָל־בְּכוֹר בְּאֶרֶץ מִצְרַיִם
מֵאָדָם וְעַד־בְּהֵמָה
וּבְכָל־אֱלֹהֵי מִצְרַיִם אֶעֱשֶׂה שְׁפָטִים
אֲנִי יהוה:

וְעָבַרְתִּי בְאֶרֶץ־מִצְרַיִם אֲנִי וְלֹא מַלְאָךְ
וְהִכֵּיתִי כָל־בְּכוֹר אֲנִי וְלֹא שָׂרָף
וּבְכָל־אֱלֹהֵי מִצְרַיִם
אֶעֱשֶׂה שְׁפָטִים אֲנִי וְלֹא הַשָּׁלִיחַ
אֲנִי יהוה אֲנִי הוּא וְלֹא אַחֵר

Our Personal *Avoda*: I Shall Pass Through the Land of Egypt

Ask that all your requests go directly to God, without passing through the angels. They didn't want us to be created, perhaps even correctly so.[170] But now we need a passing grade, and only God will agree to pass us now. He and no other.

"WITH A STRONG HAND" –

This refers to the pestilence,
as it is said:
"You shall see the *hand* of the LORD Ex. 9
among your cattle in the field,
among your horses and donkeys and camels,
in the herd and in the flock,
bringing harsh, heavy pestilence."

"AND AN OUTSTRETCHED ARM" –

This refers to the sword,
as it is said:
"And His sword 1 Chron. 21
was drawn in His hand,
stretched out over Jerusalem."

בְּיָד חֲזָקָה

זוֹ הַדֶּבֶר
כְּמָה שֶׁנֶּאֱמַר
הִנֵּה יַד־יהוה הוֹיָה בְּמִקְנְךָ אֲשֶׁר בַּשָּׂדֶה — שמות ט
בַּסּוּסִים בַּחֲמֹרִים בַּגְּמַלִּים
בַּבָּקָר וּבַצֹּאן
דֶּבֶר כָּבֵד מְאֹד:

וּבִזְרֹעַ נְטוּיָה

זוֹ הַחֶרֶב
כְּמָה שֶׁנֶּאֱמַר
וְחַרְבּוֹ שְׁלוּפָה בְּיָדוֹ — דברי הימים א׳ כא
נְטוּיָה עַל־יְרוּשָׁלָיִם

"In an awesome happening" –

This refers to the revelation of His Presence,
as it is said:
"Has any god ever tried to come *Deut. 4*
and take a nation out of the midst of another,
with trials
and with signs
and wonders,
in war
and with a strong hand,
with an outstretched arm,
inspiring *great awe,*
as the Lord your God has done all this
for you in Egypt,
before your eyes?"

וּבְמֹרָא גָּדֹל

זֶה גִּלּוּי שְׁכִינָה
כְּמָה שֶׁנֶּאֱמַר
או הֲנִסָּה אֱלֹהִים
לָבוֹא לָקַחַת לוֹ גוֹי מִקֶּרֶב גּוֹי
בְּמַסֹּת בְּאֹתֹת וּבְמוֹפְתִים וּבְמִלְחָמָה
וּבְיָד חֲזָקָה
וּבִזְרוֹעַ נְטוּיָה
וּבְמוֹרָאִים גְּדֹלִים
כְּכֹל אֲשֶׁר־עָשָׂה לָכֶם
יהוה אֱלֹהֵיכֶם בְּמִצְרַיִם
לְעֵינֶיךָ׃

דברים ד

"WITH SIGNS" –

This refers to the staff,
as it is said:
"Take this staff in your hand, *Ex. 4*
and with it you shall perform the *signs*."

"AND WITH WONDERS" –

This refers to the blood,
as it is said:
"I shall make *wonders* *Joel 3*
in the sky and on the earth –

Our Personal *Avoda*: Blood and Fire and Pillars of Smoke

As we spill wine from the cup with our finger, it is as if we are engaged in the process of bloodletting, removing the evil from within us.

It's a process of purging, the purging of the soul.

A drop of wine is spilled three times from the cup while saying:

BLOOD,

AND FIRE,

AND PILLARS OF SMOKE."

וּבְאֹתוֹת

זֶה הַמַּטֶּה

כְּמָה שֶׁנֶּאֱמַר

וְאֶת־הַמַּטֶּה הַזֶּה תִּקַּח בְּיָדֶךָ שמות ד

אֲשֶׁר תַּעֲשֶׂה־בּוֹ אֶת־הָאֹתֹת:

וּבְמֹפְתִים

זֶה הַדָּם

כְּמָה שֶׁנֶּאֱמַר

וְנָתַתִּי מוֹפְתִים בַּשָּׁמַיִם וּבָאָרֶץ יואל ג

מטיפים יין מן הכוס שלוש פעמים ואומרים:

דָּם

וָאֵשׁ

וְתִימְרוֹת עָשָׁן:

Another interpretation:

"With a strong hand"	Two.
"And an outstretched arm"	Two.
"In an awesome happening"	Two.
"With signs"	Two.
"And with wonders"	Two.

THESE WERE THE TEN PLAGUES

that the Holy One brought
upon Egypt,
and these are they –

דָּבָר אַחֵר

בְּיָד חֲזָקָה שְׁתַּיִם

וּבִזְרֹעַ נְטוּיָה שְׁתַּיִם

וּבְמֹרָא גָּדֹל שְׁתַּיִם

וּבְאֹתוֹת שְׁתַּיִם

וּבְמֹפְתִים שְׁתַּיִם

אֵלּוּ עֶשֶׂר מַכּוֹת

שֶׁהֵבִיא הַקָּדוֹשׁ בָּרוּךְ הוּא

עַל הַמִּצְרִים בְּמִצְרַיִם

וְאֵלּוּ הֵן

A drop of wine is spilled while each plague is said and then again while saying דצ״ך, עד״ש, *and* באח״ב*:*

מַכַּת בְּכוֹרוֹת.

THE STRIKING DOWN OF THE FIRSTBORN.

ספרי דברים כו, ה

רַבִּי יְהוּדָה הָיָה נוֹתֵן בָּהֶם סִמָּנִים
דְּצַ״ךְ עֲדַ״שׁ בְּאַחַ״ב

Rabbi Yehuda grouped these under acronyms – *Safrai Deut. 26:5*

DETZAKH, ADASH, BE'AḤAV.

With each plague – blood, frogs, lice – we use our finger to spill a drop of wine. The Ari HaKadosh explains that this act drains sickness and pain from the body and soul. According to the kabbalists, when we spill drops of wine as we recite the ten plagues, healing powers are created within the world, and at the same time, "all the diseases that I brought upon the Egyptians"[171] disappear from within you.

RABBI

Yossei HaGelili says:

How can you know
that the Egyptians were struck
with ten plagues in Egypt
and another fifty at the sea?

For in Egypt it is said,
"The astrologers said to Pharaoh, *Ex. 8*
'This is the *finger* of God,'"

while at the sea it is said,
"When Israel saw the great *hand* *Ex. 14*
the Lord raised against the Egyptians,
the people feared the Lord,
and they believed in the Lord
and in His servant Moshe."

רַבִּי
יוֹסֵי הַגְּלִילִי אוֹמֵר

מִנַּיִן אַתָּה אוֹמֵר
שֶׁלָּקוּ הַמִּצְרִים בְּמִצְרַיִם עֶשֶׂר מַכּוֹת
וְעַל הַיָּם לָקוּ חֲמִשִּׁים מַכּוֹת

בְּמִצְרַיִם מַה הוּא אוֹמֵר
וַיֹּאמְרוּ הַחַרְטֻמִּם אֶל־פַּרְעֹה אֶצְבַּע אֱלֹהִים הִוא — שמות ח

וְעַל הַיָּם מַה הוּא אוֹמֵר
וַיַּרְא יִשְׂרָאֵל אֶת־הַיָּד הַגְּדֹלָה — שמות יד
אֲשֶׁר עָשָׂה יהוה בְּמִצְרַיִם
וַיִּירְאוּ הָעָם אֶת־יהוה
וַיַּאֲמִינוּ בַּיהוה וּבְמֹשֶׁה עַבְדּוֹ:

If a finger struck them
with ten plagues,
conclude from this that
THEY WERE STRUCK
WITH TEN PLAGUES IN EGYPT
AND WITH FIFTY PLAGUES AT THE SEA.

Rabbi Eliezer says:

How can you know
that each and every plague
the Holy One brought
upon the Egyptians in Egypt
was in fact made up of four plagues?
For it is said,

כַּמָּה לָקוּ בְּאֶצְבַּע
עֶשֶׂר מַכּוֹת.
אֱמֹר מֵעַתָּה
בְּמִצְרַיִם לָקוּ עֶשֶׂר מַכּוֹת
וְעַל הַיָּם לָקוּ חֲמִשִּׁים מַכּוֹת.

רַבִּי אֱלִיעֶזֶר אוֹמֵר

מִנַּיִן שֶׁכָּל מַכָּה וּמַכָּה
שֶׁהֵבִיא הַקָּדוֹשׁ בָּרוּךְ הוּא
עַל הַמִּצְרִים בְּמִצְרַיִם
הָיְתָה שֶׁל אַרְבַּע מַכּוֹת
שֶׁנֶּאֱמַר:

"His fury was sent down upon them, *Ps. 78*
great anger, rage, and distress,
a company of messengers of destruction."

"Great anger" – one,
"rage" – two,
"distress" – three,
"a company of messengers of destruction" – four.

Conclude from this that
THEY WERE STRUCK WITH FORTY PLAGUES IN EGYPT
AND WITH TWO HUNDRED PLAGUES AT THE SEA.

תהלים עח

יְשַׁלַּח־בָּם חֲרוֹן אַפּוֹ
עֶבְרָה וָזַעַם וְצָרָה
מִשְׁלַחַת מַלְאֲכֵי רָעִים:

עֶבְרָה	אַחַת
וָזַעַם	שְׁתַּיִם
וְצָרָה	שָׁלוֹשׁ
מִשְׁלַחַת מַלְאֲכֵי רָעִים	אַרְבַּע

אֱמֹר מֵעַתָּה
בְּמִצְרַיִם לָקוּ אַרְבָּעִים מַכּוֹת
וְעַל הַיָּם לָקוּ מָאתַיִם מַכּוֹת.

Rabbi Akiva says:

How can you know
that each and every plague
the Holy One brought upon the Egyptians in Egypt
was in fact made up of five plagues?
For it is said,
"His fury was sent down upon them, *Ps. 78*
great anger, rage, and distress,
a company of messengers of destruction."
"His fury" – one,
"great anger" – two,
"rage" – three,
"distress" – four,
"a company of messengers
of destruction" – five.

Conclude from this that
THEY WERE STRUCK WITH FIFTY PLAGUES IN EGYPT
AND WITH TWO HUNDRED AND FIFTY PLAGUES
AT THE SEA.

רַבִּי עֲקִיבָא אוֹמֵר

מִנַּיִן שֶׁכָּל מַכָּה וּמַכָּה
שֶׁהֵבִיא הַקָּדוֹשׁ בָּרוּךְ הוּא עַל הַמִּצְרִים בְּמִצְרַיִם
הָיְתָה שֶׁל חָמֵשׁ מַכּוֹת
שֶׁנֶּאֱמַר:
יְשַׁלַּח־בָּם תהלים עח
חֲרוֹן אַפּוֹ עֶבְרָה וָזַעַם וְצָרָה, מִשְׁלַחַת מַלְאֲכֵי רָעִים:

חֲרוֹן אַפּוֹ אַחַת
עֶבְרָה שְׁתַּיִם
וָזַעַם שָׁלוֹשׁ
וְצָרָה אַרְבַּע
מִשְׁלַחַת מַלְאֲכֵי רָעִים חָמֵשׁ

אֱמֹר מֵעַתָּה
בְּמִצְרַיִם לָקוּ חֲמִשִּׁים מַכּוֹת
וְעַל הַיָּם לָקוּ חֲמִשִּׁים וּמָאתַיִם מַכּוֹת.

Our Personal *Avoda*: How Many Plagues Struck Them at Sea

How many plagues struck them at sea, how many struck them in Egypt?
This list is one of the boring parts of the Haggada.
Why does it matter? Either way it's the same miracle.

In truth, though, this section is amazing. The Haggada is saying to you: Count.

You've gotten used to so many wonderful things in your life. In the daily grind of life, you've forgotten so many moments of redemption and personal salvation. When you stop for a moment to count them out loud, like Rabbi Eliezer and Rabbi Akiva, when you list these things one by one, you'll suddenly be overwhelmed with joy. The room will become filled with confetti comprised of the small details of redemption. You'll look differently at your husband, whom you've been married to for twenty-odd years; you'll look differently at your children, your parents, your friends, your home, your place of work. Everyone has something to be thankful for; we just tend to forget. So count these things! Count them out loud! And then you'll remember.

This is the power of breaking things down into details.
We spend an entire night telling a story that can be summed up in one sentence.
What's the point of this long-winded discussion before we start *Shulḥan Orekh*?
So that we can say: Wow. We have it so good.

This detailed list doesn't only seek to praise God.
It also enables us to appreciate the redemption that we have been lucky enough to experience.

HOW MUCH GOOD,

LAYER UPON LAYER, THE OMNIPRESENT

HAS DONE FOR US.

כַּמָּה

מַעֲלוֹת
טוֹבוֹת
לַמָּקוֹם

עָלֵינוּ

Had He brought us out of Egypt
without bringing judgment upon
[our oppressors],
that would have been enough for us.

Had He brought judgment upon them
but not upon their gods,
that would have been enough for us.

Had He brought judgment upon their gods
without killing their firstborn sons,
that would have been enough for us.

Had He killed their firstborn sons
without giving us their wealth,
that would have been enough for us.

Had He given us their wealth
without splitting the sea for us,
that would have been enough for us.

Had He split the sea for us
but not brought us through it dry,
that would have been enough for us.

Had He brought us through [the sea] dry
without drowning our enemies in it,
that would have been enough for us.

אִלּוּ הוֹצִיאָֽנוּ מִמִּצְרַֽיִם
וְלֹא עָשָׂה בָהֶם שְׁפָטִים דַּיֵּֽנוּ

אִלּוּ עָשָׂה בָהֶם שְׁפָטִים
וְלֹא עָשָׂה בֵאלֹהֵיהֶם דַּיֵּֽנוּ

אִלּוּ עָשָׂה בֵאלֹהֵיהֶם
וְלֹא הָרַג אֶת בְּכוֹרֵיהֶם דַּיֵּֽנוּ

אִלּוּ הָרַג אֶת בְּכוֹרֵיהֶם
וְלֹא נָתַן לָֽנוּ אֶת מָמוֹנָם דַּיֵּֽנוּ

אִלּוּ נָתַן לָֽנוּ אֶת מָמוֹנָם
וְלֹא קָרַע לָֽנוּ אֶת הַיָּם דַּיֵּֽנוּ

אִלּוּ קָרַע לָֽנוּ אֶת הַיָּם
וְלֹא הֶעֱבִירָֽנוּ בְתוֹכוֹ בֶּחָרָבָה דַּיֵּֽנוּ

אִלּוּ הֶעֱבִירָֽנוּ בְתוֹכוֹ בֶּחָרָבָה
וְלֹא שִׁקַּע צָרֵֽינוּ בְּתוֹכוֹ דַּיֵּֽנוּ

Had He drowned our enemies in it
without providing for our needs
for forty years in the desert,
that would have been enough for us.

Had He provided for our needs
for forty years in the desert,
without feeding us with manna,
that would have been enough for us.

Had He fed us with manna
without giving us Shabbat,
that would have been enough for us.

Had He given us Shabbat
without drawing us close
around Mount Sinai,
that would have been enough for us.

Had He drawn us close around Mount Sinai
without giving us the Torah,
that would have been enough for us.

Had He given us the Torah
without bringing us to the land of Israel,
that would have been enough for us.

Had He brought us to the land of Israel
without building for us
the House He chose
that would have been enough for us.

אִלּוּ שִׁקַּע צָרֵינוּ בְּתוֹכוֹ
וְלֹא סִפֵּק צָרְכֵּנוּ בַּמִּדְבָּר אַרְבָּעִים שָׁנָה דַּיֵּנוּ

אִלּוּ סִפֵּק צָרְכֵּנוּ בַּמִּדְבָּר אַרְבָּעִים שָׁנָה
וְלֹא הֶאֱכִילָנוּ אֶת הַמָּן דַּיֵּנוּ

אִלּוּ הֶאֱכִילָנוּ אֶת הַמָּן
וְלֹא נָתַן לָנוּ אֶת הַשַּׁבָּת דַּיֵּנוּ

אִלּוּ נָתַן לָנוּ אֶת הַשַּׁבָּת
וְלֹא קֵרְבָנוּ לִפְנֵי הַר סִינַי דַּיֵּנוּ

אִלּוּ קֵרְבָנוּ לִפְנֵי הַר סִינַי
וְלֹא נָתַן לָנוּ אֶת הַתּוֹרָה דַּיֵּנוּ

אִלּוּ נָתַן לָנוּ אֶת הַתּוֹרָה
וְלֹא הִכְנִיסָנוּ לְאֶרֶץ יִשְׂרָאֵל דַּיֵּנוּ

אִלּוּ הִכְנִיסָנוּ לְאֶרֶץ יִשְׂרָאֵל
וְלֹא בָנָה לָנוּ אֶת בֵּית הַבְּחִירָה דַּיֵּנוּ

HOW MANY AND MANIFOLD THEN, THE OMNIPRESENT'S KINDNESSES ARE TO US –

for He brought us out of Egypt
and brought judgment upon
[our oppressors]
and upon their gods,
and He killed their firstborn sons
and gave us their wealth,
and He split the sea for us
and brought us through it on dry land
and drowned our enemies there,
and He provided for our needs
for forty years in the desert
and fed us manna,
and He gave us Shabbat,
and He drew us close
around Mount Sinai
and gave us the Torah,
and He brought us to the land of Israel
and built for us the House He chose,
SO WE COULD FIND
ATONEMENT [THERE]
FOR ALL OUR SINS.

Our Personal *Avoda*: That Would Have Been Enough

Pray to know how to value the here and now.

To appreciate things as they are right now, without viewing them as a means to an end.

Ask for the light of this night to shine within you the entire year.

Ask to say, "That would have been enough" for everything you have.

Tell your child you're happy with him. For once, don't talk about what has changed, and what you want him to change about himself. Instead, just tell him how good he is, how much you appreciate him.

עַל אַחַת כַּמָּה וְכַמָּה טוֹבָה כְּפוּלָה וּמְכֻפֶּלֶת לַמָּקוֹם עָלֵינוּ

שֶׁהוֹצִיאָנוּ מִמִּצְרַיִם
וְעָשָׂה בָהֶם שְׁפָטִים
וְעָשָׂה בֵאלֹהֵיהֶם
וְהָרַג בְּכוֹרֵיהֶם
וְנָתַן לָנוּ אֶת מָמוֹנָם
וְקָרַע לָנוּ אֶת הַיָּם
וְהֶעֱבִירָנוּ בְתוֹכוֹ בֶּחָרָבָה
וְשִׁקַּע צָרֵינוּ בְּתוֹכוֹ
וְסִפֵּק צָרְכֵּנוּ בַּמִּדְבָּר אַרְבָּעִים שָׁנָה
וְהֶאֱכִילָנוּ אֶת הַמָּן
וְנָתַן לָנוּ אֶת הַשַּׁבָּת
וְקֵרְבָנוּ לִפְנֵי הַר סִינַי
וְנָתַן לָנוּ אֶת הַתּוֹרָה
וְהִכְנִיסָנוּ לְאֶרֶץ יִשְׂרָאֵל
וּבָנָה לָנוּ אֶת בֵּית הַבְּחִירָה
לְכַפֵּר עַל כָּל עֲוֹנוֹתֵינוּ.

The Tales of Rebbe Nahman:

The Treasure Beneath the Bridge

Once upon a time, there was a man from a city who dreamed that beneath a bridge in Vienna lay a treasure.

He traveled there and stood by the bridge and sought advice for how to dig there, since the passersby made it impossible to dig there during the day. A soldier passed by and asked him, "What are you standing here and thinking about?"

The man thought to himself that it would be good to tell the soldier of his dream, so that he would help him, and share a portion [of the treasure with him]. So he told him.

The soldier responded and said, "Oy, foolish Jew! Why do you pay attention to dreams? I also dreamed that there is a treasure beneath the oven of a Jewish man who lives in such and such place." And he mentioned the city where this man lived and the name of this man. "Do you think I would travel there for this treasure?"

The Jew was amazed, and he traveled [back] to his house and dug beneath his oven and found the treasure.

Afterward, the Jew said: I needed to travel all the way to Vienna in order to discover that there was a treasure in my own home.

So it is with the service of God. The treasure lies within each person, but to know of the treasure, one must go to the *tzaddik*. And there are those who say that the Rebbe hinted that, in the absence of this thing, one need not travel far distances and do drastic things to find the treasure. Rather, the treasure is found within each and every person, but there are many things that conceal it, so one must search properly for it.[173]

Only after we say "Enough!" and stop thinking about what happened and what could have been – if only I had been this, if only I had done that, if only I had gone out, if only I had stood strong, if only He had split the sea for me – only then, can we say: "Enough! I have so much, right here in my home!"

Only after we undertake this journey do we understand where the treasure is really buried.

Yehuda Gizbar writes:

> It's a strange poem. What would we have done at Mount Sinai if we hadn't received the Torah? But this indicates an important perspective that goes far beyond this. We tend to judge things only in light of their ultimate result, success or failure. Let's assume that this entire story and this entire time and this entire encounter will turn out to be negative, or irrelevant, that nothing comes out of it. The spousal relationship, the life project that we are so invested in right now. Does that render it unnecessary? Irrelevant? Would it have been better not to leave Egypt?
>
> This poem tells us the exact opposite. Things find their importance in the present. Not everything should be judged by the end result. Even if nothing happens in the end, the road we traveled is still so significant. We are significant.[172]

For this reason, I repeat, these words are key to the Seder night: "Each person must see himself *as if* he himself had come out of Egypt." It's an act. We act "as if" everything is perfectly fine, and the abundance that you will experience throughout the entire year perfectly reflects this charade. Because the fact that one night a year you're able to assume this role and act as if you have been redeemed indicates that there is indeed potential for this story within your life.

Rabban Gamliel would say:
Anyone who does not say these three things on Pesaḥ has not fulfilled his obligation, and these are they: *Pesaḥim 116a*

PESAḤ,

MATZA,

AND BITTER HERBS.

רַבָּן גַּמְלִיאֵל הָיָה אוֹמֵר
כָּל שֶׁלֹּא אָמַר שְׁלוֹשָׁה דְבָרִים אֵלּוּ בַּפֶּסַח
לֹא יָצָא יְדֵי חוֹבָתוֹ, וְאֵלּוּ הֵן

פסחים קטז

Even if you have been really busy and weren't able to read the Haggada, recite "Pesaḥ, matza, and maror" to fulfill your baseline obligation.

Our Personal *Avoda*: These Bitter Herbs

Ask that we should be able to distinguish between Pesaḥ and *maror*.

That we should be able to point at the *maror* with certainty and declare: "These bitter herbs!"

That we shouldn't delude ourselves into thinking that it's the redemption.

That we shouldn't be scared to move beyond it, even if all that's waiting for us on the other side is the matza.

It's so worth it.

The
PESAḤ

is what our ancestors would eat while the Temple stood:
and what does it recall?
It recalls the Holy One's
passing over (*Pasaḥ*) the houses
of our ancestors in Egypt,
as it is said:
"You shall say:

'It is a Pesaḥ offering for the Lord, *Ex. 12*
for He passed over the houses of the children of Israel in Egypt
while He struck the Egyptians,
but saved those in our homes' –
and the people bowed and prostrated themselves."

פֶּסַח

שֶׁהָיוּ אֲבוֹתֵינוּ אוֹכְלִים
בִּזְמַן שֶׁבֵּית הַמִּקְדָּשׁ הָיָה קַיָּם
עַל שׁוּם מָה
עַל שׁוּם שֶׁפָּסַח הַקָּדוֹשׁ בָּרוּךְ הוּא
עַל בָּתֵּי אֲבוֹתֵינוּ בְּמִצְרַיִם
שֶׁנֶּאֱמַר

שמות יב

וַאֲמַרְתֶּם זֶבַח־פֶּסַח הוּא לַיהוה
אֲשֶׁר פָּסַח עַל־בָּתֵּי בְנֵי־יִשְׂרָאֵל בְּמִצְרַיִם
בְּנָגְפּוֹ אֶת־מִצְרַיִם
וְאֶת־בָּתֵּינוּ הִצִּיל
וַיִּקֹּד הָעָם וַיִּשְׁתַּחֲווּ:

The matzot are lifted and the following is said:

THIS MATZA

that we eat:
what does it recall?
It recalls the dough of our ancestors,
which did not have time to rise
before the King, King of kings, the Holy One, blessed be He,
revealed Himself and redeemed them,
as it is said:

> "They baked the dough *Ex. 12*
> that they had brought out of Egypt
> into unleavened cakes,
> for it had not risen,
> for they were cast out of Egypt
> and could not delay,
> and they made no provision
> for the way."

מגביה את המצות ואומר:

מַצָּה זוֹ

שֶׁאָנוּ אוֹכְלִים עַל שׁוּם מָה
עַל שׁוּם שֶׁלֹּא הִסְפִּיק בְּצֵקָם שֶׁל אֲבוֹתֵינוּ לְהַחֲמִיץ
עַד שֶׁנִּגְלָה עֲלֵיהֶם מֶלֶךְ מַלְכֵי הַמְּלָכִים
הַקָּדוֹשׁ בָּרוּךְ הוּא וּגְאָלָם

שֶׁנֶּאֱמַר

שמות יב

וַיֹּאפוּ אֶת־הַבָּצֵק
אֲשֶׁר הוֹצִיאוּ מִמִּצְרַיִם
עֻגֹת מַצּוֹת כִּי לֹא חָמֵץ
כִּי־גֹרְשׁוּ מִמִּצְרַיִם
וְלֹא יָכְלוּ לְהִתְמַהְמֵהַּ
וְגַם־צֵדָה לֹא־עָשׂוּ לָהֶם׃

The maror is lifted and the following is said:

THESE BITTER HERBS

that we eat:
what do they recall?
They recall the bitterness
that the Egyptians imposed
on the lives of our ancestors in Egypt,

as it is said:

"They embittered their lives *Ex. 1*
with hard labor,
with clay and with bricks
and with all field labors,
with all the work
with which
they enslaved them –
hard labor."

מגביה את המרור ואומר:

מָרוֹר זֶה

שֶׁאָנוּ אוֹכְלִים
עַל שׁוּם מָה
עַל שׁוּם שֶׁמֵּרְרוּ הַמִּצְרִים
אֶת חַיֵּי אֲבוֹתֵינוּ בְּמִצְרַיִם
שֶׁנֶּאֱמַר

וַיְמָרְרוּ אֶת־חַיֵּיהֶם שמות א
בַּעֲבֹדָה קָשָׁה
בְּחֹמֶר וּבִלְבֵנִים
וּבְכָל־עֲבֹדָה בַּשָּׂדֶה
אֵת כָּל־עֲבֹדָתָם
אֲשֶׁר־עָבְדוּ בָהֶם בְּפָרֶךְ:

GENERATION BY GENERATION,

each person must see himself
as if he himself had come out of Egypt, *Pesaḥim 116b*

as it is said:

"And you shall tell your child on that day, *Ex. 13*
'Because of this the Lord acted for me

when I came out of Egypt.'"
It was not only our ancestors
whom the Holy One redeemed;
He redeemed us too along with them,
as it is said:

"He took us *Deut. 6*
out of there,
to bring us to the land
He promised our ancestors
and to give it to us."

בְּכָל דּוֹר וָדוֹר

פסחים קטז:

חַיָּב אָדָם לִרְאוֹת אֶת עַצְמוֹ
כְּאִלּוּ הוּא יָצָא מִמִּצְרָיִם

שֶׁנֶּאֱמַר

שמות יג

וְהִגַּדְתָּ לְבִנְךָ בַּיּוֹם הַהוּא לֵאמֹר
בַּעֲבוּר זֶה עָשָׂה יהוה לִי בְּצֵאתִי מִמִּצְרָיִם:

לֹא אֶת אֲבוֹתֵינוּ בִּלְבָד
גָּאַל הַקָּדוֹשׁ בָּרוּךְ הוּא
אֶלָּא אַף אוֹתָנוּ גָּאַל עִמָּהֶם
שֶׁנֶּאֱמַר

דברים ו

וְאוֹתָנוּ הוֹצִיא מִשָּׁם
לְמַעַן הָבִיא אֹתָנוּ
לָתֶת לָנוּ אֶת־הָאָרֶץ
אֲשֶׁר נִשְׁבַּע לַאֲבֹתֵינוּ:

The matzot are covered, the cup is raised, and the following is said:

Therefore it is our duty

to thank, praise, laud,
glorify, exalt, honor,
bless, raise high, and acclaim

the One who has performed all these miracles
for our ancestors and for us;
who has brought us out from slavery to freedom,
from sorrow to joy, from grief to celebration;
from darkness to great light
and from enslavement to redemption;
and so we shall sing a new song before Him.

HALLELUYA!

The cup is put down and the matzot are uncovered.

מכסה את המצות ואוחז את הכוס ואומר:

לְפִיכָךְ אֲנַחְנוּ חַיָּבִים

לְהוֹדוֹת לְהַלֵּל לְשַׁבֵּחַ
לְפָאֵר לְרוֹמֵם לְהַדֵּר
לְבָרֵךְ לְעַלֵּה וּלְקַלֵּס

לְמִי שֶׁעָשָׂה לַאֲבוֹתֵינוּ וְלָנוּ אֶת כָּל הַנִּסִּים הָאֵלֶּה
הוֹצִיאָנוּ מֵעַבְדוּת לְחֵרוּת
מִיָּגוֹן לְשִׂמְחָה
מֵאֵבֶל לְיוֹם טוֹב
וּמֵאֲפֵלָה לְאוֹר גָּדוֹל
וּמִשִּׁעְבּוּד לִגְאֻלָּה
וְנֹאמַר לְפָנָיו שִׁירָה חֲדָשָׁה

הַלְלוּיָהּ.

מניח את הכוס מידו וחוזר ומגלה את המצות.

HALLELUYA!

Ps. 113

Servants of the Lord, give praise;
praise the name of the Lord.
Blessed be the name of the Lord
now and for evermore.
From the rising of the sun to its setting,
may the Lord's name be praised.
High is the Lord above all nations;
His glory is above the heavens.
Who is like the Lord our God, who sits enthroned so high,
yet turns so low to see the heavens and the earth?
He raises the poor from the dust
and the needy from the refuse heap,
giving them a place alongside princes,
the princes of His people.
He makes the woman in a childless house
a happy mother of children.

HALLELUYA!

תהלים קיג

הַלְלוּיָהּ

הַלְלוּ עַבְדֵי יהוה, הַלְלוּ אֶת־שֵׁם יהוה:
יְהִי שֵׁם יהוה מְבֹרָךְ, מֵעַתָּה וְעַד־עוֹלָם:
מִמִּזְרַח־שֶׁמֶשׁ עַד־מְבוֹאוֹ, מְהֻלָּל שֵׁם יהוה:
רָם עַל־כָּל־גּוֹיִם יהוה, עַל הַשָּׁמַיִם כְּבוֹדוֹ:
מִי כַּיהוה אֱלֹהֵינוּ, הַמַּגְבִּיהִי לָשָׁבֶת:
הַמַּשְׁפִּילִי לִרְאוֹת, בַּשָּׁמַיִם וּבָאָרֶץ:
מְקִימִי מֵעָפָר דָּל, מֵאַשְׁפֹּת יָרִים אֶבְיוֹן:
לְהוֹשִׁיבִי עִם־נְדִיבִים, עִם נְדִיבֵי עַמּוֹ:
מוֹשִׁיבִי עֲקֶרֶת הַבַּיִת, אֵם־הַבָּנִים שְׂמֵחָה

הַלְלוּיָהּ:

תהלים קיד

Ps. 114

When Israel came out of Egypt,

בֵּית יַעֲקֹב מֵעַם לֹעֵז:
הָיְתָה יְהוּדָה לְקָדְשׁוֹ
יִשְׂרָאֵל מַמְשְׁלוֹתָיו:
הַיָּם רָאָה וַיָּנֹס, הַיַּרְדֵּן יִסֹּב לְאָחוֹר:
הֶהָרִים רָקְדוּ כְאֵילִים
גְּבָעוֹת כִּבְנֵי־צֹאן:
מַה־לְּךָ הַיָּם כִּי תָנוּס
הַיַּרְדֵּן תִּסֹּב לְאָחוֹר:
הֶהָרִים תִּרְקְדוּ כְאֵילִים
גְּבָעוֹת כִּבְנֵי־צֹאן:
מִלִּפְנֵי אָדוֹן חוּלִי אָרֶץ
מִלִּפְנֵי אֱלוֹהַּ יַעֲקֹב:
הַהֹפְכִי הַצּוּר אֲגַם־מָיִם
חַלָּמִישׁ לְמַעְיְנוֹ־מָיִם:

the house of Yaakov from a people of
foreign tongue,
Judah became His sanctuary,
Israel His dominion.
The sea saw and fled;
the Jordan turned back.
The mountains skipped like rams,
the hills like lambs.
Why was it, sea, that you fled?
Jordan, why did you turn back? Why,
mountains, did you skip
like rams,
and you, hills, like lambs?
It was at the presence of the LORD,
Creator of the earth,
at the presence of the God of Yaakov,
who turned the rock into
a pool of water,
flint into a flowing spring.

The cup is raised and the following is said:

בָּרוּךְ Blessed are You, LORD our God,
King of the Universe, who has redeemed us
and redeemed our ancestors from Egypt,
and brought us to this night to eat matza and bitter herbs.
So may the LORD our God bring us in peace
to other seasons and festivals that are coming to us,
happy in the building of Your city
and rejoicing in Your service;
and there we shall eat
of sacrifices
and Pesaḥ offerings

[*On Motza'ei Shabbat:* of Pesaḥ offerings and sacrifices],

אוחז את הכוס ואומר:

בָּרוּךְ אַתָּה יהוה אֱלֹהֵינוּ מֶלֶךְ הָעוֹלָם
אֲשֶׁר גְּאָלָנוּ, וְגָאַל אֶת אֲבוֹתֵינוּ מִמִּצְרַיִם
וְהִגִּיעָנוּ הַלַּיְלָה הַזֶּה, לֶאֱכׇל בּוֹ מַצָּה וּמָרוֹר.
כֵּן יהוה אֱלֹהֵינוּ וֵאלֹהֵי אֲבוֹתֵינוּ
יַגִּיעֵנוּ לְמוֹעֲדִים וְלִרְגָלִים אֲחֵרִים
הַבָּאִים לִקְרָאתֵנוּ לְשָׁלוֹם
שְׂמֵחִים בְּבִנְיַן עִירֶךָ
וְשָׂשִׂים בַּעֲבוֹדָתֶךָ
וְנֹאכַל שָׁם
מִן הַזְּבָחִים
וּמִן הַפְּסָחִים

/ במוצש״ק: מִן הַפְּסָחִים וּמִן הַזְּבָחִים/

of which the blood will reach
the side of Your altar to be accepted.
And we shall thank You
in a new song
for our redemption
and for our lives' salvation.
Blessed are You, Lord, Redeemer of Israel.

I am prepared and ready to fulfill the commandment of the second of the four cups. For the sake for the unification of the Holy One, blessed be He, and His Divine Presence, through He who is hidden and unseen, in the name of all Israel.

בָּרוּךְ Blessed are You, Lord our God,
King of the Universe,
who creates the fruit of the vine.

Drink while reclining to the left.

The Second Cup
Is Symbolic of Rivka, Our Matriarch

אֲשֶׁר יַגִּיעַ דָּמָם
עַל קִיר מִזְבַּחֲךָ לְרָצוֹן
וְנוֹדֶה לְךָ
שִׁיר חָדָשׁ
עַל גְּאֻלָּתֵנוּ וְעַל פְּדוּת נַפְשֵׁנוּ
בָּרוּךְ אַתָּה יהוה, גָּאַל יִשְׂרָאֵל.

הִנְנִי מוּכָן וּמְזֻמָּן לְקַיֵּם מִצְוַת כּוֹס שֵׁנִי שֶׁל אַרְבַּע כּוֹסוֹת
לְשֵׁם יִחוּד קֻדְשָׁא בְּרִיךְ הוּא וּשְׁכִינְתֵּהּ עַל יְדֵי הַהוּא טָמִיר וְנֶעְלָם בְּשֵׁם כָּל יִשְׂרָאֵל.

בָּרוּךְ אַתָּה יהוה
אֱלֹהֵינוּ מֶלֶךְ הָעוֹלָם
בּוֹרֵא פְּרִי הַגָּפֶן.

שותים בהסבת שמאל.

כוס שנייה
כנגד רבקה אימנו

Rivka! I literally imagined her singing "One little goat, one little goat," as she removed the skin from the two little goats and tenderly draped them on the smooth neck of her beloved son Yaakov, and sent him off, laden with her prayers, with her tears, whispering quietly: "Enough. Tonight, tonight…is all yours, my son. Go!"

According to the Zohar, the story of Yaakov and Esav and the blessings actually took place on the night of the Seder. De facto, on this night, Rivka sacrificed her life. After this incident, we don't hear about her again. She disappears, fully consumed within the character of her nursemaid.[176] Rivka is engulfed by the Torah and vanishes; she sacrifices her life by fulfilling her mission.

Rivka prays for all the Yaakovs, for all our children who have been passed over, for those who have been left behind. Our hearts beat because of her.

On This Night, Rivka

One night, I delivered a talk in Kiryat Arba to a group of women who were redolent of the Garden of Eden. Many of them have at least one empty chair at their Seder table. After the talk, the man in charge of Maarat HaMakhpela (the Makhpela Cave) came and told us: "We're going to open Yitzḥak's hall in the cave tonight, special for you."

I had never been in Yitzḥak's hall before, certainly not at midnight. With a feeling of awe, we were ushered in by a group of soldiers. For the first time in my life, I saw the entrance to the Garden of Eden.[174]

"Bend down, bend down," he told us, and as I bent down, I felt an incredible breeze, a breeze that rose up through these small openings, through the entrance to the Garden of Eden.

As I stood there, I prayed so hard for the Jewish people. I stood between Yitzḥak and Rivka, "he in one corner and she in the other,"[175] and I begged Rivka to steal the blessings for us once again on the Seder night, even though we don't deserve it, even though our Father doesn't necessarily agree. Please! With the strength that only you possess,

Raḥtza / Washing

רַחְצָה

נוטלים את הידיים לסעודה ומברכים:

בָּרוּךְ אַתָּה יהוה אֱלֹהֵינוּ מֶלֶךְ הָעוֹלָם
אֲשֶׁר קִדְּשָׁנוּ בְּמִצְוֹתָיו, וְצִוָּנוּ עַל נְטִילַת יָדַיִם.

All participants wash their hands in preparation for the meal and recite the blessing:

בָּרוּךְ Blessed are You, LORD our God, King of the Universe,
who has made us holy through His commandments,
and has commanded us about washing hands.

Motzi Matza
מוֹצִיא
מַצָּה

מגביה את שלוש המצות ואומר:

הִנְנִי מוּכָן וּמְזֻמָּן לְקַיֵּם מִצְוַת אֲכִילַת מַצָּה.
לְשֵׁם יִחוּד קֻדְשָׁא בְּרִיךְ הוּא וּשְׁכִינְתֵּהּ עַל יְדֵי הַהוּא טָמִיר וְנֶעְלָם בְּשֵׁם כָּל יִשְׂרָאֵל.

בָּרוּךְ אַתָּה יהוה אֱלֹהֵינוּ מֶלֶךְ הָעוֹלָם
הַמּוֹצִיא לֶחֶם מִן הָאָרֶץ.

All the matzot are held up and the following is said:

I am prepared and ready to fulfill the commandment of eating the matza. For the sake for the unification of the Holy One, blessed be He, and His Divine Presence, through He who is hidden and unseen, in the name of all Israel.

בָּרוּךְ Blessed are You, Lord our God,
King of the Universe,
who brings forth bread from the earth.

The lowermost matza is put down while holding the uppermost and middle matzot while reciting:

בָּרוּךְ Blessed are You, Lord our God,
King of the Universe,
who has made us holy
through His commandments,
and has commanded us to eat matza.

The leader takes for himself and gives to all the participants a kezayit from the uppermost and middle matzot (or everyone takes for themselves two kezayit from the matza in front of them), all while reclining to the left.

Our Personal *Avoda*: Matza

Pray for healing and faith. Immediately!

מניח את המצה התחתונה מידו ואוחז את העליונה ואת האמצעית ומברך:

בָּרוּךְ אַתָּה יהוה
אֱלֹהֵינוּ מֶלֶךְ הָעוֹלָם
אֲשֶׁר קִדְּשָׁנוּ בְּמִצְוֹתָיו,
וְצִוָּנוּ עַל אֲכִילַת מַצָּה.

נוטל לעצמו ונותן לכל אחד מן המסובים כזית מן המצה העליונה וכזית מן האמצעית,
(או שכל אחד ואחד לוקח לעצמו כשני זיתים מן המצה השמורה שלפניו) ואוכלים בהסבת שמאל.
נוטל כזית מרור לעצמו ולכל המסובים וטובלו בחרוסת ואומר:

The mystical explanation is that on the second day of Creation, God separated the upper waters (in the heavens) from the lower waters (the wells, the seas, and the rivers). Ever since, the Midrash explains, the lower waters are referred to as "weeping water" because they sob and yearn: How come only the upper waters ascended to God and remained there? We also want to be close to God![180]

And God tells them: Don't cry. You'll also ascend to Me in the Temple, on the holiday of Sukkot, during the water libation, as the sacrifices are offered. The sacrifice is salted with salt that is saturated with seawater. As the sacrifice is consumed by the fire and ascends to God, the water ascends with it and encounters God again.

This was the first separation, the first controversy. On the second day of Creation, the word "good" does not appear at all. When will we be able to heal all the "no good" things in our lives? In the Temple.

But what happens after the destruction of the Temple? The Yismaḥ Moshe, a tremendous *ḥasid*, explains: "By the waters of Babylon, there we sat and wept."[181] Who was crying? Us and…the waters of Babylon. The rivers cried: The Temple has been destroyed, and the water libations and sacrifices have been abolished. When will we be able to ascend and appear before You? When will we be able to correct the things that are "no good"?

God reassured the water and said: Every year, when My children take the water that rested for an entire night (*mayim shelanu*) and use it to knead dough for matza, when they dip the matza in salt and moisten it in their mouths, at that moment, the ones who eat the matza together with the lower waters absorbed within it, ascend to God's throne of glory and the lower water reunites once again with the upper water.

It's impossible not to cry as we eat matza for the first time at the Seder. You cry along with the water saturated in this matza, because, in the aftermath of the Temple's destruction, this is its only opportunity this year

Our Personal *Avoda*: Further Thoughts About the Matza

God told them: As My children eat this matza, matza made from the lower waters, from the *mayim shelanu*, they are standing before God's throne of glory. "Pour out your heart like water" because now you are "before the presence of the Lord."[182]

The Hasidim explain: As the matza is eaten, we stand before God's presence and all the "no good" things in this world are rehabilitated and fixed. We encounter something that we have longed for. It's known as "the Divine Presence." Ask for everything, pray for everything, because this is such an unusual encounter, an encounter between the upper and lower worlds. It is an incredible love letter.

Matza

An Encounter Between Heaven and Earth

We have reached the moment when we will eat the matza for the very first time. Such a powerful and sublime moment! Our Sages refer to matza as "the bread of healing, the bread of faith."[177] These two concepts are connected to one another. Will you have faith that the matza is the bread of healing?

According to the Zohar HaKadosh, someone who feels that his faith is weak should eat matza. "Feed [your] faith"[178] – faith is something that needs to be nurtured and fed. Matza nurtures faith because of its simplicity; it's comprised of just flour and water. When a person eats matza, he is filled with simple understanding and simple faith, just like the matza. Said differently, at this moment, our faith grows stronger.

The great Rabbi Salman Mutzafi would hug and kiss the matza, and his son Rabbi Mutzafi writes: "When righteous people and people of stature recite the blessings on the matza, 'Who brings forth bread from the earth,' and 'has commanded us to eat matza,' after they tasted [it] they would hug the matzot in their arms and kiss them to show that mitzvot are beloved. And this custom is rooted in the words of our Sages, of blessed memory."[179]

In my home, we eat the matza in silence on the Seder night. All one can hear is the sound of the matza crunching in the mouths of others.

And cry. As the matza is eaten for the first time at the Seder, we recline to our left and cry. Actual tears.

feels like it's full of holes. But the moment that it's assigned to someone's mouth, the matza receives its missing *vav* and is transformed into a mitzva, into a joint endeavor shared with another.

So, if you feel alone, if you're waiting to get married, eat the matza, and focus on creating a unit that operates together. That your husband-to-be will find you. "I don't want to remain a matza. I want to find my missing half and function as a unit together with him. I want to fulfill the mitzva of building a Jewish home."

And if you're married? Focus on building a strong marriage and having peace in the home.

A Bite-Sized Love Letter

Focus please. There's no talking as we eat the matza, because this is the bread of oppression (*oni*), the bread which brings answers (*onim*) from God."[186]

Which questions are being answered by the heavens now?

The questions that, as a woman, are hard to ask.

Rabbi Yitzchak Hutner explains that as you eat the matza, you should note that it has rows and rows of slits, forming lines resembling those in a letter from someone who is far away. With this bite of matza, God answers all your questions. And as you eat this matza, you can sense that He is telling you "I love you, I love you, I love you."[187]

Eating the matza is an incredible moment. Hasidim had the practice of hugging and kissing the matza because it is a letter from God. It's an ancient letter. God writes to us, "I remember the kindness of your youth." I'm always inspired by the story of Rabbi Chaim Pinchas Scheinberg's wife. As they would eat the matza, this great man would look at her and sing to her, "Thus said the Lord, I remember the kindness of your youth, your love as a bride, how you followed Me in the wilderness, in a land not sown."[188] It's an incredible, incredible moment. It's a moment of closeness.

But Yemima, my teeth…my digestive issues…

Don't think about it. Think about how those things that are "no good" are disappearing. In the words of the Zohar – "the bread of healing, the bread of faith." This is the bread that heals and the bread of faith. Eat the matza and think about all the satisfaction, strength, and faith that you will receive.

Fatherhood

year to encounter God again. As you consume your first bite of matza, you will find yourself standing before God's throne of glory. Just trust your Father. Lean on Him. And you'll see that the "no good" things in your life will suddenly feel good.

This is a moment that comes only once a year. You stand before God, and He sees all your pain, your suffering, your sorrow, your loneliness, everything. It's a moment that is truly sublime.

And Now, Pray for a *Shidduch*

The moment that we eat matza for the first time at the Seder is a powerful time to pray for *shidduchim* and harmony within the home.

The Zohar explains: Rabbi Ḥiya began and said: "In the first month, on the fourteenth day of the month at evening, you shall eat matzot."[183] And it is written: "For seven days you shall eat thereafter matzot bread of oppression."[184] In the verse, the word "oppression" (*oni*) is written without the Hebrew letter *vav* and can be read *ani*, or bread of the poor. And this matter requires clarification: Why are the words written as "bread of the poor" if they are meant to be read as "bread of oppression"?

The answer is that bread of the poor refers to matza. "For a female without a male is poverty-stricken. She is like matza, and after we eat matza, meaning after she finds her match, it is read as 'mitzva,' with the addition of a *vav*. Therefore, at the first stage it's called matza and thereafter it's called mitzva."[185] In other words, what is the "bread of the poor"? It's matza without the additional "*vav*." When she's all alone, she's like a matza. The connection between the male and female happens after we put the matza in our mouths and the matza is transformed into a mitzva (like a "team" that works together), becoming two things that are connected through the addition of the Hebrew letter *vav* (we are well aware that the Zohar discusses connections and links between the upper and lower worlds).

The Hebrew words "bread of oppression" are written without the Hebrew letter *vav*. Yet as soon as you eat, the matza is transformed into a mitzva, with the *vav*. This means that you're no longer matza, stuck in a state of controversy, at odds with your other side. You've been transformed into a mitzva! You're part of a team! God has assigned you the one who shares the root of your soul.

Look at this matza. Look at its loneliness, its distress, how small and alone and dried out and crumbling it is. It

There's so much more that can be said about the incredible moment when the matza is eaten, but we'll suffice with Rabbi Wolbe's words:

> At the moment the matza is eaten, man will sense the secret of his life,
>
> and he'll sense divine providence,
>
> and the Omnipresent will reveal to him his role in life.
>
> And as he eats the matza, he'll sense that he is maximizing his talents,
>
> and he need not be jealous of another.
>
> And eating the matza removes jealousy,
>
> and suddenly he is endowed with faith, that everything he has is divine providence.
>
> This is what [divine providence] decreed, this is what [divine providence] wanted, and he should not have doubts about it.
>
> And we will be able to work with the tools we have been given.[194]

It's amazing. As you eat the matza, you're assigned your job, and you say, "I feel like I have maximized myself, like the matza. And it's okay that I'm not all pumped up and inflated and that I don't have all that 'wow.' I'm complete. I'm happy."

The moment the matza is eaten is just incredible.

Fatherhood Is Now

The Alter Rebbe explains: The Gemara states: "The child does not know how to call [his] father and mother until he tastes grain for the first time."[189] Why is the child's ability to communicate linked to the taste of food? The newborn infant does not understand that someone is loving and providing for them until they taste food for the first time.

The Alter Rebbe explains: As you eat the first taste of matza, you'll feel the presence of your Father, the taste of God. Because when the Jewish people left Egypt, they were reborn, and the first food they ate was matza, right after their moment of birth. Matza is the taste of having a mother and father. The taste of matza is the taste of a loving embrace."[190]

It's called "the bread of faith." It gives you faith – in what? Faith that someone is carefully watching over you.[191] Pesaḥ, Rabbi Wolbe explains, means that God skipped over the doors of the Egyptian homes because He wanted to redeem *me*. He deliberately skipped over the others: "Not her, not her, not her." In other words, my life is governed by meticulous divine providence.

Every Seder night, and in a more general sense throughout this entire period, we are closely watched and provided for. The Hebrew word for "spring" (*aviv*) stems from the same root word as the Hebrew word for father (*av*): Our Father is here. He's right here with us. You don't need to worry about anything.[192]

Why is matza so simple? So the only taste that you'll experience is the taste of your Father. My Father gave this to me. And perhaps it doesn't taste so good. So why am I eating it? Because it's from my Father.

Rabbi Wolbe explains that the entire Seder night seeks to communicate to us: You are carefully watched and protected. You have no idea to what extent. "It's a night of protection for the Lord."[193] You are protected. Protected, preserved, watched over. From the moment that you exited your mother's womb. Nothing about your life is incidental. Please understand that you are safeguarded. Your Father is right here.

Maror / Bitter Herbs

מָרוֹר

נוטל כזית מרור לעצמו ולכל המסובים וטובלים בחרוסת ואומר:

הִנְנִי מוּכָן וּמְזֻמָּן לְקַיֵּם מִצְוַת אֲכִילַת מָרוֹר.
לְשֵׁם יִחוּד קֻדְשָׁא בְּרִיךְ הוּא וּשְׁכִינְתֵּהּ עַל יְדֵי הַהוּא טָמִיר וְנֶעְלָם בְּשֵׁם כָּל יִשְׂרָאֵל.

בָּרוּךְ אַתָּה יהוה אֱלֹהֵינוּ מֶלֶךְ הָעוֹלָם
אֲשֶׁר קִדְּשָׁנוּ בְּמִצְוֹתָיו, וְצִוָּנוּ עַל אֲכִילַת מָרוֹר.

אוכלים בלי הסבה.

Everyone takes a kezayit of maror, dips it in ḥaroset, and says:

I am prepared and ready to fulfill the commandment of eating maror.
For the sake for the unification of the Holy One, blessed be He, and His Divine Presence, through He who is hidden and unseen, in the name of all Israel.

בָּרוּךְ Blessed are You, Lord our God,
King of the Universe,
who has made us holy through His commandments,
and has commanded us to eat bitter herbs.

Eat without reclining.

> Know that the match that is made on the night of Pesaḥ is with Raḥel [the younger sister] and there is no match with Leah at all on this night. And we need to sweeten the judgments, even though there is no match with her [with Leah] and this is done by dipping the *maror* in the *ḥaroset.*
>
> And this is the truth [inherent] in the Hebrew letters *resh, vav, tav* in the [word] *ḥaroset*, [which spell the name] Ruth, which is the element of Leah.[195]

According to Kabbala, *ḥaroset* represents three women: Leah, Raḥel, and Ruth. This is why Ruth's name can be detected in the Hebrew word *ḥaroset*. Leah is in terrible pain on this night because Yaakov remains with Raḥel, and she feels bereft and alone. But Ruth connects to Leah. Mashiaḥ derives from both of them. Ruth tells Leah that she will overcome this sorrow. Mashiaḥ will come from you. I too, Ruth says, achieved my destiny on account of bitterness.

Jealousy is a great form of sorrow; it causes terrible stress, and if the Torah uses this word, we certainly cannot deny that it was really there: There was jealousy between the sisters, Raḥel was jealous of Leah ("And Raḥel was jealous of her sister"[196]) and Leah was jealous of Raḥel ("Was it not enough for you to take away my husband?"[197]). And if God gave you this bitter pill, it's entirely legitimate for you to feel these things. Don't repress them. They're real. Family can be sticky, annoying, and make you jealous. So be jealous.

And what should you do? Chew on the pain really, really well. Don't swallow it. Chew on it. The end will be sweet. The *ḥaroset*, as we said, sweetens the jealousy, but to get there you need to really chew on the *maror*, and really taste the bitterness.

Rabbi Wolbe writes so beautifully:

> At the moment that a person chews the *maror*, he receives his unique role. Man cannot move beyond the thicket of jealousy and accept himself until he knows that this is what he was chosen for, and the secret of his life is divine providence, and this [divine providence] is what created him and this [divine providence] is what placed upon him his role in life, and there is no place for comparing himself to others or comparing the *maror* that he chews with the bitterness of others. Because "one reign does not overlap with another, even a hairbreadth."[198] And as he eats the *maror* he should not look to the right or left, but just above, because everything is the decree of divine providence, and this is his path to his redemption.[199]

This maror

Healing and Overcoming Bitterness, Competitiveness, and Infertility

Let's talk about the *ḥaroset*. Why do we eat *ḥaroset*? Why do we dip the *maror* in the *ḥaroset*? Here's my favorite explanation and it's completely mystical.

Rabbi Mutzafi explains: "Many deep truths were said about the *ḥaroset* according to Kabbala. And it comes to sweeten the bitter judgments and annul death, because on this night [one] tastes the taste of bitterness; because on this night, Raḥel came before Leah, and the *ḥaroset* sweetens jealousy."

Let's try and explain this incredible point. Not that we really understand, but we sense it: Dipping the *maror* in the sweet *ḥaroset* sweetens harsh judgments – an older sister's bitterness that her younger sister got married first/had a baby first/succeeded.

It's a painful issue that hovers ominously over many families. There's competition and a great amount of pain, and it comes to the surface on the Seder night. Because this is a night when people feel jealous of one another, because there will always be families that are more successful, sisters-in-law who are more successful, others who are better cooks.

And what's the greatest part of this sorrow? The very fact that one feels jealous. After all, it's my sister/sister-in-law. Look how far this sorrow has taken me. Look how small-minded it's made me!

Jealousy is an emotion that subjugates. It's an emotion that makes us feel so low.

The Ari HaKadosh offers the following deep explanation:

The Tales of Rebbe Nahman:

The Bitter Herb

Once a Jew and a German traveled as vagabonds together. The Jew taught the German to make believe he was a Jew.

And it wasn't hard for him, since their languages are the same, and the Jews are compassionate and would certainly have pity on him.

Since Pesaḥ was approaching, he taught him how to conduct himself in the home of the Jew who would invite him to the Seder: At first, Kiddush is recited. Afterward, hands are washed. However, he forgot to tell him about the bitter herb.

And sure enough, a Jewish man invited him to join him for the Seder. But he was hungry from the entire day and eagerly waited to eat the fine foods that the Jew had told him about.

But he saw that they gave him a piece of *karpas* dipped in salt water and the other things served at a Seder and recited the Haggada. And he sat there impatiently longing for the meal…

When he realized they were serving the matza, he was happy, because he would soon be able to placate his hunger. And suddenly – they gave him the bitter herb. And when he put it in his mouth, it was bitter to taste, and he thought this was the entire meal, and he ran from the house bitter and hungry. And he thought to himself: Cursed Jews. After this entire ceremony, they gave me something bitter to eat…

And he went to the study hall and fell asleep.

After a while, the Jew arrived, happy and satiated from eating and drinking, and asked him: How was the Seder? And he angrily told him what had happened to him.

The Jew

This *maror* that you chew-chew-chew-chew cries for the jealousy that you feel, cries that you have become a jealous person, and suddenly endows you with a taste of reconciliation. Suddenly, you're liberated from your feelings of deficiency, because you digested them, you chewed them. Because you understood: It's bitter, but it's mine. I'm not ignoring it. I'll chew it really well, I'll swallow it as best as I can, and then I'll create space for the next incredible adventure.

Rabbi Mutzafi cites the Ari HaKadosh: "And this is the reason that he needs to feel the taste of bitterness. If he swallowed it (the *maror*) – he has not fulfilled his obligation, until he chews it with his teeth. Because by grinding [it] with teeth, the forces of judgment within Leah" – the anger about the injustice of it all, the frustration that it's your sister and you're supposed to be excited for her and you can't manage it – "are sweetened and ground into small pieces by thirty-two teeth."[200]

The *maror* is dipped in the *haroset*, and ultimately, you reach a reconciliation of sorts.

And it's necessary to go through this feminine pounding and drown in this feminine mud. When you go through things in the correct order, slowly but surely, you'll heal. From the bitterness, from the competitiveness, from the childlessness, from the infertility.

Do you understand? No. I also struggle to understand. Chew and make peace. Ultimately, we swallow the *maror*. But don't move too quickly, because you'll end up regurgitating jealousy, and it will still taste repulsive. Hold onto it for a little. Chew on it. And pray for this jealousy, this anger, to be sweetened.

> And this (*ḥaroset*) comes to sweeten judgments with kindnesses, and to eradicate death from the Jewish people. And it arouses the merit of our righteous matriarchs, primarily the merit of Raḥel and Leah and Ruth, the mother of royalty.[201]

Chew on the taste of the matriarchs; literally allow yourself to be nurtured by Raḥel, Leah, and Ruth. That's all I can explain, in my inferiority. It's hard to understand, but when we listen closely, we hear the great cry that ascends from the chewing of the *maror*.

> The Jew said to him: Stupid German, If you had waited just a little longer, you would have had a fine meal, just like me.
>
> And our Rebbe told this story to say that the body is purified through bitterness. But the person thinks that things will always be just bitter. And he therefore quickly runs away. However, if he would wait for a short while, and briefly endure the bitterness that purifies his body, he would feel all types of vitality and pleasure.

The non-Jew grows desperate when the food doesn't come, and doesn't come, and doesn't come. And finally, the food comes, and he devours it and instantly realizes: This is the bitter herb. And he curses. And he leaves. And the Jew says to him: "The story is just getting started...why did you give up in the first chapter?"

And the Or HaḤayim explains beautifully that eating the bitter herb is like putting a sharp spice in our food. It adds so much flavor to the entire dish. The sharp spice cannot be eaten on its own, but when it's added to different dishes, it makes everything taste incredible.

Korekh / Wrapping

כּוֹרֵךְ

The leader takes from himself and gives to all participants a kezayit from the lowermost matza and makes a sandwich out of the matza and a kezayit of the maror. It is passed to all participants (or everyone takes from the matza and maror in front of them) and says:

זֵכֶר In memory of the Temple, in the tradition of Hillel.
This is what Hillel would do
when the Temple still stood:
he would wrap [the Pesaḥ offering] up
with matza and bitter herbs
and eat them together,
to fulfill what is said:
"You shall eat it with matza and bitter herbs." *Num. 9*

Eat while leaning to the left.

Our Personal *Avoda: Korekh*

Pray that we will know
how to wait for the
last page of the story.
Patiently, just like Hillel.

בוצע את המצה התחתונה, נוטל ממנה כזית וכורך עמה כזית מן המרור, מחלק למסובים
(או שכל אחד מהם נוטל מן המצה השמורה שלפניו וכורך) ואומר:

זֵכֶר לַמִּקְדָּשׁ כְּהִלֵּל.
כֵּן עָשָׂה הִלֵּל בִּזְמַן שֶׁבֵּית הַמִּקְדָּשׁ הָיָה קַיָּם
הָיָה כּוֹרֵךְ פֶּסַח, מַצָּה וּמָרוֹר,
וְאוֹכֵל בְּיַחַד
לְקַיֵּם מַה שֶּׁנֶּאֱמַר:
עַל־מַצּוֹת וּמְרֹרִים יֹאכְלֻהוּ: במדבר ט

אוכלים בהסבת שמאל.

Because I taught the members of my household not to scream. When something happens, we simply wait for the next chapter of the story.

Write the chapter of your book that describes your coming of age. The chapter when you get everything you ever wanted. Decide what the cover will look like now. In my experience, as someone who published several books, this is the hard part. On the back cover, you need to summarize the plot and include a brief character sketch about you, and on the front cover you need to include a picture that will somehow tell the story in just a few lines. And, give your book a title.

And then you need to decide if it should be hardcover or softcover (this is so symbolic!).

And it's worth it! It's really worth it. When the book is finally bound, you can look from the side at everything you've gone through, and here too, the choice is all yours.

But Yemima, my story isn't just one volume. It's a long and complicated series. How many seasons will God let this show run for?

This is a fantastic question that you need to pose to Mashiaḥ. How many seasons will this show go on, if only we knew…

Look at the Story from Beginning to End

In *Korekh*, we take the *maror* (think about the most bitter thing in your life), wrap it in redemption (matza, *ḥaroset*), and proclaim: "I know that something good will come out of this bitterness. This bitterness is just one of the early chapters, and, from the get-go, I'm looking at the entire story. 'Who knows one?' I know; everything is one. Many happy chapters of this story await me."

At *Korekh* simply ask God to see the ending of your story. The happy ending, obviously.

More often than not, people ask me "Yemima, why? Why not me?" as opposed to "Yemima, when?" At *Korekh*, as we put the *maror* between two matzot, we must ask God to enable us to see the story in its entirety, from cover to cover. To help us understand that although we might be in the middle of an especially suspense-filled chapter right now, and the storyline isn't moving along so nicely, we need to look at the story in its entirety. To put things in context, between two matzot, like in *Korekh*.

"This is what Hillel would do when the Temple still stood: he would wrap [the Pesaḥ offering] up with the matza and bitter herbs and eat them together" – why? If they would hear a scream in the city, Hillel would say: "I am certain that [the scream] is not coming from my house."[202] I know, beyond a shadow of doubt, that this scream did not come from my home.

Why are you so sure?

Shulḥan Orekh / Table Setting

שֻׁלְחַן עוֹרֵךְ

אוכלים ושותים כברכת ה׳.

The festive meal is now eaten, with God's blessing.

Our Personal *Avoda: Shulḥan Orekh*

At *Shulḥan Orekh*, we should ask for the ability to appreciate.

We ask God for abundance, unity, and graciousness.

We ask that our human heart be nurtured and satisfied by this bread of oppression.

We ask to appreciate the one who prepared this meal for hours on end, and the one who went out to buy everything, and the one who showed up at the Seder tonight, even though it was hard for her.

Gratitude and appreciation are the best preparation.

Then he signaled for regular food from the table. The wise man then asked the prince, "What makes you think that you will stop being a turkey if you eat good food? You can eat whatever you want and still be a turkey!" They both ate food.

Finally, the wise man said, "What makes you think a turkey must sit under the table? Even a turkey can sit at the table." The wise man continued in this manner until the prince was completely cured.

You might find it surprising, but for some people, the hardest part is taking their eyes off the text and eating together! Our Sages teach us that eating brings people closer together,[203] and for this reason, the real drama unfolds under the table.

Who looks like he might want to disappear under the table right now?

Who looks like she's suffering from emotional anorexia?

Who is scared to have a real encounter? "You must open for him!" Descend to Egypt with him, lift him up, and bring him to this table, where the rest of the family has gathered together. Explain to him that this is also part of freedom.

The table is already a bit of a mess, and the wine stains and matza crumbs are everywhere. Even so, we can't forget about aesthetics tonight! Set the table again, and set the stage for an incredible redemption! Part of our preparation for the meal should necessarily include complimenting the people who spent hours getting everything ready, the one who cooked and prepared, the one who just wanted you to enjoy everything.

The Tales of Rebbe Nahman:

The Turkey Prince

A prince once became insane and thought that he was a turkey called Hindik. He felt compelled to sit naked under the table, pecking at bones and pieces of bread, like a turkey. All the royal physicians gave up hope of curing him of this madness. The king grieved tremendously, until one day, when a wise man arrived and said, "I take it upon myself to cure him."

The wise man undressed and sat naked under the table, next to the prince, pecking at crumbs and bones. "Who are you?" asked the prince. "What are you doing here?" "And you?" replied the wise man. "What are you doing here?" "I'm a turkey," said the prince. "I'm also a turkey," answered the wise man. They sat together like this for some time, until they became good friends.

One day, the wise man signaled to the king's servants to throw him shirts. He said to the prince, "What makes you think that a turkey can't wear a shirt? You can wear a shirt and still be a turkey." With that, the two of them put on shirts.

After a while, the wise man again signaled and they threw him pants. As before, he asked, "What makes you think that you can't be a turkey if you wear pants?" The wise man continued in this manner until they were both completely dressed.

Tzafun / Hidden

צָפוּן

בגמר הסעודה מוציא את פרוסת המצה שהצפין לאפיקומן, נוטל כשני זיתים
(שיעור אכילת אפיקומן כשני זיתים. כזית אחד - זכר לפסח, ואחד - זכר למצה הנאכלת עמו)
ונותן גם למסובים (או שהם נוטלים מן המצה השמורה שלפניהם), ואומרים:

הִנְנִי מוּכָן וּמְזֻמָּן לְקַיֵּם מִצְוַת אֲכִילַת אֲפִיקוֹמָן.
לְשֵׁם יִחוּד קֻדְשָׁא בְּרִיךְ הוּא וּשְׁכִינְתֵּהּ עַל יְדֵי הַהוּא
טָמִיר וְנֶעְלָם בְּשֵׁם כָּל יִשְׂרָאֵל.

אוכלים בהסבת שמאל.

At the end of the meal, the remaining piece of the matza which had been hidden for the afikoman, is now eaten (one kezayit for remembering the korban and the other in remembrance of the matza that was eaten with the korban) by everyone (they can also take from the matza in front of them) and say:

I am prepared and ready to fulfill the commandment of eating the afikoman. For the sake for the unification of the Holy One, blessed be He, and His Divine Presence, through He who is hidden and unseen, in the name of all Israel.

Eat while reclining to the left.

Our Personal *Avoda: Tzafun*

Ask to have faith that your other half, your missing half, is out there, hidden away somewhere.

Far more than the children want to find it, it wants to be found.

The Tales of Rebbe Nahman:

Hungarian Wine

He said a parable: Once, an important trader was traveling with a consignment of fine Hungarian wine. His assistant and the carriage driver said to him: Here we are traveling along this road with all this wine, and we're really suffering. Give us a little taste of the wine. He agreed to let them have a small taste.

A few days later the assistant happened to be sitting with a party of drinkers in a small town. The people he was with were drinking wine and praising the wine extravagantly. They said it was Hungarian wine. The assistant said: Let me have a taste. They gave him some.

He said: This isn't fine Hungarian wine at all!

They were highly offended and told him to get out.

He said: I know very well this isn't Hungarian wine! Because I was with a big merchant who really had Hungarian wine, and he gave me some to try. But they paid no attention to him.

The Rebbe concluded: However, in the future, when Mashiaḥ comes, then they will know. The time will come for them to serve the fine old wine stored up [for the righteous]. Other people they will be able to fool. They will give them inferior Romanian wines, Wallachsians and Strovitsarians, and tell them it is the fine old vintage wine.

But they won't be able to fool any of my followers, because we have already tasted the good wine.[204]

After we have tasted the *afikoman*, we cannot be misled by something that is inferior or fake.

Other people may be satisfied with less, but us?

We'll be hungry for freedom, hungry for love, ravenous for redemption! And we won't allow ourselves to be satisfied with anything less.

The time has come to give each person sitting around the table a piece of the *afikoman* that was hidden earlier in the night. These moments carry incredible power; this is a time of deep favor.

When the head of the home dispenses the *afikoman*, he must ask each and every person "What do you ask for?" and bless him with his request.

Rabbi Shlomo Carlebach used to conduct giant Seders for hundreds of people. When the time came to give out the *afikoman*, he would go from person to person, find out what they pined for, and bless them. Hundreds of people.

One year he came to a couple. A childless couple. A couple that had been married for years without children.

What do you want? He asked. They broke down in tears.

May you be blessed with a wonderful baby, he blessed them. Indeed, nine months later, a wonderful baby boy was born to this couple.

The *afikoman* is the essence of the blessing that Yitzḥak gave to Yaakov on this night. Don't let your father (or whoever dispenses the *afikoman*) give you your piece without blessing you with everything that you need and want.

"A time of favor" is a time when God can give you everything – why? Because at this moment, tremendous desire and willpower rise within *you*. At a time of favor, your desire and your willpower appear clearly and have the capacity to create change.

Don't sit there quietly and passively. Use these incredible moments. They appear only once each year. And ask, request, and pray for the things that are important to you.

The Zohar HaKadosh notes that when Esav cried and said, "Father, just show me which blessings Yaakov received," his father showed him the *afikoman*. These are the blessings that were meant for Esav and were redirected to Yaakov. All the stolen blessings are epitomized and embodied by the *afikoman*, this small piece of matza. There is so much healing and faith that radiates throughout your body as you eat the matza, and especially the *afikoman*. Faith in the power of skipping, and in the redemption that happens in an illogical order, faith in God who directs everything in the most surprising of ways.

Barekh / Blessing

בָּרֵךְ

The third cup of wine is poured and those who wash for mayim aḥronim wash now. The cup is raised and the following is said:

I am prepared and ready to fulfill the commandment of Birkat HaMazon.
You will eat and be satisfied, then you shall bless the Lord your God for the good land He has given you *Deut. 8*
For the sake for the unification of the Holy One, blessed be He, and His Divine Presence, through He who is hidden and unseen, in the name of all Israel.

שִׁיר הַמַּעֲלוֹת A song of ascents. When the LORD brought back the exiles of Zion we were like people who dream. Then were our mouths filled with laughter, and our tongues with songs of joy. Then was it said among the nations, "The LORD has done great things for them." The LORD did do great things for us and we rejoiced. Bring back our exiles, LORD, like streams in a dry land. May those who sowed in tears, reap in joy. May one who goes out weeping, carrying a bag of seed, come back with songs of joy, carrying his sheaves. *Ps. 126*

Some add:

תְּהִלַּת My mouth shall speak the praise of God, and *Ps. 145*
all creatures shall bless His holy name for ever and all
time. We will bless God now and for ever. Halleluya! *Ps. 115*
Thank the LORD for He is good: His loving-kindness *Ps. 136*
is for ever. Who can tell of the LORD's mighty acts and *Ps. 106*
make all His praise be heard?

מוזגים כוס שלישי ונוטלים מים אחרונים. אוחז את הכוס בימינו ואומר:

הִנְנִי מוּכָן וּמְזֻמָּן לְקַיֵּם מִצְוַת עֲשֵׂה שֶׁל בִּרְכַּת הַמָּזוֹן כְּמוֹ שֶׁכָּתוּב בַּתּוֹרָה
וְאָכַלְתָּ וְשָׂבָעְתָּ, וּבֵרַכְתָּ אֶת־יהוה אֱלֹהֶיךָ עַל־הָאָרֶץ הַטֹּבָה אֲשֶׁר נָתַן־לָךְ: דברים ח
לְשֵׁם יִחוּד קֻדְשָׁא בְּרִיךְ הוּא וּשְׁכִינְתֵּהּ עַל יְדֵי הַהוּא טָמִיר וְנֶעְלָם בְּשֵׁם כָּל יִשְׂרָאֵל.

שִׁיר הַמַּעֲלוֹת בְּשׁוּב יהוה אֶת־שִׁיבַת צִיּוֹן, הָיִינוּ תהלים קכו
כְּחֹלְמִים: אָז יִמָּלֵא שְׂחוֹק פִּינוּ וּלְשׁוֹנֵנוּ רִנָּה אָז יֹאמְרוּ
בַגּוֹיִם הִגְדִּיל יהוה לַעֲשׂוֹת עִם־אֵלֶּה: הִגְדִּיל יהוה
לַעֲשׂוֹת עִמָּנוּ, הָיִינוּ שְׂמֵחִים: שׁוּבָה יהוה אֶת־שְׁבִיתֵנוּ,
כַּאֲפִיקִים בַּנֶּגֶב: הַזֹּרְעִים בְּדִמְעָה, בְּרִנָּה יִקְצֹרוּ: הָלוֹךְ
יֵלֵךְ וּבָכֹה נֹשֵׂא מֶשֶׁךְ־הַזָּרַע בֹּא־יָבֹא בְרִנָּה נֹשֵׂא אֲלֻמֹּתָיו:

יש מוסיפים:

תְּהִלַּת יהוה יְדַבֶּר פִּי תהלים קמה
וִיבָרֵךְ כָּל־בָּשָׂר שֵׁם קָדְשׁוֹ לְעוֹלָם וָעֶד:
וַאֲנַחְנוּ נְבָרֵךְ יָהּ מֵעַתָּה וְעַד־עוֹלָם, הַלְלוּיָהּ: תהלים קטו
הוֹדוּ לַיהוה כִּי־טוֹב, כִּי לְעוֹלָם חַסְדּוֹ: תהלים קלו
מִי יְמַלֵּל גְּבוּרוֹת יהוה, יַשְׁמִיעַ כָּל־תְּהִלָּתוֹ: תהלים קו

Birkat Hamazon – Nusaḥ Ashkenaz

When three or more men dined together, the following must be said:

Leader Gentlemen, let us say grace.

Others May the name of the Lord be blessed from now and for ever. *Ps. 113*

Leader May the name of the Lord be blessed from now and for ever.

With your permission, (my father and teacher / my mother and teacher / the Kohanim present / our teacher the Rabbi / the master of this house / the mistress of this house)

my masters and teachers, let us bless (*in a minyan:* our God,) the One from whose food we have eaten.

Others Blessed be (*in a minyan:* our God,) the One from whose food we have eaten, and by whose goodness we live.

Leader Blessed be (*in a minyan:* our God,) the One from whose food we have eaten, and by whose goodness we live. Blessed be He, and blessed be His name.

Our Personal *Avoda*: Profound Prayers

This blessing includes so many profound prayers: Pray that all creatures will have what to eat. Pray that this home will be filled with abundant blessing.

Pray to arrive at the "holidays that await us in peace." Pray that the blessing that seems overwhelmingly long at times will not be cut short: "May the compassionate One bless my father, my teacher, and my mother, my teacher." May we always be fortunate enough to bless them.

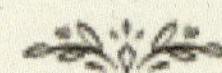

ברכת המזון בנוסח אשכנז

שלושה שאכלו כאחד חייבים לזמן:

המזמן: רַבּוֹתַי, נְבָרֵךְ.

המסובים: יְהִי שֵׁם יהוה מְבֹרָךְ מֵעַתָּה וְעַד־עוֹלָם: תהלים קיג

המזמן: יְהִי שֵׁם יהוה מְבֹרָךְ מֵעַתָּה וְעַד־עוֹלָם:

בִּרְשׁוּת (אָבִי מוֹרִי / אִמִּי מוֹרָתִי / כֹּהֲנִים / מוֹרֵנוּ הָרַב / בַּעַל הַבַּיִת הַזֶּה / בַּעֲלַת הַבַּיִת הַזֶּה)

מָרָנָן וְרַבָּנָן וְרַבּוֹתַי נְבָרֵךְ (במניין: אֱלֹהֵינוּ) שֶׁאָכַלְנוּ מִשֶּׁלּוֹ.

המסובים: בָּרוּךְ (במניין: אֱלֹהֵינוּ) שֶׁאָכַלְנוּ מִשֶּׁלּוֹ וּבְטוּבוֹ חָיִינוּ.

המזמן: בָּרוּךְ (במניין: אֱלֹהֵינוּ) שֶׁאָכַלְנוּ מִשֶּׁלּוֹ וּבְטוּבוֹ חָיִינוּ.
בָּרוּךְ הוּא וּבָרוּךְ שְׁמוֹ.

BLESSING OF NOURISHMENT

בָּרוּךְ Blessed are You, LORD our God,
King of the Universe,
who in His goodness feeds the whole world
with grace, kindness and compassion.
He gives food to all living things,
for His kindness is for ever.
Because of His continual great goodness,
we have never lacked food,
nor may we ever lack it,
for the sake of His great name.
For He is God who feeds and sustains all,
does good to all,
and prepares food for all creatures He has created. Ps. 145
Blessed are You, LORD, who feeds all.

BLESSING OF LAND

נוֹדֶה We thank You, LORD our God,
for having granted as a heritage to our ancestors
a desirable, good and spacious land;
for bringing us out, LORD our God, from the land of Egypt,
freeing us from the house of slavery;

ברכת הזן

בָּרוּךְ אַתָּה יהוה אֱלֹהֵינוּ מֶלֶךְ הָעוֹלָם
הַזָּן אֶת הָעוֹלָם כֻּלּוֹ בְּטוּבוֹ
בְּחֵן בְּחֶסֶד וּבְרַחֲמִים
הוּא נוֹתֵן לֶחֶם לְכָל בָּשָׂר כִּי לְעוֹלָם חַסְדּוֹ.
וּבְטוּבוֹ הַגָּדוֹל, תָּמִיד לֹא חָסַר לָנוּ
וְאַל יֶחְסַר לָנוּ מָזוֹן לְעוֹלָם וָעֶד
בַּעֲבוּר שְׁמוֹ הַגָּדוֹל.
כִּי הוּא אֵל זָן וּמְפַרְנֵס לַכֹּל וּמֵטִיב לַכֹּל
וּמֵכִין מָזוֹן לְכָל בְּרִיּוֹתָיו אֲשֶׁר בָּרָא.
כָּאָמוּר, פּוֹתֵחַ אֶת־יָדֶךָ וּמַשְׂבִּיעַ לְכָל־חַי רָצוֹן: תהלים קמה
בָּרוּךְ אַתָּה יהוה, הַזָּן אֶת הַכֹּל.

ברכת הארץ

נוֹדֶה לְּךָ יהוה אֱלֹהֵינוּ עַל שֶׁהִנְחַלְתָּ לַאֲבוֹתֵינוּ
אֶרֶץ חֶמְדָּה טוֹבָה וּרְחָבָה
וְעַל שֶׁהוֹצֵאתָנוּ יהוה אֱלֹהֵינוּ מֵאֶרֶץ מִצְרַיִם
וּפְדִיתָנוּ מִבֵּית עֲבָדִים

for Your covenant which You sealed in our flesh;
for Your Torah which You taught us;
for Your laws which You made known to us;
for the life, grace and kindness You have bestowed on us;
and for the food by which You continually feed and sustain us,
every day, every season, every hour.

For all this, Lord our God,
we thank and bless You.
May Your name be blessed continually
by the mouth of all that lives, for ever and all time –
for so it is written: "You will eat and be satisfied, then you shall *Deut. 8*
bless the Lord your God for the good land He has given you."
Blessed are You, Lord, for the land and for the food.

וְעַל בְּרִיתְךָ שֶׁחָתַמְתָּ בִּבְשָׂרֵנוּ
וְעַל תּוֹרָתְךָ שֶׁלִּמַּדְתָּנוּ וְעַל חֻקֶּיךָ שֶׁהוֹדַעְתָּנוּ
וְעַל חַיִּים חֵן וָחֶסֶד שֶׁחוֹנַנְתָּנוּ
וְעַל אֲכִילַת מָזוֹן שָׁאַתָּה זָן וּמְפַרְנֵס אוֹתָנוּ תָּמִיד
בְּכָל יוֹם וּבְכָל עֵת וּבְכָל שָׁעָה.

וְעַל הַכֹּל יהוה אֱלֹהֵינוּ,
אֲנַחְנוּ מוֹדִים לָךְ וּמְבָרְכִים אוֹתָךְ
יִתְבָּרַךְ שִׁמְךָ בְּפִי כָּל חַי תָּמִיד לְעוֹלָם וָעֶד
כַּכָּתוּב: וְאָכַלְתָּ וְשָׂבָעְתָּ, וּבֵרַכְתָּ אֶת־יהוה אֱלֹהֶיךָ דברים ח
עַל־הָאָרֶץ הַטֹּבָה אֲשֶׁר נָתַן־לָךְ:
בָּרוּךְ אַתָּה יהוה, עַל הָאָרֶץ וְעַל הַמָּזוֹן.

BLESSING FOR JERUSALEM

רַחֵם נָא Have compassion,
please, Lord our God,
on Israel Your people,
on Jerusalem Your city,
on Zion the dwelling place of Your glory,
on the royal house of David Your anointed,
and on the great and holy House
that bears Your name.
Our God, our Father,
tend us, feed us, sustain us and support us,
relieve us and send us relief,
Lord our God, swiftly from all our troubles.
Please, Lord our God,
do not make us dependent
on the gifts or loans of other people,
but only on Your full, open, holy and generous hand
so that we may suffer neither shame nor humiliation
for ever and all time.

ברכת ירושלים

רַחֶם נָא יהוה אֱלֹהֵינוּ
עַל יִשְׂרָאֵל עַמֶּךָ
וְעַל יְרוּשָׁלַיִם עִירֶךָ
וְעַל צִיּוֹן מִשְׁכַּן כְּבוֹדֶךָ
וְעַל מַלְכוּת בֵּית דָּוִד מְשִׁיחֶךָ
וְעַל הַבַּיִת הַגָּדוֹל וְהַקָּדוֹשׁ שֶׁנִּקְרָא שִׁמְךָ עָלָיו.
אֱלֹהֵינוּ, אָבִינוּ
רְעֵנוּ, זוּנֵנוּ, פַּרְנְסֵנוּ וְכַלְכְּלֵנוּ
וְהַרְוִיחֵנוּ, וְהַרְוַח לָנוּ
יהוה אֱלֹהֵינוּ מְהֵרָה מִכָּל צָרוֹתֵינוּ.
וְנָא אַל תַּצְרִיכֵנוּ, יהוה אֱלֹהֵינוּ
לֹא לִידֵי מַתְּנַת בָּשָׂר וָדָם וְלֹא לִידֵי הַלְוָאָתָם
כִּי אִם לְיָדְךָ הַמְּלֵאָה, הַפְּתוּחָה, הַקְּדוֹשָׁה וְהָרְחָבָה
שֶׁלֹּא נֵבוֹשׁ וְלֹא נִכָּלֵם לְעוֹלָם וָעֶד.

On Shabbat, say: רְצֵה Favor and strengthen us, Lord our God,
through Your commandments,
especially through the commandment of the seventh day,
this great and holy Sabbath.
For it is, for You, a great and holy day.
On it we cease work and rest in love
in accord with Your will's commandment.
May it be Your will, Lord our God,
to grant us rest without distress,
grief, or lament on our day of rest.
May You show us the consolation of Zion Your city,
and the rebuilding of Jerusalem Your holy city,
for You are the Master of salvation and consolation.

אֱלֹהֵינוּ Our God and God of our ancestors,
may there rise, come, reach, appear, be favored,
heard, regarded
and remembered before You, our recollection and remembrance,
as well as the remembrance of our ancestors,
and of the Messiah son of David Your servant,
and of Jerusalem Your holy city,
and of all Your people the house of Israel –

בשבת:

רְצֵה וְהַחֲלִיצֵנוּ
יהוה אֱלֹהֵינוּ, בְּמִצְוֹתֶיךָ
וּבְמִצְוַת יוֹם הַשְּׁבִיעִי
הַשַּׁבָּת הַגָּדוֹל וְהַקָּדוֹשׁ הַזֶּה
כִּי יוֹם זֶה גָּדוֹל וְקָדוֹשׁ הוּא לְפָנֶיךָ
לִשְׁבָּת בּוֹ, וְלָנוּחַ בּוֹ בְּאַהֲבָה כְּמִצְוַת רְצוֹנֶךָ
וּבִרְצוֹנְךָ הָנִיחַ לָנוּ, יהוה אֱלֹהֵינוּ
שֶׁלֹּא תְהֵא צָרָה וְיָגוֹן וַאֲנָחָה בְּיוֹם מְנוּחָתֵנוּ
וְהַרְאֵנוּ, יהוה אֱלֹהֵינוּ, בְּנֶחָמַת צִיּוֹן עִירֶךָ
וּבְבִנְיַן יְרוּשָׁלַיִם עִיר קָדְשֶׁךָ
כִּי אַתָּה הוּא בַּעַל הַיְשׁוּעוֹת וּבַעַל הַנֶּחָמוֹת.

אֱלֹהֵינוּ וֵאלֹהֵי אֲבוֹתֵינוּ
יַעֲלֶה וְיָבוֹא וְיַגִּיעַ, וְיֵרָאֶה וְיֵרָצֶה וְיִשָּׁמַע
וְיִפָּקֵד, וְיִזָּכֵר זִכְרוֹנֵנוּ וּפִקְדוֹנֵנוּ,
וְזִכְרוֹן אֲבוֹתֵינוּ
וְזִכְרוֹן מָשִׁיחַ בֶּן דָּוִד עַבְדֶּךָ וְזִכְרוֹן יְרוּשָׁלַיִם עִיר קָדְשֶׁךָ
וְזִכְרוֹן כָּל עַמְּךָ בֵּית יִשְׂרָאֵל

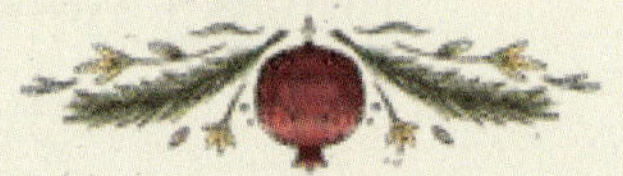

for deliverance and well-being, grace, loving-kindness
and compassion, life and peace, on this day of the festival of Matzot.
On it remember us, LORD our God, for good;
recollect us for blessing, and deliver us for life.
In accord with Your promise of salvation and compassion,
spare us and be gracious to us; have compassion on us and deliver us,
for our eyes are turned to You because You are God,
gracious and compassionate.

And may Jerusalem the holy city be rebuilt soon, in our time.
Blessed are You, LORD, who in His compassion
will rebuild Jerusalem.

Amen.

לְפָנֶיךָ, לִפְלֵיטָה לְטוֹבָה, לְחֵן וּלְחֶסֶד וּלְרַחֲמִים
לְחַיִּים וּלְשָׁלוֹם בְּיוֹם חַג הַמַּצּוֹת הַזֶּה.
זָכְרֵנוּ יהוה אֱלֹהֵינוּ בּוֹ לְטוֹבָה וּפָקְדֵנוּ בוֹ לִבְרָכָה
וְהוֹשִׁיעֵנוּ בוֹ לְחַיִּים טוֹבִים.
וּבִדְבַר יְשׁוּעָה וְרַחֲמִים חוּס וְחָנֵּנוּ וְרַחֵם עָלֵינוּ, וְהוֹשִׁיעֵנוּ
כִּי אֵלֶיךָ עֵינֵינוּ, כִּי אֵל מֶלֶךְ חַנּוּן וְרַחוּם אָתָּה.

וּבְנֵה יְרוּשָׁלַיִם עִיר הַקֹּדֶשׁ בִּמְהֵרָה בְיָמֵינוּ.
בָּרוּךְ אַתָּה יהוה, בּוֹנֶה בְרַחֲמָיו יְרוּשָׁלָיִם

אָמֵן.

BLESSING OF GOD'S GOODNESS

בָּרוּךְ Blessed are You, LORD our God,
King of the Universe –
God our Father, our King, our Sovereign,
our Creator, our Redeemer, our Maker,
our Holy One, the Holy One of Yaakov.
He is our Shepherd, Israel's Shepherd,
the good King who does good to all.
Every day He has done, is doing,
and will do good to us.
He has acted, is acting,
and will always act kindly toward us for ever,
granting us grace, kindness and compassion,
relief and rescue,
prosperity, blessing,
redemption and comfort,
sustenance and support, compassion, life,
peace and all good things,
and of all good things
may He never let us lack.

ברכת הטוב והמטיב

בָּרוּךְ אַתָּה יהוה אֱלֹהֵינוּ מֶלֶךְ הָעוֹלָם
הָאֵל אָבִינוּ, מַלְכֵּנוּ, אַדִּירֵנוּ
בּוֹרְאֵנוּ, גּוֹאֲלֵנוּ, יוֹצְרֵנוּ, קְדוֹשֵׁנוּ
קְדוֹשׁ יַעֲקֹב רוֹעֵנוּ, רוֹעֵה יִשְׂרָאֵל
הַמֶּלֶךְ הַטּוֹב וְהַמֵּיטִיב לַכֹּל, שֶׁבְּכָל יוֹם וָיוֹם
הוּא הֵיטִיב, הוּא מֵיטִיב, הוּא יֵיטִיב לָנוּ
הוּא גְמָלָנוּ, הוּא גוֹמְלֵנוּ
הוּא יִגְמְלֵנוּ לָעַד
לְחֵן וּלְחֶסֶד וּלְרַחֲמִים
וּלְרֶוַח, הַצָּלָה וְהַצְלָחָה
בְּרָכָה וִישׁוּעָה
נֶחָמָה, פַּרְנָסָה וְכַלְכָּלָה
וְרַחֲמִים וְחַיִּים וְשָׁלוֹם וְכָל טוֹב
וּמִכָּל טוּב
לְעוֹלָם אַל יְחַסְּרֵנוּ.

ADDITIONAL REQUESTS

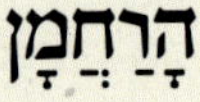

May the Compassionate One reign over us
for ever and all time.

May the Compassionate One be blessed
in heaven and on earth.

May the Compassionate One be praised
from generation to generation,
be glorified by us to all eternity,
and honored among us for ever and all time.

May the Compassionate One
grant us an honorable livelihood.

May the Compassionate One
break the yoke from our neck
and lead us upright to our land.

May the Compassionate One
send us many blessings to this house
and this table at which we have eaten.

May the Compassionate One
send us Eliyahu the prophet –
may he be remembered for good –
to bring us good tidings
of salvation and consolation.

May the Compassionate One
bless the State of Israel,
first flowering of our redemption.

May the Compassionate One
bless the members of Israel's Defense Forces,
who stand guard over our land.

בקשות נוספות

הָרַחֲמָן הוּא יִמְלֹךְ עָלֵינוּ לְעוֹלָם וָעֶד.

הָרַחֲמָן הוּא יִתְבָּרַךְ בַּשָּׁמַיִם וּבָאָרֶץ.

הָרַחֲמָן הוּא יִשְׁתַּבַּח לְדוֹר דּוֹרִים
וְיִתְפָּאַר בָּנוּ לָעַד וּלְנֵצַח נְצָחִים
וְיִתְהַדַּר בָּנוּ לָעַד וּלְעוֹלְמֵי עוֹלָמִים.

הָרַחֲמָן הוּא יְפַרְנְסֵנוּ בְּכָבוֹד.

הָרַחֲמָן הוּא יִשְׁבֹּר עֻלֵּנוּ מֵעַל צַוָּארֵנוּ
וְהוּא יוֹלִיכֵנוּ קוֹמְמִיּוּת לְאַרְצֵנוּ.

הָרַחֲמָן הוּא יִשְׁלַח לָנוּ בְּרָכָה מְרֻבָּה בַּבַּיִת הַזֶּה
וְעַל שֻׁלְחָן זֶה שֶׁאָכַלְנוּ עָלָיו.

הָרַחֲמָן הוּא יִשְׁלַח לָנוּ
אֶת אֵלִיָּהוּ הַנָּבִיא זָכוּר לַטּוֹב
וִיבַשֶּׂר לָנוּ בְּשׂוֹרוֹת טוֹבוֹת
יְשׁוּעוֹת וְנֶחָמוֹת.

הָרַחֲמָן הוּא יְבָרֵךְ אֶת מְדִינַת יִשְׂרָאֵל
רֵאשִׁית צְמִיחַת גְּאֻלָּתֵנוּ.

הָרַחֲמָן הוּא יְבָרֵךְ אֶת חַיָּלֵי צְבָא הַהֲגָנָה לְיִשְׂרָאֵל
הָעוֹמְדִים עַל מִשְׁמַר אַרְצֵנוּ.

A guest says:

May it be Your will that the master of this house shall not suffer shame in this world, nor humiliation in the World to Come. May all he owns prosper greatly, and may his and our possessions be successful and close to hand. Let not the Accuser hold sway over his deeds or ours, and may no thought of sin, iniquity or transgression enter him or us from now and for evermore.

הָרַחֲמָן May the Compassionate One bless –

When eating at one's own table, say (include the words in parentheses that apply):

me, (my wife / husband / my father, my teacher / my mother, my teacher / my children)
and all that is mine,

Children at their parents' table say (include the words in parentheses that apply):

my father, my teacher (master of this house), and my mother,
my teacher (mistress of this house), them, their household,
their children, and all that is theirs.

A guest at someone else's table says (include the words in parentheses that apply):

the master of this house, him
(and his wife, the mistress of this house / and his children)
and all that is his,

ברכת האורח:

יְהִי רָצוֹן שֶׁלֹּא יֵבוֹשׁ בַּעַל הַבַּיִת בָּעוֹלָם הַזֶּה, וְלֹא יִכָּלֵם לָעוֹלָם הַבָּא, וְיִצְלַח מְאֹד בְּכָל נְכָסָיו, וְיִהְיוּ נְכָסָיו וּנְכָסֵינוּ מֻצְלָחִים וּקְרוֹבִים לָעִיר, וְאַל יִשְׁלֹט שָׂטָן לֹא בְּמַעֲשֵׂה יָדָיו וְלֹא בְּמַעֲשֵׂה יָדֵינוּ. וְאַל יִזְדַּקֵּק לֹא לְפָנָיו וְלֹא לְפָנֵינוּ שׁוּם דְּבַר הִרְהוּר חֵטְא, עֲבֵירָה וְעָוֹן, מֵעַתָּה וְעַד עוֹלָם.

בעל הבית ובעלת הבית אומרים:

הָרַחֲמָן הוּא יְבָרֵךְ אוֹתִי

(וְאֶת אִשְׁתִּי / וְאֶת בַּעֲלִי / וְאֶת אָבִי מוֹרִי / וְאֶת אִמִּי מוֹרָתִי / וְאֶת זַרְעִי)

וְאֶת כָּל אֲשֶׁר לִי

ילדים האוכלים על שולחן הוריהם אומרים:

הָרַחֲמָן הוּא יְבָרֵךְ אֶת אָבִי מוֹרִי (בַּעַל הַבַּיִת הַזֶּה)**,**
וְאֶת אִמִּי מוֹרָתִי (בַּעֲלַת הַבַּיִת הַזֶּה)**, אוֹתָם וְאֶת בֵּיתָם וְאֶת זַרְעָם**
וְאֶת כָּל אֲשֶׁר לָהֶם

אורח אומר:

הָרַחֲמָן הוּא יְבָרֵךְ אֶת בַּעַל הַבַּיִת הַזֶּה
וְאֶת בַּעֲלַת הַבַּיִת הַזֶּה אוֹתָם וְאֶת בֵּיתָם וְאֶת זַרְעָם וְאֶת
כָּל אֲשֶׁר לָהֶם

For all other guests, add:

and all the diners here,
them, their household,
their children, and all that is theirs

אוֹתָנוּ together with us and all that is ours.
Just as our forefathers Avraham, Yitzḥak and Yaakov
were blessed in all, from all, with all, so may He
bless all of us together with a complete blessing,

and let us say: Amen.

בַּמָּרוֹם On high, may grace be invoked for them and for us,
as a safeguard of peace.
May we receive a blessing from the Lord
and a just reward from the God of our salvation,
and may we find grace and good favor
in the eyes of God and man.

אם יש אורחים נוספים, מוסיפים:

וְאֶת כָּל הַמְּסֻבִּין כָּאן
אוֹתָם וְאֶת בֵּיתָם וְאֶת זַרְעָם
וְאֶת כָּל אֲשֶׁר לָהֶם

אוֹתָֽנוּ וְאֶת כָּל אֲשֶׁר לָֽנוּ כְּמוֹ שֶׁנִּתְבָּֽרְכוּ אֲבוֹתֵֽינוּ
אַבְרָהָם יִצְחָק וְיַֽעֲקֹב, בַּכֹּל, מִכֹּל, כֹּל
כֵּן יְבָרֵךְ אוֹתָֽנוּ כֻּלָּֽנוּ יַֽחַד בִּבְרָכָה שְׁלֵמָה

וְנֹאמַר אָמֵן.

בַּמָּרוֹם יְלַמְּדוּ עֲלֵיהֶם וְעָלֵֽינוּ
זְכוּת שֶׁתְּהֵא לְמִשְׁמֶֽרֶת שָׁלוֹם
וְנִשָּׂא בְרָכָה מֵאֵת יהוה וּצְדָקָה
מֵאֱלֹהֵי יִשְׁעֵֽנוּ וְנִמְצָא חֵן וְשֵֽׂכֶל טוֹב
בְּעֵינֵי אֱלֹהִים וְאָדָם.

On Shabbat: May the Compassionate One
let us inherit the time, that will be entirely Shabbat
and rest for life everlasting.

May the Compassionate One
let us inherit the day that is all good.

May the Compassionate One
make us worthy
of the messianic age and life in the World to Come.

He is a tower of salvation to His king,
showing kindness to His anointed,
to David and his descendants for ever.

He who makes peace in His high places,
may He make peace for us and all Israel,
and let us say: Amen.

בשבת: הָרַחֲמָן הוּא יַנְחִילֵנוּ יוֹם שֶׁכֻּלּוֹ שַׁבָּת
וּמְנוּחָה לְחַיֵּי הָעוֹלָמִים.

הָרַחֲמָן הוּא יַנְחִילֵנוּ יוֹם שֶׁכֻּלּוֹ טוֹב.

הָרַחֲמָן הוּא יְזַכֵּנוּ לִימוֹת הַמָּשִׁיחַ
וּלְחַיֵּי הָעוֹלָם הַבָּא.

מִגְדּוֹל יְשׁוּעוֹת מַלְכּוֹ
וְעֹשֶׂה־חֶסֶד לִמְשִׁיחוֹ
לְדָוִד וּלְזַרְעוֹ עַד־עוֹלָם: שמואל ב׳ כב

עֹשֶׂה שָׁלוֹם בִּמְרוֹמָיו הוּא יַעֲשֶׂה שָׁלוֹם
עָלֵינוּ וְעַל כָּל יִשְׂרָאֵל
וְאִמְרוּ אָמֵן.

יְראוּ Fear the LORD, you His holy ones; *Ps. 34*
those who fear Him lack nothing.
Young lions may grow weak and hungry,
but those who seek the LORD lack no good thing.
Thank the LORD for He is good: His loving-kindness is for ever. *Ps. 118*
You open Your hand and satisfy the desire of every living thing. *Ps. 145*
Blessed is the person who trusts in the LORD, *Jer. 17*
whose trust is in the LORD alone.
Once I was young, and now I am old, *Ps. 37*
yet I have never watched a righteous man forsaken
or his children begging for bread.
The LORD will give His people strength.
The LORD will bless His people with peace. *Ps. 29*

תהלים לד **יִרְאוּ** אֶת־יהוה קְדֹשָׁיו כִּי־אֵין מַחְסוֹר לִירֵאָיו:
כְּפִירִים רָשׁוּ וְרָעֵבוּ
וְדֹרְשֵׁי יהוה לֹא־יַחְסְרוּ כָל־טוֹב:

תהלים קיח הוֹדוּ לַיהוה כִּי־טוֹב, כִּי לְעוֹלָם חַסְדּוֹ:

תהלים קמה פּוֹתֵחַ אֶת־יָדֶךָ, וּמַשְׂבִּיעַ לְכָל־חַי רָצוֹן:

ירמיה יז בָּרוּךְ הַגֶּבֶר אֲשֶׁר יִבְטַח בַּיהוה, וְהָיָה יהוה מִבְטַחוֹ:

תהלים לז נַעַר הָיִיתִי גַּם־זָקַנְתִּי
וְלֹא־רָאִיתִי צַדִּיק נֶעֱזָב, וְזַרְעוֹ מְבַקֶּשׁ־לָחֶם:

תהלים כט יהוה עֹז לְעַמּוֹ יִתֵּן, יהוה יְבָרֵךְ אֶת־עַמּוֹ בַשָּׁלוֹם:

Birkat Hamazon – Nusaḥ Edot Hamizraḥ

Before saying Birkat Hamazon, there are those that wash their hands with a bit of water to rid any residue from their hands. The following is said:

I will bless the Lord at all times; His praise will be always on my lips. The final word: *Ps. 34*
it has all been said. Hold God in awe; heed His commands for that is all man has. *Eccl. 12*
My mouth shall speak the praise of the Lord, and all creatures shall bless His holy name for ever and *Ps. 145*
all time. We will bless the Lord now and for ever. Halleluya! He spoke to me: *Ps. 115*
"This is the table placed before the Lord." *Ez. 41*

When three or more men dined together, the following must be said . If a minyan is present, add "Our God.":

All: Let us bless the Holy, Supreme King.

Leader: [with the permission of] Heaven,
With the permission of the Holy Supreme King,
With the permission of the Shabbat Queen
With the permission of the holy Good Day
And with the permission of the seven holy supreme guests,
With the permission of my teachers and rabbis,
And with your permission, with heaven's permission,
Let us bless (our God), from whose food we have eaten.

All: Blessed is (our God) He from whose food we have eaten
and by whose goodness we live.

Leader: Blessed is (our God) He from whose food we have eaten
and by whose goodness we live.
Blessed be He, blessed be His name, and blessed be His memory forever and ever.

ברכת המזון בנוסח עדות המזרח

קודם ברכת המזון יש ליטול את הידיים במעט מים כדי להעביר את הלכלוך שעליהן.

יש אומרים:

אֲבָרְכָה אֶת־יְהוָה בְּכָל־עֵת, תָּמִיד תְּהִלָּתוֹ בְּפִי: סוֹף דָּבָר הַכֹּל נִשְׁמָע, אֶת־הָאֱלֹהִים יְרָא וְאֶת־ תהלים לד קהלת יב
מִצְוֹתָיו שְׁמוֹר, כִּי־זֶה כָּל־הָאָדָם: תְּהִלַּת יְהוָה יְדַבֶּר פִּי, וִיבָרֵךְ כָּל־בָּשָׂר שֵׁם קָדְשׁוֹ, לְעוֹלָם תהלים קמה
וָעֶד: וַאֲנַחְנוּ נְבָרֵךְ יָהּ, מֵעַתָּה וְעַד־עוֹלָם, הַלְלוּיָהּ: וַיְדַבֵּר אֵלַי, זֶה הַשֻּׁלְחָן, אֲשֶׁר לִפְנֵי יְהוָה: תהלים קטו יחזקאל מא

שלושה שאכלו כאחד חיבים לזמן. אם עשרה אכלו יחד, מזמנים בשם.

המזמן: הַב לָן וְנִבְרִיךְ לְמַלְכָּא עִלָּאָה קַדִּישָׁא

המסובין: שָׁמַיִם

המזמן: בִּרְשׁוּת מַלְכָּא עִלָּאָה קַדִּישָׁא

וּמַמְשִׁיכִים 'וּבִרְשׁוּת מוֹרַי וְרַבּוֹתַי'.

ויש המתחילים מכאן:

המזמן: בִּרְשׁוּת מוֹרַי וְרַבּוֹתַי וּבִרְשׁוּתְכֶם

והשומעים עונים: בִּרְשׁוּת שָׁמַיִם

המזמן: נְבָרֵךְ (במניין: אֱלֹהֵינוּ) שֶׁאָכַלְנוּ מִשֶּׁלּוֹ.

המסובין: בָּרוּךְ (במניין: אֱלֹהֵינוּ) שֶׁאָכַלְנוּ מִשֶּׁלּוֹ וּבְטוּבוֹ חָיִינוּ.

המסובין: בָּרוּךְ (במניין: אֱלֹהֵינוּ) שֶׁאָכַלְנוּ מִשֶּׁלּוֹ וּבְטוּבוֹ חָיִינוּ.

יש אומרים: בָּרוּךְ הוּא וּבָרוּךְ שְׁמוֹ, וּבָרוּךְ זִכְרוֹ לְעוֹלְמֵי עַד.

בָּרוּךְ Blessed are You, Lord our God, King of the Universe,
(Who feeds us not from our deeds, who sustains us not
because we deserve it, who favors us with His goodness)
(The God) who feeds us
and the whole world in His goodness
with grace, kindness, abundance and much compassion.
He gives food to all living things, for His kindness is for ever. *Ps. 136*
Because of His great goodness,
we have never lacked food, nor may we ever lack it.
For He is God who feeds and sustains all,
and His table is set for all,
and He prepares sustenance and food
for all creatures He has created,

בָּרוּךְ אַתָּה יְהֹוָה
אֱלֹהֵינוּ מֶלֶךְ הָעוֹלָם
(הַזָּנֵנוּ וְלֹא מִמַּעֲשֵׂינוּ, הַמְפַרְנְסֵנוּ וְלֹא מִצִּדְקוֹתֵינוּ, הַמַּעֲדִיף טוּבוֹ עָלֵינוּ)
הָאֵל הַזָּן אוֹתָנוּ וְאֶת הָעוֹלָם כֻּלּוֹ בְּטוּבוֹ
בְּחֵן בְּחֶסֶד בְּרֶוַח וּבְרַחֲמִים רַבִּים
נֹתֵן לֶחֶם לְכָל־בָּשָׂר כִּי לְעוֹלָם חַסְדּוֹ: תהלים קלו
וּבְטוּבוֹ הַגָּדוֹל, תָּמִיד לֹא חָסַר לָנוּ
וְאַל יֶחְסַר לָנוּ מָזוֹן תָּמִיד לְעוֹלָם וָעֶד
כִּי הוּא אֵל זָן וּמְפַרְנֵס לַכֹּל, וְשֻׁלְחָנוֹ עָרוּךְ לַכֹּל
וְהִתְקִין מִחְיָה וּמָזוֹן לְכָל בְּרִיּוֹתָיו אֲשֶׁר בָּרָא

in His compassion and great loving-kindness.
As it is said: You open Your hand, *Ps. 145*
and satisfy every living thing with favor.
Blessed are You, Lord, who (in His mercy) feeds all.
(For our land and the portion of our ancestors)
We thank You, Lord our God,
for having granted as a heritage to our ancestors
a desirable, good and spacious land;
covenant and Torah, life and food;
for bringing us out from the land of Egypt,
freeing us from the house of slavery;
for Your covenant which You sealed in our flesh;
for Your Torah which You taught us;
for Your laws of Your will which You made known to us;
for the life and food by which You continually feed
and sustain us.
(And) for all this, Lord our God,
we thank and bless Your name.
As it says: "You will eat and be satisfied, *Deut 8*
then you shall bless (Pour the cup) the Lord your God
for the good land He has given you."
Blessed are You, Lord, for the land and for the food.

בְּרַחֲמָיו וּבְרֹב חֲסָדָיו

תהלים קמה
כָּאָמוּר: פּוֹתֵחַ אֶת־יָדֶךָ וּמַשְׂבִּיעַ לְכָל־חַי רָצוֹן:

בָּרוּךְ אַתָּה יְהוָה, הַזָּן (בְּרַחֲמָיו) אֶת הַכֹּל.

(עַל אַרְצֵנוּ וְעַל נַחֲלַת אֲבוֹתֵינוּ)

נוֹדֶה לְךָ, יְהוָה אֱלֹהֵינוּ

עַל שֶׁהִנְחַלְתָּ לַאֲבוֹתֵינוּ אֶרֶץ חֶמְדָּה טוֹבָה וּרְחָבָה

בְּרִית וְתוֹרָה חַיִּים וּמָזוֹן

עַל שֶׁהוֹצֵאתָנוּ מֵאֶרֶץ מִצְרַיִם

וּפְדִיתָנוּ מִבֵּית עֲבָדִים

וְעַל בְּרִיתְךָ שֶׁחָתַמְתָּ בִּבְשָׂרֵנוּ

וְעַל תּוֹרָתְךָ שֶׁלִּמַּדְתָּנוּ

וְעַל חֻקֵּי רְצוֹנָךְ שֶׁהוֹדַעְתָּנוּ

וְעַל חַיִּים וּמָזוֹן שֶׁאַתָּה זָן וּמְפַרְנֵס אוֹתָנוּ.

(וְ)עַל הַכֹּל, יְהוָה אֱלֹהֵינוּ

אֲנַחְנוּ מוֹדִים לָךְ וּמְבָרְכִים אֶת שְׁמָךְ

דברים ח
כָּאָמוּר: וְאָכַלְתָּ וְשָׂבָעְתָּ

וּבֵרַכְתָּ אֶת־יְהוָה אֱלֹהֶיךָ עַל־הָאָרֶץ הַטֹּבָה אֲשֶׁר נָתַן־לָךְ:

בָּרוּךְ אַתָּה יְהוָה, עַל הָאָרֶץ וְעַל הַמָּזוֹן.

רַחֵם Have compassion on us, Lord our God,
and on Israel Your people,
on Jerusalem Your city,
on Mount Zion the dwelling place of Your glory,
on Your Temple, on Your dwelling place,
on Your sanctuary,
and on the great and holy House that bears Your name.
Our Father, tend us, feed us, sustain us and support us,
relieve us and send us relief
swiftly from all our troubles.
O Lord our God, do not make us dependent
on the gifts or loans of other people –
(for their gifts are meager and their disgrace is great) –
but only on Your full, generous, rich and open hand.
May it be Your will that we not suffer shame
in this world, nor
humiliation in the World to Come,
and may You restore the royal house
of David Your anointed to
its place, swiftly in our time.

רַחֵם יְהֹוָה אֱלֹהֵינוּ עָלֵינוּ וְעַל יִשְׂרָאֵל עַמֶּךָ
וְעַל יְרוּשָׁלַיִם עִירֶךָ
וְעַל הַר צִיּוֹן מִשְׁכַּן כְּבוֹדֶךָ
וְעַל הֵיכָלֶךָ וְעַל מְעוֹנֶךָ וְעַל דְּבִירֶךָ
וְעַל הַבַּיִת הַגָּדוֹל וְהַקָּדוֹשׁ שֶׁנִּקְרָא שִׁמְךָ עָלָיו
אָבִינוּ, רְעֵנוּ, זוּנֵנוּ, פַּרְנְסֵנוּ, כַּלְכְּלֵנוּ
הַרְוִיחֵנוּ, הַרְוַח לָנוּ מְהֵרָה מִכָּל צָרוֹתֵינוּ
וְאַל תַּצְרִיכֵנוּ, יְהֹוָה אֱלֹהֵינוּ לִידֵי מַתְּנוֹת בָּשָׂר וָדָם
וְלֹא לִידֵי הַלְוָאָתָם (שֶׁמַּתְּנָתָם מְעוּטָה וְחֶרְפָּתָם מְרֻבָּה)
אֶלָּא לְיָדְךָ הַמְּלֵאָה וְהָרְחָבָה, הָעֲשִׁירָה וְהַפְּתוּחָה.
שֶׁלֹּא נֵבוֹשׁ בָּעוֹלָם הַזֶּה, וְלֹא נִכָּלֵם לָעוֹלָם הַבָּא
וּמַלְכוּת בֵּית דָּוִד מְשִׁיחָךְ תַּחֲזִירֶנָּה
לִמְקוֹמָהּ בִּמְהֵרָה בְיָמֵינוּ.

On Shabbat, say:

רְצֵה Favor and strengthen us, Lord our God,
throug Your commandments,
especially through the commandment of the seventh day,
this great and holy Sabbath.
For it is, for You, a great and holy day.
On it we cease work and rest (and delight in it)
in accord with Your will's commandment.
May there be no grief or lament on our day of rest,
and may You show us the consolation of Zion soon, in our time,
for You are the Master of consolation.
For though we have eaten and drunk,
we have not forgotten the destruction
of Your great and holy House.
Do not forget us forever, and do not forsake us for eternity,
for You, God, are a great and holy King.

בשבת:

רְצֵה וְהַחֲלִיצֵנוּ יְהוָֹה אֱלֹהֵינוּ בְּמִצְוֹתֶיךָ
וּבְמִצְוַת יוֹם הַשְּׁבִיעִי הַשַּׁבָּת
הַגָּדוֹל וְהַקָּדוֹשׁ הַזֶּה.
כִּי יוֹם גָּדוֹל וְקָדוֹשׁ הוּא מִלְּפָנֶיךָ
נִשְׁבּוֹת בּוֹ וְנָנוּחַ בּוֹ וְנִתְעַנֵּג בּוֹ
כְּמִצְוַת חֻקֵּי רְצוֹנָךְ.
וְאַל תְּהִי צָרָה וְיָגוֹן בְּיוֹם מְנוּחָתֵנוּ
וְהַרְאֵנוּ בְּנֶחָמַת צִיּוֹן
בִּמְהֵרָה בְּיָמֵינוּ כִּי אַתָּה הוּא
בַּעַל הַנֶּחָמוֹת וְגַם שֶׁאָכַלְנוּ וְשָׁתִינוּ חָרְבַּן בֵּיתְךָ
הַגָּדוֹל וְהַקָּדוֹשׁ לֹא שָׁכַחְנוּ אַל תִּשְׁכָּחֵנוּ לָנֶצַח
וְאַל תִּזְנָחֵנוּ לָעַד כִּי אֵל מֶלֶךְ גָּדוֹל וְקָדוֹשׁ אָתָּה.

Our God and God of our ancestors,
may there rise, come, reach, appear, be favored,heard, regarded and
remembered before You, our remembrance
and the remembrance of our ancestors, and of Jerusalem
Your city, and of the Messiah son of David Your servant,
and of all Your people the house of Israel – for deliverance and
well-being, grace, loving-kindness and compassion,
(for good life and peace),
on this day of:
the Festival of Matzot, this holy day of assembly
this holy day of assembly
Remembrance, this holy day of assembly
to show compassion to us and to save us.
On it remember us, Lord our God, for good;
recollect us for blessing,
and deliver us for good life,
in accord with Your promise of salvation and compassion.
Spare us and be gracious to us; have mercy and compassion
on us, and deliver us,
for our eyes are turned to You because You, God,
are a gracious and compassionate King.

הָרַחֲמָן הוּא יִשְׁתַּבַּח עַל כִּסֵּא כְבוֹדוֹ.

הָרַחֲמָן הוּא יִשְׁתַּבַּח בַּשָּׁמַיִם וּבָאָרֶץ.

הָרַחֲמָן הוּא יִשְׁתַּבַּח בָּנוּ לְדוֹר דּוֹרִים.

הָרַחֲמָן הוּא קֶרֶן לְעַמּוֹ יָרִים.

הָרַחֲמָן הוּא יִתְפָּאַר בָּנוּ לָנֵצַח נְצָחִים.

הָרַחֲמָן הוּא יְפַרְנְסֵנוּ בְּכָבוֹד וְלֹא בְּבִזּוּי (בְּהֶתֵּר וְלֹא בְּאִסּוּר)
בְּנַחַת וְלֹא בְּצַעַר (בְּרֶוַח וְלֹא בְּצִמְצוּם).

הָרַחֲמָן הוּא יִתֵּן שָׁלוֹם בֵּינֵינוּ.

הָרַחֲמָן הוּא יִשְׁלַח בְּרָכָה רְוָחָה וְהַצְלָחָה בְּכָל מַעֲשֵׂה יָדֵינוּ.

הָרַחֲמָן הוּא יַצְלִיחַ אֶת דְּרָכֵינוּ.

הָרַחֲמָן הוּא יִשְׁבֹּר עֹל הַגּוֹיִם מְהֵרָה מֵעַל צַוָּארֵנוּ.

הָרַחֲמָן הוּא יוֹלִיכֵנוּ מְהֵרָה קוֹמְמִיּוּת לְאַרְצֵנוּ.

May the Compassionate One soon heal us
for complete healing – healing of both soul and body.

May the Compassionate One open His hand wide for us.

May the Compassionate One bless each and every one of us
with His great name, just as our (holy and pure)
forefathers Abraham, Yitzḥak and Yaakov
were blessed in all, from all, with all,
so may He bless us together with a
complete blessing, and so may it be His will,
and let us say: Amen.

May the Compassionate One spread over us His canopy of
peace.

On Shabbat: May the Compassionate One let us inherit the time, that
will be entirely Shabbat and rest for life everlasting.

May the Compassionate One let us inherit the day
that is all good.

May the Compassionate One implant knowledge of and love for
His Torah in our hearts; and may His awe be upon us
so that we do not sin; and may all our deeds
be for the sake of Heaven.

הָרַחֲמָן הוּא יְרַפְּאֵנוּ רְפוּאָה שְׁלֵמָה
רְפוּאַת הַנֶּפֶשׁ וּרְפוּאַת הַגּוּף.

הָרַחֲמָן הוּא יִפְתַּח לָנוּ אֶת יָדוֹ הָרְחָבָה.

הָרַחֲמָן הוּא יְבָרֵךְ כָּל אֶחָד וְאֶחָד מִמֶּנּוּ בִּשְׁמוֹ הַגָּדוֹל
כְּמוֹ שֶׁנִּתְבָּרְכוּ אֲבוֹתֵינוּ הַקְּדוֹשִׁים וְהַטְּהוֹרִים
אַבְרָהָם יִצְחָק וְיַעֲקֹב, בַּכֹּל, מִכֹּל, כֹּל
כֵּן יְבָרֵךְ אוֹתָנוּ יַחַד בְּרָכָה שְׁלֵמָה
וְכֵן יְהִי רָצוֹן וְנֹאמַר אָמֵן.

הָרַחֲמָן הוּא יִפְרֹשׂ עָלֵינוּ סֻכַּת שְׁלוֹמוֹ.

בשבת: הָרַחֲמָן הוּא יַנְחִילֵנוּ יוֹם שֶׁכֻּלּוֹ שַׁבָּת
וּמְנוּחָה לְחַיֵּי הָעוֹלָמִים.

הָרַחֲמָן הוּא יַנְחִילֵנוּ יוֹם שֶׁכֻּלּוֹ טוֹב.

הָרַחֲמָן הוּא יִטַּע תּוֹרָתוֹ וְאַהֲבָתוֹ בְּלִבֵּנוּ
וְתִהְיֶה יִרְאָתוֹ עַל פָּנֵינוּ לְבִלְתִּי נֶחֱטָא
וְיִהְיוּ כָּל מַעֲשֵׂינוּ לְשֵׁם שָׁמָיִם.

A guest says:

May the Compassionate One bless this table upon which we have eaten, and place upon it all of the delights of the world. Let it be like the table of Avraham, our father: let all who are hungry eat from it and all who are thirsty drink from it, and let it not lack any good things for ever and ever, Amen.

May the Compassionate One bless the master of this house and the master of this meal, his children, his wife and all that he has with descendants who will survive, and with abundant possessions.

Bless, O Lord, his substance and accept the work of his hands. *Deut. 33* And let his possessions and ours be successful and close to home. Let no thought of sin, iniquity or transgression enter him or us, and let him rejoice and be happy for all time, with wealth and honor from now and for evermore. Let him not be shamed in this world nor humiliated in the

World to Come. Amen; may it be His will.

May the Compassionate One give us life, make us worthy and bring us close to the Messianic Age, the building of the Temple and life in the World to Come.

אורח אומר:

הָרַחֲמָן הוּא יְבָרֵךְ אֶת הַשֻּׁלְחָן הַזֶּה שֶׁאָכַלְנוּ עָלָיו
וִיסַדֵּר בּוֹ כָּל מַעֲדַנֵּי עוֹלָם, וְיִהְיֶה כְּשֻׁלְחָנוֹ שֶׁל
אַבְרָהָם אָבִינוּ כָּל רָעֵב מִמֶּנּוּ יֹאכַל וְכָל צָמֵא
מִמֶּנּוּ יִשְׁתֶּה וְאַל יֶחְסַר מִמֶּנּוּ כָּל טוּב לָעַד
וּלְעוֹלְמֵי עוֹלָמִים, אָמֵן.

הָרַחֲמָן הוּא יְבָרֵךְ אֶת בַּעַל הַבַּיִת הַזֶּה וּבַעַל הַסְּעֻדָּה
הַזֹּאת הוּא וּבָנָיו וְאִשְׁתּוֹ וְכָל אֲשֶׁר לוֹ, בְּבָנִים
שֶׁיִּחְיוּ וּבִנְכָסִים שֶׁיִּרְבּוּ. בָּרֵךְ יְהֹוָה חֵילוֹ, וּפֹעַל דברים לג
יָדָיו תִּרְצֶה: וְיִהְיוּ נְכָסָיו וּנְכָסֵינוּ מֻצְלָחִים וּקְרוֹבִים
לָעִיר וְאַל יִזְדַּקֵּק לְפָנָיו וְלֹא לְפָנֵינוּ שׁוּם דְּבַר חֵטְא
וְהִרְהוּר עָוֹן. וְיִהְיֶה שָׂשׂ וְשָׂמֵחַ כָּל הַיָּמִים, בְּעֹשֶׁר
וְכָבוֹד, מֵעַתָּה וְעַד עוֹלָם. לֹא יֵבוֹשׁ בָּעוֹלָם הַזֶּה
וְלֹא יִכָּלֵם לָעוֹלָם הַבָּא. אָמֵן כֵּן יְהִי רָצוֹן.

הָרַחֲמָן הוּא יְחַיֵּינוּ וִיזַכֵּנוּ וִיקָרְבֵנוּ לִימוֹת הַמָּשִׁיחַ
וּלְבִנְיַן בֵּית הַמִּקְדָּשׁ וּלְחַיֵּי הָעוֹלָם הַבָּא.

He is a tower of salvation to His king,
showing kindness to His anointed,
to David and his descendants for ever.
Young lions may grow weak and hungry, *Ps. 34*
but those who seek the Lord
lack no good thing.
I was once young; now I am old, yet I have never *Ps. 37*
seen the righteous forsaken, with their children
begging for bread.
They are always generous, lending freely,
and their children become a blessing.
May what we have eaten be for satiation,
may what we have drunk be for health,
and may what we have left over be for a blessing,

מִגְדּוֹל יְשׁוּעוֹת מַלְכּוֹ
וְעֹשֶׂה־חֶסֶד לִמְשִׁיחוֹ
לְדָוִד וּלְזַרְעוֹ עַד־עוֹלָם:
כְּפִירִים רָשׁוּ וְרָעֵבוּ, וְדֹרְשֵׁי יְהֹוָה תהלים לד
לֹא־יַחְסְרוּ כָל־טוֹב:
נַעַר הָיִיתִי גַּם־זָקַנְתִּי, וְלֹא־רָאִיתִי צַדִּיק נֶעֱזָב תהלים לז
וְזַרְעוֹ מְבַקֶּשׁ־לָחֶם:
כָּל־הַיּוֹם חוֹנֵן וּמַלְוֶה, וְזַרְעוֹ לִבְרָכָה:
מַה שֶּׁאָכַלְנוּ יִהְיֶה לְשָׂבְעָה
וּמַה שֶּׁשָּׁתִינוּ יִהְיֶה לִרְפוּאָה
וּמַה שֶּׁהוֹתַרְנוּ יִהְיֶה לִבְרָכָה

as it is written:
So he set it before them, *II Kings 4*
and they ate,
and left over, according to the word of the Lord.
May you be blessed by the Lord, *Ps. 115*
Maker of heaven and earth.
Blessed is the person *Jer. 17*
who trusts in the Lord,
whose trust is in the Lord alone.
The Lord will give His people strength, *Ps. 29*
the Lord will bless His people with peace.
May He who makes peace in His high places,
in His compassion
make peace for us and all His people Israel,
and let us say: Amen.

כִּדְכְתִיב:

וַיִּתֵּן לִפְנֵיהֶם וַיֹּאכְלוּ וַיּוֹתִרוּ כִּדְבַר יְהוָה: מלכים ב׳ ד

בְּרוּכִים אַתֶּם לַיהוָה, תהלים קטו

עֹשֵׂה שָׁמַיִם וָאָרֶץ:

בָּרוּךְ הַגֶּבֶר אֲשֶׁר יִבְטַח בַּיהוָה, ירמיה יז

וְהָיָה יְהוָה מִבְטַחוֹ:

יְהוָה עֹז לְעַמּוֹ יִתֵּן, תהלים כט

יְהוָה יְבָרֵךְ אֶת־עַמּוֹ בַשָּׁלוֹם:

עוֹשֶׂה שָׁלוֹם בִּמְרוֹמָיו

הוּא בְּרַחֲמָיו יַעֲשֶׂה שָׁלוֹם

עָלֵינוּ וְעַל כָּל עַמּוֹ יִשְׂרָאֵל

(וְאִמְרוּ) אָמֵן.

I am prepared and ready to fulfill the commandment of the third of the four cups. For the sake for the unification of the Holy One, blessed be He, and His Divine Presence, through He who is hidden and unseen, in the name of all Israel.

בָּרוּךְ Blessed are You, Lord our God,
King of the Universe,
who creates the fruit of the vine.

Drink while reclining to the left.

The Third Cup
Is Symbolic of Raḥel, Our Matriarch

הִנְנִי מוּכָן וּמְזֻמָּן לְקַיֵּם מִצְוַת כּוֹס שְׁלִישִׁי שֶׁל אַרְבַּע כּוֹסוֹת
לְשֵׁם יִחוּד קֻדְשָׁא בְּרִיךְ הוּא וּשְׁכִינְתֵּהּ עַל יְדֵי הַהוּא טָמִיר וְנֶעְלָם בְּשֵׁם כָּל יִשְׂרָאֵל.

בָּרוּךְ אַתָּה יהוה
אֱלֹהֵינוּ מֶלֶךְ הָעוֹלָם
בּוֹרֵא פְּרִי הַגָּפֶן.

שותים כוס שלישי בהסבת שמאל.

כוס שלישית
כנגד רחל אימנו.

A cup of wine is poured for Eliyahu the prophet, the door is opened, and the following is said:

POUR OUT *Ps. 79*
Your rage
upon the nations
that do not know You,
and on regimes that
have not called upon Your name.
For Yaakov is devoured;
they have laid his places waste.

Pour out Your great anger upon them, *Ps. 69*
and let Your blazing fury overtake them.
Pursue them in Your fury *Lam. 3*
and destroy them
from under the heavens of the Lord.

מוזגים כוסו של אליהו, פותחים את הדלת ואומרים:

תהלים עט

שְׁפֹךְ חֲמָתְךָ אֶל־הַגּוֹיִם
אֲשֶׁר לֹא־יְדָעוּךָ
וְעַל מַמְלָכוֹת
אֲשֶׁר בְּשִׁמְךָ לֹא קָרָאוּ:
כִּי אָכַל אֶת־יַעֲקֹב
וְאֶת־נָוֵהוּ הֵשַׁמּוּ:

תהלים סט

שְׁפָךְ־ עֲלֵיהֶם זַעְמֶךָ
וַחֲרוֹן אַפְּךָ יַשִּׂיגֵם:

איכה ג

תִּרְדֹּף בְּאַף וְתַשְׁמִידֵם
מִתַּחַת שְׁמֵי יהוה:

She pushes him toward Yitzḥak and storms the heavens with prayers. Yitzḥak, blind to the drama unfolding around him (the mom knows what the father doesn't know and will never know), blesses him. Which blessing does he receive? "May God give you of the dew of heaven and the fat of the earth, abundance of new grain and wine.... Let peoples serve you."[208]

The door slowly opens. This is the moment that the door opens in "Pour out Your rage." Yaakov hides behind the door. Esav walks in. It's a moment fraught with danger, and it's a moment that takes place in every Jewish home on the Seder night. He says: "Let my father get up."[209] I have prepared something delicious for you to eat. "Have you not reserved a blessing for me?"[210]

"Your brother came with guile and took your blessing,"[211] Yaakov says.

But didn't you save a blessing for me? Didn't you save something for me?

No. I gave him everything. "What then can I still do for you, my son?"[212]

It was an awful moment. At this moment, three tears roll down Esav's cheeks, and these three tears continue to haunt us and castigate us today. It's a moment in which our enemies are empowered. The terror attacks that immediately precede Pesaḥ are unfortunately a well-known phenomenon.

Rivka stands there. "Standing means nothing [other] than prayer."[213] But "it was not only one man who rose up [stood]." Two mighty powers faced off against each other: Esav's tears versus the people of Israel. And Rivka continued to stand there, in the kitchen, pleading: "For it was not only one man who rose up [stood] to destroy us!" Master of the world, he isn't just one man alone. He's a twin. Esav is also in the picture. His twin brother rose up to destroy us. Save us from his hands![214]

Who will be the last man standing?

Esav's tears threaten to castigate us at "Pour out Your rage." For this reason, precisely at this moment, *Pirkei DeRabbi Eliezer* tells us to cry out, "Pour out Your rage upon the nations that do not know You, and on regimes that have not called in Your name." Father, don't allow them to mislead You. Don't believe Esav. Yitzḥak was misled, but Rivka knew the truth. Yaakov didn't steal it – "Yaakov is devoured [by Esav]!" Our enemies' insistent claims of "They're terrible, they hurt us, they killed us" have resonated with the world on many occasions, but really it's just fake news, an optical illusion. "They have laid his places waste" – Your Temple is desolate and abandoned because of them. "Pour Your great anger upon them and let Your blazing fury overtake them from under the heavens of the Lord."[215] It might not be politically correct, but this is our blessing!

The moment

Pour Out Your Rage

An Encounter with the Divine Presence

Are You Ready to Accept God's Gifts?

At least once during the Seder, Rabbi Wolbe explains, you need to feel a profound sense of excitement. And when this happens, you should know that God has just entered your home. Rabbi Wolbe refers to this moment as *heimishkeit*, a moment of incredible family closeness – when? According to the kabbalists, this happens as we open the door and say: "Pour out Your rage." At this moment, the Divine Presence enters, laden with gifts and blessings for your entire home. This is the moment you've been waiting for.

Now, right now, you should snatch all those blessings – for you, for your loved ones, for the entire Jewish people. It's an extraordinary moment.

Let's learn a little Kabbala and *Pirkei DeRabbi Eliezer*. What happens on the Seder night? On this exact date, thousands and thousands of years ago, Yitzḥak called Esav and told him: "My son, tonight the upper worlds recite song, on this night the treasuries of dew are opened; 'make me savory meat…and I will bless you.'[205]"

"And Rivka hears."[206] And she calls Yaakov and tells him: "My son, tonight the upper worlds recite song, on this night the treasuries of dew are opened, 'make savory meat for your father, so he will bless you!'[207]"

She takes two goats, "one little goat, one little goat." She places the goat skins on Yaakov's smooth neck and arms and tells him: Go quickly, my son. If you don't steal the *afikoman* now, we'll be licking our wounds for generations to come.

The moment the door is opened is critical. Yaakov, our patriarch, is behind the door. Inside the home is Yitzḥak, dispensing blessing after blessing after blessing. The Divine Presence enters and bestows incredible abundance upon this home. What does this home need – a *shidduch*? Here, take. Livelihood? Here you go. Health? Take it. Peace? Happiness? Take it![216]

It's mystical, and it's not especially polite, but these blessings belong to you. All you need to do is ask. It's a moment when prayers are graciously accepted. The Divine Presence enters our homes. At this moment, each and every one of us can steal blessings that weren't really intended for us, and receive things that defy our predestined lot in life, because on this night we, the Jewish people, received blessings that (seemingly) weren't intended for us. It's a sublime moment of divine favor.

Hallel / Praising

הַלֵּל

The fourth cup of wine is poured, and the following is said:

Not to us, LORD, not to us, Ps. 115
but to Your name give glory,
for Your love, for Your faithfulness.
Why should the nations say, "Where now is their God?"
Our God is in heaven; whatever He wills He does.
Their idols are silver and gold, made by human hands.
They have mouths but cannot speak; eyes but cannot see.
They have ears but cannot hear; noses but cannot smell.
They have hands but cannot feel; feet but cannot walk.
No sound comes from their throat.
Those who make them become like them;
so will all who trust in them.
Israel, trust in the LORD –
He is their Help and their Shield.
House of Aharon, trust in the LORD –
He is their Help and their Shield.
You who fear the LORD,
trust in the LORD –
He is their Help and their Shield.

מוזגים כוס רביעי וגומרים עליו את ההלל:

תהלים קטו

לֹא לָנוּ יהוה, לֹא לָנוּ

כִּי־לְשִׁמְךָ תֵּן כָּבוֹד, עַל־חַסְדְּךָ עַל־אֲמִתֶּךָ:

לָמָּה יֹאמְרוּ הַגּוֹיִם אַיֵּה־נָא אֱלֹהֵיהֶם:

וֵאלֹהֵינוּ בַשָּׁמָיִם, כֹּל אֲשֶׁר־חָפֵץ עָשָׂה:

עֲצַבֵּיהֶם כֶּסֶף וְזָהָב, מַעֲשֵׂה יְדֵי אָדָם:

פֶּה־לָהֶם וְלֹא יְדַבֵּרוּ, עֵינַיִם לָהֶם וְלֹא יִרְאוּ:

אָזְנַיִם לָהֶם וְלֹא יִשְׁמָעוּ, אַף לָהֶם וְלֹא יְרִיחוּן:

יְדֵיהֶם וְלֹא יְמִישׁוּן, רַגְלֵיהֶם וְלֹא יְהַלֵּכוּ

לֹא־יֶהְגּוּ בִּגְרוֹנָם:

כְּמוֹהֶם יִהְיוּ עֹשֵׂיהֶם, כֹּל אֲשֶׁר־בֹּטֵחַ בָּהֶם:

יִשְׂרָאֵל בְּטַח בַּיהוה, עֶזְרָם וּמָגִנָּם הוּא:

בֵּית אַהֲרֹן בִּטְחוּ בַיהוה, עֶזְרָם וּמָגִנָּם הוּא:

יִרְאֵי יהוה בִּטְחוּ בַיהוה, עֶזְרָם וּמָגִנָּם הוּא:

The Lord remembers us and will bless us.
He will bless the house of Israel.
He will bless the house of Aharon.
He will bless those who fear the Lord, small and great alike.
May the Lord give you increase: you and your children.
May you be blessed by the Lord, Maker of heaven and earth.
The heavens are the Lord's,
but the earth He has given over to mankind.
It is not the dead who praise the Lord,
nor those who go down to the silent grave.
But we will bless the Lord, now and for ever.

HALLELUYA!

יהוה זְכָרָנוּ יְבָרֵךְ
יְבָרֵךְ אֶת־בֵּית יִשְׂרָאֵל, יְבָרֵךְ אֶת־בֵּית אַהֲרֹן:
יְבָרֵךְ יִרְאֵי יהוה, הַקְּטַנִּים עִם־הַגְּדֹלִים:
יֹסֵף יהוה עֲלֵיכֶם, עֲלֵיכֶם וְעַל־בְּנֵיכֶם:
בְּרוּכִים אַתֶּם לַיהוה, עֹשֵׂה שָׁמַיִם וָאָרֶץ:
הַשָּׁמַיִם שָׁמַיִם לַיהוה, וְהָאָרֶץ נָתַן לִבְנֵי־אָדָם:
לֹא הַמֵּתִים יְהַלְלוּ־יָהּ, וְלֹא כָּל־יֹרְדֵי דוּמָה:
וַאֲנַחְנוּ נְבָרֵךְ יָהּ, מֵעַתָּה וְעַד־עוֹלָם

הַלְלוּיָהּ:

I love the LORD, *Ps. 116*
for He hears my voice, my pleas.
He turns His ear to me whenever I call.
The bonds of death encompassed me,
the anguish of the grave came upon me,
I was overcome by trouble and sorrow.
Then I called on the name of the LORD:
"LORD, I pray, save my life."
Gracious is the LORD, and righteous;
our God is full of compassion.
The LORD protects the simple hearted.
When I was brought low, He saved me.
My soul, be at peace once more,
for the LORD has been good to you.
For You have rescued me from death,
my eyes from weeping, my feet from stumbling.
I shall walk in the presence of the LORD
in the land of the living.
I had faith, even when I said, "I am greatly afflicted,"
even when I said rashly, "All men are liars."

תהלים קטז

אָהַבְתִּי, כִּי־יִשְׁמַע יהוה, אֶת־קוֹלִי תַּחֲנוּנָי:
כִּי־הִטָּה אָזְנוֹ לִי, וּבְיָמַי אֶקְרָא:
אֲפָפוּנִי חֶבְלֵי־מָוֶת, וּמְצָרֵי שְׁאוֹל מְצָאוּנִי
צָרָה וְיָגוֹן אֶמְצָא:
וּבְשֵׁם־יהוה אֶקְרָא, אָנָּה יהוה מַלְּטָה נַפְשִׁי:
חַנּוּן יהוה וְצַדִּיק, וֵאלֹהֵינוּ מְרַחֵם:
שֹׁמֵר פְּתָאִים יהוה, דַּלּוֹתִי וְלִי יְהוֹשִׁיעַ:
שׁוּבִי נַפְשִׁי לִמְנוּחָיְכִי, כִּי־יהוה גָּמַל עָלָיְכִי:
כִּי חִלַּצְתָּ נַפְשִׁי מִמָּוֶת אֶת־עֵינִי מִן־דִּמְעָה
אֶת־רַגְלִי מִדֶּחִי:
אֶתְהַלֵּךְ לִפְנֵי יהוה, בְּאַרְצוֹת הַחַיִּים:
הֶאֱמַנְתִּי כִּי אֲדַבֵּר, אֲנִי עָנִיתִי מְאֹד:
אֲנִי אָמַרְתִּי בְחָפְזִי, כָּל־הָאָדָם כֹּזֵב:

How can I repay the Lord for all His goodness to me?
I will lift the cup of salvation and call on the name of the Lord.
I will fulfill my vows to the Lord
in the presence of all His people.
Grievous in the Lord's sight is the death of His devoted ones.
Truly, Lord, I am Your servant;
I am Your servant, the son of Your maidservant.
You set me free from my chains.
To You I shall bring a thanksgiving-offering
and call on the Lord by name.
I will fulfill my vows to the Lord in the presence of all His people,
in the courts of the House of the Lord,
in your midst, Jerusalem.

HALLELUYA!

מָה־אָשִׁיב לַיהוה

כָּל־תַּגְמוּלוֹהִי עָלָי:

כּוֹס־יְשׁוּעוֹת אֶשָּׂא, וּבְשֵׁם יהוה אֶקְרָא:

נְדָרַי לַיהוה אֲשַׁלֵּם, נֶגְדָה־נָּא לְכָל־עַמּוֹ:

יָקָר בְּעֵינֵי יהוה, הַמָּוְתָה לַחֲסִידָיו:

אָנָּה יהוה כִּי־אֲנִי עַבְדֶּךָ, אֲנִי־עַבְדְּךָ בֶּן־אֲמָתֶךָ, פִּתַּחְתָּ לְמוֹסֵרָי:

לְךָ־אֶזְבַּח זֶבַח תּוֹדָה, וּבְשֵׁם יהוה אֶקְרָא:

נְדָרַי לַיהוה אֲשַׁלֵּם, נֶגְדָה־נָּא לְכָל־עַמּוֹ:

בְּחַצְרוֹת בֵּית יהוה, בְּתוֹכֵכִי יְרוּשָׁלָיִם

הַלְלוּיָהּ:

Praise the LORD,

Ps. 117

all nations; acclaim Him, all you peoples;
for His loving-kindness to us is strong,
and the LORD's faithfulness is everlasting.

HALLELUYA!

Thank the LORD for He is good, His loving-kindness is for ever. *Ps. 118*
Let Israel say His loving-kindness is for ever.
Let the house of Aharon say His loving-kindness is for ever.
Let those who fear the LORD say His loving-kindness is for ever.

תהלים קיז

הַלְלוּ

אֶת־יהוה כָּל־גּוֹיִם, שַׁבְּחוּהוּ כָּל־הָאֻמִּים:
כִּי גָבַר עָלֵינוּ חַסְדּוֹ, וֶאֱמֶת־יהוה לְעוֹלָם

הַלְלוּיָהּ:

תהלים קיח

הוֹדוּ לַיהוה כִּי־טוֹב — כִּי לְעוֹלָם חַסְדּוֹ:
יֹאמַר־נָא יִשְׂרָאֵל — כִּי לְעוֹלָם חַסְדּוֹ:
יֹאמְרוּ־נָא בֵית־אַהֲרֹן — כִּי לְעוֹלָם חַסְדּוֹ:
יֹאמְרוּ־נָא יִרְאֵי יהוה — כִּי לְעוֹלָם חַסְדּוֹ:

In my distress I called on the LORD.
The LORD answered me
and set me free.

מִן־הַמֵּצַר קָרָאתִי יָּהּ
עָנָנִי בַמֶּרְחָב יָהּ:

The Lord is with me; I will not be afraid.
What can man do to me? The Lord is with me.
He is my Helper. I will see the downfall of my enemies.
It is better to take refuge in the Lord than to trust in man.
It is better to take refuge in the Lord than to trust in princes.
The nations all surrounded me,
but in the Lord's name I drove them off.
They surrounded me on every side,
but in the Lord's name I drove them off.
They surrounded me like bees, they attacked me as fire attacks brushwood, but in the Lord's name I drove them off.
They thrust so hard against me, I nearly fell,
but the Lord came to my help.
The Lord is my strength and my song;
He has become my salvation.
Sounds of song and salvation resound in the tents of the righteous:
"The Lord's right hand has done mighty deeds.
The Lord's right hand is lifted high.
The Lord's right hand has done mighty deeds."
I will not die but live, and tell what the Lord has done.
The Lord has chastened me severely,
but He has not given me over to death.
Open for me the gates of righteousness
that I may enter them and thank the Lord.
This is the gateway to the Lord; through it,
the righteous shall enter.

יהוה לִי לֹא אִירָא, מַה־יַּעֲשֶׂה לִי אָדָם:
יהוה לִי בְּעֹזְרָי, וַאֲנִי אֶרְאֶה בְשֹׂנְאָי:
טוֹב לַחֲסוֹת בַּיהוה, מִבְּטֹחַ בָּאָדָם:
טוֹב לַחֲסוֹת בַּיהוה, מִבְּטֹחַ בִּנְדִיבִים:
כָּל־גּוֹיִם סְבָבוּנִי, בְּשֵׁם יהוה כִּי אֲמִילַם:
סַבּוּנִי גַם־סְבָבוּנִי, בְּשֵׁם יהוה כִּי אֲמִילַם:
סַבּוּנִי כִדְבֹרִים, דֹּעֲכוּ כְּאֵשׁ קוֹצִים
בְּשֵׁם יהוה כִּי אֲמִילַם:
דָּחֹה דְחִיתַנִי לִנְפֹּל, וַיהוה עֲזָרָנִי:
עָזִּי וְזִמְרָת יָהּ, וַיְהִי־לִי לִישׁוּעָה:
קוֹל רִנָּה וִישׁוּעָה בְּאָהֳלֵי צַדִּיקִים, יְמִין יהוה עֹשָׂה חָיִל:
יְמִין יהוה רוֹמֵמָה, יְמִין יהוה עֹשָׂה חָיִל:
לֹא־אָמוּת כִּי־אֶחְיֶה, וַאֲסַפֵּר מַעֲשֵׂי יָהּ:
יַסֹּר יִסְּרַנִּי יָּהּ, וְלַמָּוֶת לֹא נְתָנָנִי:
פִּתְחוּ־לִי שַׁעֲרֵי־צֶדֶק, אָבֹא־בָם אוֹדֶה יָהּ:
זֶה־הַשַּׁעַר לַיהוה, צַדִּיקִים יָבֹאוּ בוֹ:

I will thank You, for You answered me, and became my salvation.
I will thank You, for You answered me, and became my salvation.

The stone the builders rejected has become the main cornerstone.
The stone the builders rejected has become the main cornerstone.

This is the LORD's doing. It is wondrous in our eyes.
This is the LORD's doing. It is wondrous in our eyes.

This is the day the LORD has made. Let us rejoice and be glad in it.
This is the day the LORD has made. Let us rejoice and be glad in it.

אוֹדְךָ כִּי עֲנִיתָנִי, וַתְּהִי־לִי לִישׁוּעָה:

אוֹדְךָ כִּי עֲנִיתָנִי, וַתְּהִי־לִי לִישׁוּעָה:

אֶבֶן מָאֲסוּ הַבּוֹנִים, הָיְתָה לְרֹאשׁ פִּנָּה:

אֶבֶן מָאֲסוּ הַבּוֹנִים, הָיְתָה לְרֹאשׁ פִּנָּה:

מֵאֵת יהוה הָיְתָה זֹּאת, הִיא נִפְלָאת בְּעֵינֵינוּ:

מֵאֵת יהוה הָיְתָה זֹּאת, הִיא נִפְלָאת בְּעֵינֵינוּ:

זֶה־הַיּוֹם עָשָׂה יהוה, נָגִילָה וְנִשְׂמְחָה בוֹ:

זֶה־הַיּוֹם עָשָׂה יהוה, נָגִילָה וְנִשְׂמְחָה בוֹ:

אָנָּא יהוה הוֹשִׁיעָה נָּא:
אָנָּא יהוה הוֹשִׁיעָה נָּא:
אָנָּא יהוה הַצְלִיחָה נָא:
אָנָּא יהוה הַצְלִיחָה נָא:

LORD, PLEASE, SAVE US.

LORD, PLEASE, SAVE US.

LORD, PLEASE, GRANT US SUCCESS.

LORD, PLEASE, GRANT US SUCCESS.

בָּרוּךְ הַבָּא בְּשֵׁם יהוה, בֵּרַכְנוּכֶם מִבֵּית יהוה:

בָּרוּךְ הַבָּא בְּשֵׁם יהוה, בֵּרַכְנוּכֶם מִבֵּית יהוה:

Blessed is one who comes
in the name of the LORD;
we bless you from the House of the LORD.

Blessed is one who comes in the name of the LORD;
we bless you from the House of the LORD.

אֵל יהוה וַיָּאֶר לָנוּ
אִסְרוּ־חַג בַּעֲבֹתִים
עַד־קַרְנוֹת הַמִּזְבֵּחַ:

אֵל יהוה וַיָּאֶר לָנוּ, אִסְרוּ־חַג בַּעֲבֹתִים
עַד־קַרְנוֹת הַמִּזְבֵּחַ:

The LORD is God; He has given us light.
Bind the festival offering with thick cords [and bring it] to the horns of the altar.

The LORD is God; He has given us light.
Bind the festival offering with thick cords [and bring it]
to the horns of the altar.

אֵלִי אַתָּה וְאוֹדֶךָּ, אֱלֹהַי אֲרוֹמְמֶךָּ:

אֵלִי אַתָּה וְאוֹדֶךָּ, אֱלֹהַי אֲרוֹמְמֶךָּ:

You are my God and I will thank You;
You are my God, I will exalt You.

You are my God and I will thank You; You are my God,
I will exalt You.

הוֹדוּ לַיהוה כִּי־טוֹב,
כִּי לְעוֹלָם חַסְדּוֹ:

הוֹדוּ לַיהוה כִּי־טוֹב, כִּי לְעוֹלָם חַסְדּוֹ:

Thank the LORD for He is good,
His loving-kindness is for ever.

Thank the LORD for He is good,
His loving-kindness is for ever.

ALL YOUR WORKS WILL PRAISE YOU,

LORD our God,
and Your devoted ones –
the righteous who do Your will,
together with all Your people
the house of Israel –
will joyously thank, bless, praise,
glorify, exalt, revere, sanctify,
and proclaim the sovereignty of Your name, our King.
For it is good to thank You
and fitting to sing psalms to Your name,
for from eternity to eternity You are God.

יְהַלְלוּךָ

יהוה אֱלֹהֵינוּ כָּל מַעֲשֶׂיךָ
וַחֲסִידֶיךָ צַדִּיקִים עוֹשֵׂי רְצוֹנֶךָ
וְכָל עַמְּךָ בֵּית יִשְׂרָאֵל
בְּרִנָּה יוֹדוּ
וִיבָרְכוּ וִישַׁבְּחוּ
וִיפָאֲרוּ וִירוֹמְמוּ וְיַעֲרִיצוּ
וְיַקְדִּישׁוּ וְיַמְלִיכוּ אֶת שִׁמְךָ מַלְכֵּנוּ
כִּי לְךָ טוֹב לְהוֹדוֹת וּלְשִׁמְךָ נָאֶה לְזַמֵּר
כִּי מֵעוֹלָם וְעַד עוֹלָם
אַתָּה אֵל.

Hallel HaGadol

Ps. 136

Thank

the Lord, for He is good,

His loving-kindness is for ever.

הלל הגדול:

תהלים קלו

הוֹדוּ

לַיהוה
כִּי־טוֹב

כִּי לְעוֹלָם חַסְדּוֹ:

Thank the God of gods, His loving-kindness is for ever.

Thank the Lord of lords, His loving-kindness is for ever.

To the One who alone
works great wonders, His loving-kindness is for ever.

Who made the heavens
with wisdom, His loving-kindness is for ever.

Who spread the earth
upon the waters, His loving-kindness is for ever.

Who made the great lights, His loving-kindness is for ever.

The sun to rule by day, His loving-kindness is for ever.

The moon and the stars
to rule by night; His loving-kindness is for ever.

Who struck Egypt
through their firstborn, His loving-kindness is for ever.

And brought out Israel
from their midst, His loving-kindness is for ever.

With a strong hand
and outstretched arm, His loving-kindness is for ever.

Who split the Reed Sea
into parts, His loving-kindness is for ever.

Hallel – An Encounter with Those Who Recited Hallel Long Ago

Remember when Rabbi Akiva and Rabbi Eliezer argued about the precise number of plagues that took place and we discussed the importance of counting each and every detail of the miracle? This is what Hallel is all about.

הוֹדוּ לֵאלֹהֵי הָאֱלֹהִים   כִּי לְעוֹלָם חַסְדּוֹ:
הוֹדוּ לַאֲדֹנֵי הָאֲדֹנִים   כִּי לְעוֹלָם חַסְדּוֹ:
לְעֹשֵׂה נִפְלָאוֹת גְּדֹלוֹת לְבַדּוֹ   כִּי לְעוֹלָם חַסְדּוֹ:
לְעֹשֵׂה הַשָּׁמַיִם בִּתְבוּנָה   כִּי לְעוֹלָם חַסְדּוֹ:
לְרֹקַע הָאָרֶץ עַל־הַמָּיִם   כִּי לְעוֹלָם חַסְדּוֹ:
לְעֹשֵׂה אוֹרִים גְּדֹלִים   כִּי לְעוֹלָם חַסְדּוֹ:
אֶת־הַשֶּׁמֶשׁ לְמֶמְשֶׁלֶת בַּיּוֹם   כִּי לְעוֹלָם חַסְדּוֹ:
אֶת־הַיָּרֵחַ וְכוֹכָבִים
לְמֶמְשְׁלוֹת בַּלָּיְלָה   כִּי לְעוֹלָם חַסְדּוֹ:
לְמַכֵּה מִצְרַיִם בִּבְכוֹרֵיהֶם   כִּי לְעוֹלָם חַסְדּוֹ:
וַיּוֹצֵא יִשְׂרָאֵל מִתּוֹכָם   כִּי לְעוֹלָם חַסְדּוֹ:
בְּיָד חֲזָקָה וּבִזְרוֹעַ נְטוּיָה   כִּי לְעוֹלָם חַסְדּוֹ:
לְגֹזֵר יַם־סוּף לִגְזָרִים   כִּי לְעוֹלָם חַסְדּוֹ:
וְהֶעֱבִיר יִשְׂרָאֵל בְּתוֹכוֹ   כִּי לְעוֹלָם חַסְדּוֹ:
וְנִעֵר פַּרְעֹה וְחֵילוֹ בְיַם־סוּף   כִּי לְעוֹלָם חַסְדּוֹ:

And made Israel pass through it, His loving-kindness is for ever.

Casting Pharaoh and his army
into the Reed Sea; His loving-kindness is for ever.

Who led His people through the wilderness; His loving-kindness is for ever.

Who struck down great kings, His loving-kindness is for ever.

And slew mighty kings, His loving-kindness is for ever.

Siḥon, king of the Amorites, His loving-kindness is for ever.

And Og, king of Bashan, His loving-kindness is for ever.

And gave their land as a heritage, His loving-kindness is for ever.

A heritage for His servant Israel; His loving-kindness is for ever.

Who remembered us in our lowly state, His loving-kindness is for ever.

And rescued us from our tormentors, His loving-kindness is for ever.

Who gives food to all flesh, His loving-kindness is for ever.

Give thanks to the God of heaven. His loving-kindness is for ever.

לְמוֹלִיךְ עַמּוֹ בַּמִּדְבָּר   כִּי לְעוֹלָם חַסְדּוֹ:
לְמַכֵּה מְלָכִים גְּדֹלִים   כִּי לְעוֹלָם חַסְדּוֹ:
וַיַּהֲרֹג מְלָכִים אַדִּירִים   כִּי לְעוֹלָם חַסְדּוֹ:
לְסִיחוֹן מֶלֶךְ הָאֱמֹרִי   כִּי לְעוֹלָם חַסְדּוֹ:
וּלְעוֹג מֶלֶךְ הַבָּשָׁן   כִּי לְעוֹלָם חַסְדּוֹ:
וְנָתַן אַרְצָם לְנַחֲלָה   כִּי לְעוֹלָם חַסְדּוֹ:
נַחֲלָה לְיִשְׂרָאֵל עַבְדּוֹ   כִּי לְעוֹלָם חַסְדּוֹ:
שֶׁבְּשִׁפְלֵנוּ זָכַר לָנוּ   כִּי לְעוֹלָם חַסְדּוֹ:
וַיִּפְרְקֵנוּ מִצָּרֵינוּ   כִּי לְעוֹלָם חַסְדּוֹ:
נֹתֵן לֶחֶם לְכָל־בָּשָׂר   כִּי לְעוֹלָם חַסְדּוֹ:
הוֹדוּ לְאֵל הַשָּׁמָיִם   כִּי לְעוֹלָם חַסְדּוֹ:

Blessing of Song

THE SOUL

of all that lives shall bless Your name,
Lord our God,
and the spirit of all flesh shall always glorify
and exalt Your remembrance, our King.
From eternity to eternity You are God.
Without You, we have no King, Redeemer or Savior,
who liberates, rescues, sustains
and shows compassion
in every time of trouble and distress.
We have no King but You,
God of the first and last,
God of all creatures,
Master of all ages,
extolled by a multitude of praises,
who guides His world with loving-kindness
and His creatures with compassion.
The Lord neither slumbers nor sleeps.
He rouses the sleepers and wakens the slumberers.

נִשְׁמַת

כָּל חַי תְּבָרֵךְ אֶת שִׁמְךָ, יהוה אֱלֹהֵינוּ
וְרוּחַ כָּל בָּשָׂר תְּפָאֵר וּתְרוֹמֵם זִכְרְךָ מַלְכֵּנוּ תָּמִיד
מִן הָעוֹלָם וְעַד הָעוֹלָם אַתָּה אֵל.
וּמִבַּלְעָדֶיךָ אֵין לָנוּ מֶלֶךְ
גּוֹאֵל וּמוֹשִׁיעַ, פּוֹדֶה וּמַצִּיל וּמְפַרְנֵס וְעוֹנֶה וּמְרַחֵם
בְּכָל עֵת צָרָה וְצוּקָה
אֵין לָנוּ מֶלֶךְ עוֹזֵר וְסוֹמֵךְ אֶלָּא אָתָּה.
אֱלֹהֵי הָרִאשׁוֹנִים וְהָאַחֲרוֹנִים
אֱלוֹהַּ כָּל בְּרִיּוֹת
אֲדוֹן כָּל תּוֹלָדוֹת הַמְהֻלָּל בְּרֹב הַתִּשְׁבָּחוֹת
הַמְנַהֵג עוֹלָמוֹ בְּחֶסֶד וּבְרִיּוֹתָיו בְּרַחֲמִים.
וַיהוה עֵר
הִנֵּה לֹא יָנוּם וְלֹא יִישָׁן
הַמְעוֹרֵר יְשֵׁנִים וְהַמֵּקִיץ נִרְדָּמִים
וְהַמֵּשִׂיחַ אִלְּמִים וְהַמַּתִּיר אֲסוּרִים

He makes the dumb speak, sets the bound free,
supports the fallen,
and raises those bowed down.
To You alone we give thanks:
If our mouths were as full of song as the sea,
and our tongue with jubilation as its myriad waves,
if our lips were full of praise like the spacious heavens,
and our eyes shone like the sun and moon,
if our hands were outstretched like eagles of the sky,
and our feet as swift as hinds –
still we could not thank You enough,
LORD our God and God of our ancestors,
or bless Your name
for even one of the thousand thousands
and myriad myriads of favors
You did for our ancestors and for us.
You redeemed us from Egypt, LORD our God,
and freed us from the house of bondage.
In famine You nourished us; in times of plenty You sustained us.

וְהַסּוֹמֵךְ נוֹפְלִים וְהַזּוֹקֵף כְּפוּפִים וְהַמְפַעְנֵחַ נֶעְלָמִים
וּלְךָ לְבַדְּךָ אֲנַחְנוּ מוֹדִים
וְאִלּוּ פִינוּ מָלֵא שִׁירָה כַּיָּם
וּלְשׁוֹנֵנוּ רִנָּה כַּהֲמוֹן גַּלָּיו
וְשִׂפְתוֹתֵינוּ שֶׁבַח כְּמֶרְחֲבֵי רָקִיעַ
וְעֵינֵינוּ מְאִירוֹת כַּשֶּׁמֶשׁ וְכַיָּרֵחַ
וְיָדֵינוּ פְרוּשׂוֹת כְּנִשְׁרֵי שָׁמָיִם
וְרַגְלֵינוּ קַלּוֹת כָּאַיָּלוֹת
אֵין אֲנַחְנוּ מַסְפִּיקִים לְהוֹדוֹת לְךָ
יהוה אֱלֹהֵינוּ וֵאלֹהֵי אֲבוֹתֵינוּ
וּלְבָרֵךְ אֶת שִׁמְךָ, מַלְכֵּנוּ
עַל אַחַת מֵאֶלֶף אֶלֶף אַלְפֵי אֲלָפִים וְרִבֵּי רְבָבוֹת פְּעָמִים
הַטּוֹבוֹת, נִסִּים וְנִפְלָאוֹת שֶׁעָשִׂיתָ עִם אֲבוֹתֵינוּ וְעִמָּנוּ
מִלְּפָנִים מִמִּצְרַיִם גְּאַלְתָּנוּ, יהוה אֱלֹהֵינוּ
וּמִבֵּית עֲבָדִים פְּדִיתָנוּ
בְּרָעָב זַנְתָּנוּ וּבְשָׂבָע כִּלְכַּלְתָּנוּ

You delivered us from the sword, saved us from the plague,
and spared us from serious and lasting illness.
Until now Your mercies have helped us.
Your love has not forsaken us.
May You, LORD our God, never abandon us.
Therefore the limbs You formed within us,
the spirit and soul You breathed into our nostrils,
and the tongue You placed in our mouth –
they will thank and bless, praise and glorify,
exalt and esteem,
hallow and do homage to Your name, O our King.
For every mouth shall give thanks to You,
every tongue vow allegiance to You,
every knee shall bend to You,
every upright body shall bow to You,
all hearts shall fear You,
and our innermost being sing praises to Your name,

מֵחֶרֶב הִצַּלְתָּנוּ וּמִדֶּבֶר מִלַּטְתָּנוּ
וּמֵחֳלָיִים רָעִים וְרַבִּים וְנֶאֱמָנִים דִּלִּיתָנוּ.
עַד הֵנָּה עֲזָרוּנוּ רַחֲמֶיךָ וְלֹא עֲזָבוּנוּ חֲסָדֶיךָ, יהוה אֱלֹהֵינוּ
וְאַל תִּטְּשֵׁנוּ, יהוה אֱלֹהֵינוּ, לָנֶצַח.
עַל כֵּן אֵבָרִים שֶׁפִּלַּגְתָּ בָּנוּ
וְרוּחַ וּנְשָׁמָה שֶׁנָּפַחְתָּ בְּאַפֵּנוּ
וְלָשׁוֹן אֲשֶׁר שַׂמְתָּ בְּפִינוּ
הֵן הֵם יוֹדוּ וִיבָרְכוּ וִישַׁבְּחוּ וִיפָאֲרוּ וִישׁוֹרְרוּ
וִירוֹמְמוּ וְיַעֲרִיצוּ וְיַקְדִּישׁוּ וְיַמְלִיכוּ
אֶת שִׁמְךָ מַלְכֵּנוּ תָמִיד
כִּי כָל פֶּה לְךָ יוֹדֶה, וְכָל לָשׁוֹן לְךָ תִשָּׁבַע
וְכָל עַיִן לְךָ תְצַפֶּה
וְכָל בֶּרֶךְ לְךָ תִכְרַע, וְכָל קוֹמָה לְפָנֶיךָ תִשְׁתַּחֲוֶה
וְכָל הַלְּבָבוֹת יִירָאוּךָ, וְכָל קֶרֶב וּכְלָיוֹת יְזַמְּרוּ לִשְׁמֶךָ

as is written:

"All my bones shall say: LORD, who is like You? *Ps. 35*
You save the poor from one stronger than him,
the poor and needy from one who would rob him."

Who is like You? Who is equal to You?
Who can be compared to You?

O great, mighty and awesome God, *Deut. 10*
God Most High,
Maker of heaven and earth. *Gen. 14*

We will laud, praise and glorify
You and bless Your holy name,
as it is said:

"Of David. Bless the LORD, O my soul, *Ps. 103*
and all that is within me bless His holy name."

כַּדָּבָר שֶׁכָּתוּב

כָּל עַצְמֹתַי תֹּאמַרְנָה יהוה תהלים לה

מִי כָמוֹךָ

מַצִּיל עָנִי מֵחָזָק מִמֶּנּוּ, וְעָנִי וְאֶבְיוֹן מִגֹּזְלוֹ:

שַׁוְעַת עֲנִיִּים אַתָּה תִשְׁמַע

צַעֲקַת הַדַּל תַּקְשִׁיב וְתוֹשִׁיעַ.

מִי יִדְמֶה לָּךְ וּמִי יִשְׁוֶה לָּךְ וּמִי יַעֲרָךְ לָךְ.

הָאֵל הַגָּדוֹל, הַגִּבּוֹר וְהַנּוֹרָא דברים י

אֵל עֶלְיוֹן, קֹנֵה שָׁמַיִם וָאָרֶץ: בראשית יד

נְהַלֶּלְךָ וּנְשַׁבֵּחֲךָ וּנְפָאֶרְךָ וּנְבָרֵךְ אֶת שֵׁם קָדְשֶׁךָ

כָּאָמוּר

לְדָוִד בָּרְכִי נַפְשִׁי אֶת־יהוה תהלים קג

וְכָל־קְרָבַי אֶת־שֵׁם קָדְשׁוֹ:

God in Your absolute power,
Great in the glory of Your name,
Mighty for ever,
Awesome in Your awe-inspiring deeds,

The King – who sits on a throne.
High and lofty
He inhabits eternity; exalted and holy is His name.

And it is written:
Sing joyfully to the LORD, you righteous, *Ps. 33*
for praise from the upright is seemly

By the mouth of the upright You shall be praised.
By the words of the righteous You shall be blessed.
By the tongue of the devout You shall be extolled,
And in the midst of the holy You shall be sanctified.

הָאֵל בְּתַעֲצוּמוֹת עֻזֶּךָ
הַגָּדוֹל בִּכְבוֹד שְׁמֶךָ
הַגִּבּוֹר לָנֶצַח
וְהַנּוֹרָא בְּנוֹרְאוֹתֶיךָ

הַמֶּלֶךְ הַיּוֹשֵׁב עַל כִּסֵּא.

רָם וְנִשָּׂא

שׁוֹכֵן עַד מָרוֹם וְקָדוֹשׁ שְׁמוֹ

וְכָתוּב

רַנְּנוּ צַדִּיקִים בַּיהוה, לַיְשָׁרִים נָאוָה תְהִלָּה: תהלים לג

בְּפִי יְשָׁרִים תִּתְרוֹמָם
וּבְשִׂפְתֵי צַדִּיקִים תִּתְבָּרַךְ
וּבִלְשׁוֹן חֲסִידִים תִּתְקַדָּשׁ
וּבְקֶרֶב קְדוֹשִׁים תִּתְהַלָּל

And in the assemblies
of tens of thousands of Your people, the house of Israel,
with joyous song shall Your name, our King,
be glorified in every generation.
For this is the duty of all creatures before You,
Lord our God and God of our ancestors:

to thank, praise, laud, glorify, exalt,
honor, bless, raise high and acclaim –
even beyond all the words
of song and praise
of David, son of Jesse,
Your servant, Your anointed.

וּבְמַקְהֲלוֹת רִבְבוֹת עַמְּךָ בֵּית יִשְׂרָאֵל
בְּרִנָּה יִתְפָּאַר שִׁמְךָ מַלְכֵּנוּ בְּכָל דּוֹר וָדוֹר
שֶׁכֵּן חוֹבַת כָּל הַיְצוּרִים לְפָנֶיךָ
יהוה אֱלֹהֵינוּ וֵאלֹהֵי אֲבוֹתֵינוּ

לְהוֹדוֹת, לְהַלֵּל, לְשַׁבֵּחַ, לְפָאֵר, לְרוֹמֵם לְהַדֵּר וּלְנַצֵּחַ, לְבָרֵךְ לְעַלֵּה וּלְקַלֵּס עַל כָּל דִּבְרֵי שִׁירוֹת וְתִשְׁבְּחוֹת, דָּוִד בֶּן יִשַׁי עַבְדְּךָ מְשִׁיחֶךָ.

May Your name be praised for ever, our King,
the great and holy God, King in heaven and on earth.
For to You, Lord our God and God of our ancestors,
it is right to offer song and praise,
hymn and psalm, strength and dominion,
eternity, greatness and power,
song of praise and glory,
holiness and kingship,
blessings and thanks, from now and for ever.
Blessed are You, Lord,
God and King, exalted in praises,
God of thanksgivings,
Master of wonders,
who delights in hymns of song,
King, God, Giver of life to the worlds.

וּבְכֵן יִשְׁתַּבַּח שִׁמְךָ לָעַד מַלְכֵּנוּ
הָאֵל, הַמֶּלֶךְ, הַגָּדוֹל וְהַקָּדוֹשׁ
בַּשָּׁמַיִם וּבָאָרֶץ
כִּי לְךָ נָאֶה, יהוה אֱלֹהֵינוּ וֵאלֹהֵי אֲבוֹתֵינוּ
שִׁיר וּשְׁבָחָה, הַלֵּל וְזִמְרָה, עֹז וּמֶמְשָׁלָה
נֶצַח, גְּדֻלָּה וּגְבוּרָה
תְּהִלָּה וְתִפְאֶרֶת, קְדֻשָּׁה וּמַלְכוּת
בְּרָכוֹת וְהוֹדָאוֹת לְשִׁמְךָ הַגָּדוֹל וְהַקָּדוֹשׁ
וּמֵעוֹלָם וְעַד עוֹלָם אַתָּה אֵל.
בָּרוּךְ אַתָּה יהוה
אֵל מֶלֶךְ גָּדוֹל וּמְהֻלָּל בַּתִּשְׁבָּחוֹת
אֵל הַהוֹדָאוֹת, אֲדוֹן הַנִּפְלָאוֹת
בּוֹרֵא כָּל הַנְּשָׁמוֹת, רִבּוֹן כָּל הַמַּעֲשִׂים
הַבּוֹחֵר בְּשִׁירֵי זִמְרָה
מֶלֶךְ, יָחִיד אֵל, חֵי הָעוֹלָמִים.

> throughout, from beginning to end, and there is no truth here whatsoever! And he began to retell all the falsehood of the country. When the king heard his words, he bent his ear to the veil to listen to hear his words, for it was a great wonder to the king that there should exist a man who would know all the falsehood of the country....
>
> The wise man spoke up: One could say that the king is also like them, that he likes falsehood as the country does. But on the contrary, one sees what a man of truth you are, and because of this you keep your distance from them, since you cannot bear the falsehood of the country. And he began to praise the king very, very much. And the king, because he was very humble, and in the place of his greatness is his humility, for that is the way of a humble man, that the more he is praised and extolled, the smaller to himself and the humbler he becomes, so on account of the wise man's great praise and exultation of the king, the king entered into great humility and extreme smallness, until he became absolutely nothing, and he could no longer withhold himself, and he threw aside the veil to see the wise man, who it is that knows and understands all this. And the king's face was revealed. And the wise man saw him, depicted his portrait, and brought it back to the king.

The king calls his trusted confidant, the wise man, and tells him: I have portraits of all the kings in the world, aside from one. Can you bring me a picture of this king? And his trusted confidant went to this king's country, a country filled with liars and swindlers and cynical people and evil people. He searches for their king, and discovers that the king hides behind a veil.

So this wise man goes to the veil and tells the king about all the corruption, and evil, and deceit in his country. But it doesn't help. The king still hides behind the veil. The king will not reveal his face to one who speaks about evil all the time.

And the wise man understands: If this king is covered by a veil, it means that he is the antithesis to the rest of the country. I tried to tell him about everything that is bad in this deceitful country, but it didn't cause the king to reveal himself. What should I do now? Now, I'll begin to tell him about everything that is good about him.

And he begins to praise and extol and extol and praise, and he goes on and on, and as he praises, the king comes closer and closer to the veil that covers him, and suddenly the veil is lifted and the king himself is revealed.

As long

The Tales of Rebbe Nahman:

The Tale of the Humble King

There was once a king who had a wise man. The king said to the wise man, "I know that there is a king who is a great man of might, truth, and humility... I want you to bring me this king's portrait, for I have portraits of all the kings but this one, whose portrait is nowhere to be found. For he is concealed from all as he sits beyond a veil, far from the eyes of his people."

The wise man went to that country. The wise man said to himself that he must come to know the essence of the country. And how can he find out the country's essence? By way of the country's jests. Because when one needs to know [the essence of] something, one must know its jesting.

He understood from the jests that the country is full of falsehood through and through. For he saw them making fun of how people are cheated in business.... The wise man understood from this jesting that the country is full of lies and deceit, lacking any truth in the land whatsoever.

So he went and conducted some commerce in the country...until he came to the king himself. When he came to the king he spoke up and said: Over whom are you king? The entire country is full of falsehood

"Because the God of this nation is busy doing miracles for them on this night as they say Hallel."

"And Sanḥeriv mocked and said: For this small city, I'm troubling my entire army? And he said to his soldiers: Go to sleep tonight and in the morning, I will take it [apart] stone by stone, and we'll leave."

What did God do? "An angel of God went and struck the Assyrian camp. That very night, was the night of Pesaḥ and this miracle was done by Ḥizkiya, one of the sons of Leah,"[220] in essence the incredible and powerful Hallel recited by the Jewish people at the Seder. "And they awoke the next morning, and behold, they were all dead corpses."[221]

Sanḥeriv's army was defeated by a song of gratitude. You probably never thought of Hallel as a weapon. But it's deadly. Who knows how many tunnels it caused to collapse. Sing!

As long as the wise man speaks about how terrible everything is in this unscrupulous country and describes its corrupt legal system, he's not able to encounter the king. He is wise, and this is an accurate reflection of the land. The state of the union. But the king remains hidden.

And then the wise man thinks to himself: Perhaps I should try something else. Perhaps praising the good things proves that we are well aware of the bad things that we need to avoid! "For silver the crucible, for gold the furnace, and man is tested by his praise."[217] Tell me what you praise and hold in high esteem, and I'll tell you who you are.

And the veil is lifted.

The veil is lifted precisely at the stage that our Sages describe as "and the Hallel breaks the roof."[218] Hallel is recited and the roof breaks! Rabbi Hutner likes to explain that Hallel includes everything. In the words of David in Psalms: "I will tell all Your praise."[219] It includes everything, and for this reason it exceeds all boundaries of time and space. At this point, there are no more partitions that stand between us. We have an unmediated encounter with the King.

Hallel, and the Roof Flies Off

We ate, we told the story, and though there's a strong chance that we're exhausted, we won't skip Hallel. We recite the entire Hallel on Pesaḥ night, the *Hallel gamur* – whose Gematria value is equivalent to God's name Shaddai, the name that describes God's capacity to override the natural world and bring about miracles. Indeed, Hallel is an incredible prayer of gratitude that has the capacity to vanquish the sworn (human) enemies of the Jewish people.

"That night," the Midrash tells the story of Sanḥeriv, king of Assyria, who wanted to capture Jerusalem on the day before Pesaḥ: "And Rav-Shakeh was there [Rav-Shakeh was one of Sanḥeriv's senior officers]. He went and he peeked at the opening of the wall of Jerusalem and heard them reciting Hallel. He said to Sanḥeriv: Turn around and go back."

Why?

I am prepared and ready to fulfill the commandment of the fourth of the four cups. For the sake for the unification of the Holy One, blessed be He, and His Divine Presence, through He who is hidden and unseen, in the name of all Israel.

בָּרוּךְ Blessed are You, Lord our God,
King of the Universe,
who creates the fruit of the vine.

Drink while reclining to the left.

The Fourth Cup
Is Symbolic of Leah, Our Matriarch

בָּרוּךְ Blessed are You, Lord our God,
King of the Universe,
for the vine and the fruit of the vine,
and for the produce of the field;
for the desirable, good
and spacious land that You willingly gave as heritage to our ancestors, that they might eat of its fruit
and be satisfied with its goodness.

הִנְנִי מוּכָן וּמְזֻמָּן לְקַיֵּם מִצְוַת כּוֹס רְבִיעִי שֶׁל אַרְבַּע כּוֹסוֹת.
לְשֵׁם יִחוּד קֻדְשָׁא בְּרִיךְ הוּא וּשְׁכִינְתֵּהּ עַל יְדֵי הַהוּא טָמִיר וְנֶעְלָם בְּשֵׁם כָּל יִשְׂרָאֵל.

בָּרוּךְ אַתָּה יהוה
אֱלֹהֵינוּ מֶלֶךְ הָעוֹלָם
בּוֹרֵא פְּרִי הַגָּפֶן.

שותים בהסבת שמאל.

כוס רביעית
כנגד לאה אימנו

בָּרוּךְ אַתָּה יהוה אֱלֹהֵינוּ מֶלֶךְ הָעוֹלָם
עַל הַגֶּפֶן וְעַל פְּרִי הַגֶּפֶן
וְעַל תְּנוּבַת הַשָּׂדֶה
וְעַל אֶרֶץ חֶמְדָּה טוֹבָה וּרְחָבָה
שֶׁרָצִיתָ וְהִנְחַלְתָּ לַאֲבוֹתֵינוּ
לֶאֱכֹל מִפִּרְיָהּ וְלִשְׂבֹּעַ מִטּוּבָהּ.

Have compassion, Lord our God,
on Israel Your people, on Jerusalem,
Your city, on Zion the home of Your glory,
on Your altar and Your Temple.
May You rebuild Jerusalem,
the holy city swiftly in our time,
and may You bring us back there,
rejoicing in its rebuilding,
eating from its fruit,
satisfied by its goodness,
and blessing You for it in holiness and purity.
(*On Shabbat:* Be pleased to refresh us on this Sabbath Day.)
Grant us joy on this festival of Matzot.
For You, God, are good and do good to all
and we thank You for the land
and for the fruit of the vine.
Blessed are You, Lord,
for the land and for the fruit of the vine.

רַחֵם נָא יהוה אֱלֹהֵינוּ עַל יִשְׂרָאֵל עַמֶּךָ
וְעַל יְרוּשָׁלַיִם עִירֶךָ וְעַל צִיּוֹן מִשְׁכַּן כְּבוֹדֶךָ
וְעַל מִזְבְּחֶךָ וְעַל הֵיכָלֶךָ.
וּבְנֵה יְרוּשָׁלַיִם עִיר הַקֹּדֶשׁ בִּמְהֵרָה בְיָמֵינוּ
וְהַעֲלֵנוּ לְתוֹכָהּ וְשַׂמְּחֵנוּ בְּבִנְיָנָהּ
וְנֹאכַל מִפִּרְיָהּ וְנִשְׂבַּע מִטּוּבָהּ
וּנְבָרֶכְךָ עָלֶיהָ בִּקְדֻשָּׁה וּבְטָהֳרָה.
בשבת: וּרְצֵה וְהַחֲלִיצֵנוּ בְּיוֹם הַשַּׁבָּת הַזֶּה
וְשַׂמְּחֵנוּ בְּיוֹם חַג הַמַּצּוֹת הַזֶּה
כִּי אַתָּה יהוה טוֹב וּמֵטִיב לַכֹּל, וְנוֹדֶה לְּךָ
עַל הָאָרֶץ וְעַל פְּרִי גַפְנָהּ / אם היין מחו״ל: הַגָּפֶן/.
בָּרוּךְ אַתָּה יהוה
עַל הָאָרֶץ וְעַל פְּרִי גַפְנָהּ / אם היין מחו״ל: הַגָּפֶן/.

Nirtza / Parting

נִרְצָה

Who Is Pleased?

Look around you. Do the people sitting next to you look pleased and fulfilled?

You should know that even if you can't wait for the guests to finally leave ("Go home already! The Seder's over!"), right now, at this very moment, God is so pleased with your Seder.

As you should be, too. You, too, deserve to feel pleased and fulfilled.

You should also be. You deserve to feel pleased and fulfilled.

Our Personal *Avoda: Nirtza*

Ask to believe that the heavens are pleased with us right now.

Pray that we should also reconcile and be pleased with one another.

"May this moment be a moment of compassion and a time of favor before You."

"Next year in Jerusalem rebuilt."

חֲסַל סִדּוּר פֶּסַח כְּהִלְכָתוֹ
כְּכָל מִשְׁפָּטוֹ וְחֻקָּתוֹ
כַּאֲשֶׁר זָכִינוּ לְסַדֵּר אוֹתוֹ, כֵּן נִזְכֶּה לַעֲשׂוֹתוֹ
זָךְ שׁוֹכֵן מְעוֹנָה, קוֹמֵם קְהַל עֲדַת מִי מָנָה
קָרֵב נַהֵל נִטְעֵי כַנָּה
פְּדוּיִם לְצִיּוֹן בְּרִנָּה.

The Pesaḥ service is finished, as it was meant to be
performed, in accordance with all its rules and laws.
Just as we have been privileged to lay out its order so may
we be privileged to perform it [in the Temple].
Pure One, dwelling in Your heaven, raise up this people,
too abundant to be counted.
Soon, lead the shoots of [Israel's] stock, redeemed, into
Zion with great joy.

NEXT YEAR
לַשָּׁנָה הַבָּאָה

IN JERUSALEM REBUILT
בִּירוּשָׁלַיִם הַבְּנוּיָה.

exactly how illogical our Father is. How He created man despite the fact that man "is full of lies and full of discord."[223] How He favors us and gives us preferential treatment, even though we don't deserve it. How God loves His children and "casts truth earthward"[224] as the celestial angels cry from a different world.

And in this way, a father, perhaps the greatest one of all, comes along in the springtime and declares unapologetically: "I will set [them] apart."[225] Because "Israel is My firstborn son."[226] It's an unreasonable deal. To primarily identify as "the father of so-and-so" is unreasonable. In my mind, there is an intrinsic connection between the Hebrew word for "springtime" (*aviv*) and the Hebrew word for "his father" (*aviv*), even though they're spelled differently. Springtime is emblematic of the small father, the dad who is wholly and irrationally committed to his son.

I find myself searching again, through the nooks and crannies, for the father who favors me and shows me preferential treatment. Each Seder night, I light a candle for him. I search for my great father on *Shabbat HaGadol* (the "great Shabbat" that precedes the holiday of Pesaḥ). My father of German descent, who was fond of saying *Alles ist in ordnung*, "Everything is in order," but for me, would defy my mother's unequivocal instructions, which were all about organization and order. Shortly before Pesaḥ, after my mother had finished polishing the terrace clean, my father decided to explain springtime to me. He took a permanent marker and drew a sundial on the gleaming floor of our terrace and outlined the different positions that the sun and shade pass through all day long. This is how the sun travels in the spring, he explained to me, as my mother looked on in shock.... At that point I was his daughter, a free woman, once again unfairly discriminating against my wonderful mother.

Immediately afterward, my father and I boarded the number 12 bus that took us from Bayit Vegan directly to the Zaharei Ḥama Synagogue by the Mahane Yehuda marketplace. My father showed me the sundial there, the ancient one, and I felt so good about myself and my relationship with him. I literally felt like the sun.

This was how my father showed me spring. And even though I knew in my heart of hearts that life isn't always so beautiful, this was me and not an angel, and therefore my father cast truth toward the ground and redeemed me again and again for far more than my true value and told me "in your blood live."[227]

As the Seder reaches its climax, I seek to sing the battle of this father, the great father who fought for me. When my heart is about to burst, I sing *Ḥad Gadya* to my father's special tune, knowing that this song doesn't sing about the return of the little goat who is attacked again and again and again as much as the return of a father, who paid two *zuz* for one little goat in a boundless display of fatherly love, and was eaten by a cat and bitten by a dog and hit by a stick and burned by a fire and extinguished by water and drunk by an ox and slaughtered by a slaughterer and killed by the angel of death and is still a father.

And I long to redeem this father, the great father who was taken advantage of. I seek to redeem him for more than

his true

Abba's Little Girl

At my Seder table, the empty chair is reserved for my father.

Throughout the past week, I have found myself speaking compassionately about fathers. Fathers who try so hard, fathers who are often underappreciated. The father who will always be "too small" in our eyes, or too great to actually be interested in us. But the truth is, these fathers are incredibly devoted.

One of the most contested prisoner exchanges ever conducted was the deal that secured Gilad Shalit's release in exchange for many terrorists. Gilad's father, Noam Shalit, who turned the world upside down to secure his son's release, passed away the day before Pesaḥ. I remember that I was asked why I didn't speak about him – the father who was endlessly devoted to his son – in my talks. And I thought to myself that perhaps the reason is that this was the sum total of what he was. His father. He was only his father.

And then perhaps I understood for the very first time, the deeper meaning of this time period, the Festival of the Spring. The time period that cries the cry of fatherhood, which maintains that as a prisoner exchange loses its legitimacy, fatherhood assumes its absolute legitimacy.

The extent that a father redeems his son for far more than his true value is the extent to which this love is defined as an "illogical" love, in the words of Rebbe Nahman. Because a father is illogical. A father's love does not take anything else into account; a father has eyes only for his children.

God also redeemed us from Egypt for far more than our true worth. The angels themselves protested the deal and declared to God: "It's not worth it! They're basically worth the exact same amount as the Egyptians! "These [people] are idol worshippers, and these [people] are idol worshippers!"[222]

I love this celestial objection. Each time this angelic grievance appears in rabbinic literature, it seeks to highlight

> excommunication was valid, because this liturgical poem is redemption and satisfaction for the entire year.[234]

The songs sung at the end of the Seder should not be mocked. They have tremendous power.

What is *Ḥad Gadya*? And what is "*Eḥad Mi Yode'a*"?

Ḥad Gadya means "one goat." The Hebrew word for goat (*gedi*) also means "good fortune.". In Egypt, they believed in *gad*, in fortune. The Jewish people, though, add one letter to this word – the Hebrew letter *yod*, which is emblematic of God. We believe in the Master of the world. It's easy to get confused. Sometimes I hear great speakers talking about faith in God as though it were a matter of fate, like a fortune or a zodiac sign: "If it will happen to you – it will happen to you." In this New Age generation it's easy to start worshipping the stars and the zodiac signs, more than ever before.

And God says to you: It doesn't matter what you went through. You can always start over again from the very beginning.

Look at the little goat in the song. He's swallowed and engulfed and devoured again and again in a tragic chain of events. What will be? Where is the little goat? Rabbi Mutzafi explains that *Ḥad Gadya* is a "hidden and incredible parable."[235] God stands at the end of this food chain and slaughters the angel of death, and who comes back? The little goat returns.

And you will also return on this night, on this night.

In *Eḥad Mi Yode'a*, we come to understand that all the frightening details are part of the same story. And behind all of this is One, our God is One. And there is one, one little goat. Just wait.

"Then came the Holy One, and slew the angel of death." Slaying the angel of death and restoring someone to life, starting again from the very beginning, is an exclusively divine capacity. For this reason, the *haftara* chanted on Pesaḥ discusses the dry bones that come back to life. This is something that lies far beyond the domain of any zodiac sign.

> For this reason, every individual should take to his heart and look closely, during both *Ḥad Gadya* and also *Eḥad Mi Yode'a*, and it is written in code to remove the evil eye and accusatory angels. They would read these songs on an actual parchment, and they have the capacity to console brokenhearted and sad people and bring comfort to hearts, that they should not despair of redemption. Because we have promises that we will soon reach our redemption and our lives' salvation. And when we recite this song, we offer a defense of Israel: the merit of the Tablets of the Covenant, the merit of the three patriarchs, the merit of circumcision, "the kindness of the Lord that has not ended" (Lam. 3:22).[236]

his true value, for more than what he really was, for what I imagined him to be, and in the aftermath of his death, he becomes greater, since there is nobody else to favor me and there is nobody else to draw a sundial for me and placate the winter that I hold in my heart, even with the onset of spring.

On these days I sing to you, Abba. I remember the goat that you passionately told me about, I remember the way you moved mountains for me with two *zuz*, and explained to me complex things that were far beyond my years.

I want to give back to you, in a big way. I want to restore the hearts of the fathers to their children and reconcile daughters with their fathers.[228] All the fathers, the great ones and the small ones alike.

Happy Pesaḥ, my dear father. Sharp as a razor, one of a kind, one little goat, one little goat.

A Note About the Songs and Poems Recited at the Seder

Ki Lo Na'eh, *Dayeinu*, etc. – Women aren't obligated to recite these words, and perhaps you might prefer to do without them, but these songs keep God with you in your home. Naturally, He is distant for most of the year; "He who is enthroned in heaven laughs,"[229] but when it comes to songs, He "is enthroned, the praise of Israel."[230] God sits by your side at the Seder table.[231]

And these moments are also extremely sublime. *Ḥad Gadya* and *Eḥad Mi Yode'a* are emblematic of the exclusive encounter between a bride and groom![232] And what happens when we sing these songs – "it breaks the roof."[233] The roof breaks, and it's not there anymore. There are no windows, no doors. It's just you and Him and Him and you, without any barriers dividing you. And He can see even the most trivial of your sorrows. And He delivers salvation.

Rabbi Mutzafi writes:

> We have the custom of reciting the liturgical poem *Ḥad Gadya*, which is attributed to Rabbi Elazar of Worms, the author of the *Sefer HaRoke'aḥ*, a leading rabbi of his time. And it alludes to the order of events that happened to the Jewish people throughout the generations, until the arrival of the redeemer, speedily in our days.
>
> And once there was a man who mocked this liturgical poem, and he opened his mouth wide and said that the ones who recite it are foolish and occupy themselves with nonsense. And a member of the congregation excommunicated him. And Maran [Rabbi Ovadia Yosef] agreed that the

Outside of Israel, this poem is recited on the first night of Pesaḥ only.

AND SO – IT HAPPENED AT MIDNIGHT.

Ex. 12

Many were the miracles You performed long ago, at night.
At the beginning of the watch, on this night,
You won [Avraham's] battle, when [his men were] split, and the night
IT HAPPENED AT MIDNIGHT.

You judged the king of Gerar in his dream at night.
You put dread into [Lavan] the Aramean's heart that night.
And Israel struggled with an angel and overcame him at night
IT HAPPENED AT MIDNIGHT.

You crushed the firstborns of Patros [Egypt] in the middle of the night.
They could not find their strength, when they rose up
[against Israel] at night.
You flung [Sisera] the commander of Ḥaroshet
off course with the stars of night
IT HAPPENED AT MIDNIGHT.

בחוץ לארץ אומרים פיוט זה רק בלילה הראשון של פסח.

וּבְכֵן וַיְהִי בַּחֲצִי הַלַּיְלָה

שמות יב

אָז רֹב נִסִּים הִפְלֵאתָ בַּלַּיְלָה
בְּרֹאשׁ אַשְׁמוּרוֹת זֶה הַלַּיְלָה
גֵּר צֶדֶק נִצַּחְתּוֹ, כְּנֶחֱלַק לוֹ לַיְלָה
וַיְהִי בַּחֲצִי הַלַּיְלָה

דַּנְתָּ מֶלֶךְ גְּרָר בַּחֲלוֹם הַלַּיְלָה
הִפְחַדְתָּ אֲרַמִּי בְּאֶמֶשׁ לַיְלָה
וַיִּשְׂרָאֵל יָשַׁר לָאֵל, וַיּוּכַל לוֹ לַיְלָה
וַיְהִי בַּחֲצִי הַלַּיְלָה

זֶרַע בְּכוֹרֵי פַתְרוֹס מָחַצְתָּ בַּחֲצִי הַלַּיְלָה
חֵילָם לֹא מָצְאוּ בְּקוּמָם בַּלַּיְלָה
טִיסַת נְגִיד חֲרֹשֶׁת סִלִּיתָ בְּכוֹכְבֵי לַיְלָה
וַיְהִי בַּחֲצִי הַלַּיְלָה

[Sanḥeriv] the blasphemer thought to raise his hand
against the beloved [city];
but You dried up the bodies of his fallen in the night.

You overthrew Bel, idol and pedestal together, in the dead of night.

To [Daniel] the beloved man were revealed
the secrets of that vision of the night

IT HAPPENED AT MIDNIGHT.

[Belshazzar], who drank himself merry
from the holy vessels, was killed on that same night.

[Daniel] was brought out unharmed from the
lions' den; he who had explained those terrors of the night.

[Haman] the Agagite bore his hatred and wrote his orders at night

IT HAPPENED AT MIDNIGHT.

You awakened Your might against him, disturbing
[King Aḥashverosh's] sleep at night.

You shall tread the winepress of [Se'ir],
who asks anxiously, "What of the night?"

You will cry out like the watchman, calling,
"Morning is come, and also night"

IT HAPPENED AT MIDNIGHT.

יָעַץ מְחָרֵף לְנוֹפֵף אִוּוּי, הוֹבַשְׁתָּ פְגָרָיו בַּלַּיְלָה
כָּרַע בֵּל וּמַצָּבוֹ בְּאִישׁוֹן לַיְלָה
לְאִישׁ חֲמוּדוֹת נִגְלָה רָז חֲזוּת לַיְלָה
וַיְהִי בַּחֲצִי הַלַּיְלָה

מִשְׁתַּכֵּר בִּכְלֵי קֹדֶשׁ נֶהֱרַג בּוֹ בַּלַּיְלָה
נוֹשַׁע מִבּוֹר אֲרָיוֹת, פּוֹתֵר בִּעֲתוּתֵי לַיְלָה
שִׂנְאָה נָטַר אֲגָגִי, וְכָתַב סְפָרִים בַּלַּיְלָה
וַיְהִי בַּחֲצִי הַלַּיְלָה

עוֹרַרְתָּ נִצְחֲךָ עָלָיו בְּנֶדֶד שְׁנַת לַיְלָה
פּוּרָה תִדְרוֹךְ לְשׁוֹמֵר מַה מִּלַּיְלָה
צָרַח כַּשּׁוֹמֵר, וְשָׂח אָתָא בֹקֶר וְגַם לַיְלָה
וַיְהִי בַּחֲצִי הַלַּיְלָה

Draw near the day that will be neither day nor night.
Highest One, make known that day is Yours and also night.
Appoint watchmen [to guard] Your city all day long and all night,
Light up like daylight the darkness of night
IT HAPPENED AT MIDNIGHT.

Outside of Israel, this poem is recited on the second night of Pesaḥ only.

TELL [your children]:
"THIS IS
THE PESAḤ."

קָרֵב יוֹם אֲשֶׁר הוּא לֹא יוֹם וְלֹא לַיְלָה
רָם הוֹדַע כִּי לְךָ הַיּוֹם אַף לְךָ הַלַּיְלָה
שׁוֹמְרִים הַפְקֵד לְעִירְךָ כָּל הַיּוֹם וְכָל הַלַּיְלָה
תָּאִיר כְּאוֹר יוֹם חֶשְׁכַת לַיְלָה
וַיְהִי בַּחֲצִי הַלַּיְלָה

בחוץ לארץ אומרים פיוט זה רק בלילה השני של פסח.

וּבְכֵן
וַאֲמַרְתֶּם
זֶבַח פֶּסַח

You showed Your immense power in wonders on Pesaḥ; *Ex. 4–14*
to the head of all seasons You have raised up Pesaḥ.
You revealed to [Avraham] the Ezraḥi what would come
at midnight on Pesaḥ.
TELL [your children]: "THIS IS THE PESAḤ."

You knocked at his doors in the heat of the day on Pesaḥ;
he gave Your shining [messengers] unleavened cakes to eat on Pesaḥ;
and he ran to the herd, hinting at the ox in the Torah reading of Pesaḥ.
TELL [your children]: "THIS IS THE PESAḤ."

The men of Sedom raged and burned in fire on Pesaḥ.
Lot was saved; he baked matzot at the end of Pesaḥ.
You swept bare the land of Mof and Nof [Egypt]
in Your great rage on Pesaḥ.
TELL [your children]: "THIS IS THE PESAḤ."

שמות ד-יד

אֹמֶץ גְּבוּרוֹתֶיךָ הִפְלֵאתָ בַּפֶּסַח
בְּרֹאשׁ כָּל מוֹעֲדוֹת נִשֵּׂאתָ פֶּסַח
גִּלִּיתָ לְאֶזְרָחִי חֲצוֹת לֵיל פֶּסַח
וַאֲמַרְתֶּם זֶבַח פֶּסַח

דְּלָתָיו דָּפַקְתָּ כְּחֹם הַיּוֹם בַּפֶּסַח
הִסְעִיד נוֹצְצִים עֻגוֹת מַצּוֹת בַּפֶּסַח
וְאֶל הַבָּקָר, רָץ זֵכֶר לְשׁוֹר עֵרֶךְ פֶּסַח
וַאֲמַרְתֶּם זֶבַח פֶּסַח

זֹעֲמוּ סְדוֹמִים, וְלֹהֲטוּ בָּאֵשׁ בַּפֶּסַח
חֻלַּץ לוֹט מֵהֶם, וּמַצּוֹת אָפָה בְּקֵץ פֶּסַח
טִאטֵאתָ אַדְמַת מֹף וְנֹף בְּעָבְרְךָ בַּפֶּסַח
וַאֲמַרְתֶּם זֶבַח פֶּסַח

The firstborns of [Egypt's] vigor You crushed, Lord,
on the night of guarding, on Pesaḥ.

[But,] Mighty One, You passed over Your firstborn son
when You saw the blood of the Pesaḥ,

allowing no destruction through my doors on Pesaḥ.
TELL [your children]: "THIS IS THE PESAḤ."

The walled city [of Yeriḥo] was closed [for fear] when it was Pesaḥ.

Midyan was destroyed in the din, [after a dream of]
Omer barley on Pesaḥ.
The fat ones of [Assyria; of] Pul and Lud were
burned away in fires on Pesaḥ.
TELL [your children]: "THIS IS THE PESAḤ."

This day [Sanḥeriv] halted at Nov [and laid siege]
until the time of Pesaḥ.

A hand wrote Babylonia's doom on the wall at Pesaḥ:

the lamp was lit, the table was laid on Pesaḥ.
TELL [your children]: "THIS IS THE PESAḤ."

יָהּ, רֹאשׁ כָּל אוֹן מָחַצְתָּ בְּלֵיל שִׁמּוּר פֶּסַח
כַּבִּיר, עַל בֵּן בְּכוֹר פָּסַחְתָּ בְּדַם פֶּסַח
לְבִלְתִּי תֵּת מַשְׁחִית לָבֹא בִּפְתָחַי בַּפֶּסַח
וַאֲמַרְתֶּם זֶבַח פֶּסַח

מְסֻגֶּרֶת סֻגָּרָה בְּעִתּוֹתֵי פֶּסַח
נִשְׁמְדָה מִדְיָן בִּצְלִיל שְׂעוֹרֵי עֹמֶר פֶּסַח
שֹׂרְפוּ מִשְׁמַנֵּי פּוּל וְלוּד, בִּיקַד יְקוֹד פֶּסַח
וַאֲמַרְתֶּם זֶבַח פֶּסַח

עוֹד הַיּוֹם בְּנֹב לַעֲמֹד, עַד גָּעָה עוֹנַת פֶּסַח
פַּס יָד כָּתְבָה לְקַעֲקֵעַ צוּל בַּפֶּסַח
צָפֹה הַצָּפִית עָרוֹךְ הַשֻּׁלְחָן בַּפֶּסַח
וַאֲמַרְתֶּם זֶבַח פֶּסַח

Hadassa gathered the people to fast three days at Pesaḥ;

You crushed [Haman,] the head of that evil family,
on a gallows fifty cubits high on Pesaḥ.

[Loss and widowhood –] You will bring these two
in a moment to [Edom, which rules us now,] on Pesaḥ.

Strengthen Your hand, raise Your right hand,
as on the night first sanctified as Pesaḥ.

TELL [your children]: "THIS IS THE PESAḤ."

קָהָל כִּנְסָה הֲדַסָּה, צוֹם לְשַׁלֵּשׁ   בַּפֶּסַח
רֹאשׁ מִבֵּית רָשָׁע מָחַצְתָּ בְּעֵץ חֲמִשִּׁים   בַּפֶּסַח
שְׁתֵּי אֵלֶּה, רֶגַע תָּבִיא לְעוּצִית   בַּפֶּסַח
תָּעֹז יָדְךָ, תָּרוּם יְמִינֶךָ, כְּלֵיל הִתְקַדֵּשׁ חַג   פֶּסַח

וַאֲמַרְתֶּם זֶבַח פֶּסַח

FOR HIM IT IS FITTING

Majestic in Kingship, truly chosen: His legions say to Him:
"Yours and Yours; Yours, for it is Yours; Yours, only Yours;
Yours, LORD, is the Kingdom." *1 Chron. 29*

FOR HIM IT IS FITTING, FOR HIM IT IS RIGHT.

Unmistakable in His Kingship, truly glorious:
His venerable ones say to Him:
"Yours and Yours; Yours, for it is Yours; Yours, only Yours;
Yours, LORD, is the kingdom."

FOR HIM IT IS FITTING, FOR HIM IT IS RIGHT.

Worthy of Kingship, truly mighty: His officers say to Him:
"Yours and Yours; Yours, for it is Yours; Yours, only Yours;
Yours, LORD, is the kingdom."

FOR HIM IT IS FITTING, FOR HIM IT IS RIGHT.

One in Kingship, truly omnipotent: His learned ones say to Him:
"Yours and Yours; Yours, for it is Yours; Yours, only Yours;
Yours, LORD, is the kingdom."

כִּי לוֹ נָאֶה, כִּי לוֹ יָאֶה

אַדִּיר בִּמְלוּכָה בָּחוּר כַּהֲלָכָה גְּדוּדָיו יֹאמְרוּ לוֹ
לְךָ וּלְךָ, לְךָ כִּי לְךָ, לְךָ אַף לְךָ, לְךָ יהוה הַמַּמְלָכָה דברי הימים א׳ כט

כִּי לוֹ נָאֶה, כִּי לוֹ יָאֶה

דָּגוּל בִּמְלוּכָה הָדוּר כַּהֲלָכָה וָתִיקָיו יֹאמְרוּ לוֹ
לְךָ וּלְךָ, לְךָ כִּי לְךָ, לְךָ אַף לְךָ, לְךָ יהוה הַמַּמְלָכָה

כִּי לוֹ נָאֶה, כִּי לוֹ יָאֶה

זַכַּאי בִּמְלוּכָה חָסִין כַּהֲלָכָה טַפְסְרָיו יֹאמְרוּ לוֹ
לְךָ וּלְךָ, לְךָ כִּי לְךָ, לְךָ אַף לְךָ, לְךָ יהוה הַמַּמְלָכָה

כִּי לוֹ נָאֶה, כִּי לוֹ יָאֶה

יָחִיד בִּמְלוּכָה כַּבִּיר כַּהֲלָכָה לִמּוּדָיו יֹאמְרוּ לוֹ
לְךָ וּלְךָ, לְךָ כִּי לְךָ, לְךָ אַף לְךָ, לְךָ יהוה הַמַּמְלָכָה

FOR HIM IT IS FITTING, FOR HIM IT IS RIGHT.

King in His Kingship, truly awesome:
those surrounding Him say to Him:
"Yours and Yours; Yours, for it is Yours; Yours, only Yours;
Yours, LORD, is the kingdom."

FOR HIM IT IS FITTING, FOR HIM IT IS RIGHT.

Humble in Kingship, truly the Redeemer, His righteous ones say to Him:
"Yours and Yours; Yours, for it is Yours; Yours, only Yours;
Yours, LORD, is the kingdom."

FOR HIM IT IS FITTING, FOR HIM IT IS RIGHT.

Holy in Kingship, truly compassionate, His angels say to Him:
"Yours and Yours; Yours, for it is Yours; Yours, only Yours;
Yours, LORD, is the kingdom."

FOR HIM IT IS FITTING, FOR HIM IT IS RIGHT.

Powerful in Kingship, truly our Support, His perfect ones say to Him:
"Yours and Yours; Yours, for it is Yours; Yours, only Yours;
Yours, LORD, is the kingdom."

FOR HIM IT IS FITTING,
FOR HIM IT IS RIGHT.

כִּי לוֹ נָאֶה, כִּי לוֹ יָאֶה

מֶלֶךְ בִּמְלוּכָה נוֹרָא כַּהֲלָכָה סְבִיבָיו יֹאמְרוּ לוֹ
לְךָ וּלְךָ, לְךָ כִּי לְךָ, לְךָ אַף לְךָ, לְךָ יהוה הַמַּמְלָכָה

כִּי לוֹ נָאֶה, כִּי לוֹ יָאֶה

עָנָו בִּמְלוּכָה פּוֹדֶה כַּהֲלָכָה צַדִּיקָיו יֹאמְרוּ לוֹ
לְךָ וּלְךָ, לְךָ כִּי לְךָ, לְךָ אַף לְךָ, לְךָ יהוה הַמַּמְלָכָה

כִּי לוֹ נָאֶה, כִּי לוֹ יָאֶה

קָדוֹשׁ בִּמְלוּכָה רַחוּם כַּהֲלָכָה שִׁנְאַנָּיו יֹאמְרוּ לוֹ
לְךָ וּלְךָ, לְךָ כִּי לְךָ, לְךָ אַף לְךָ, לְךָ יהוה הַמַּמְלָכָה

כִּי לוֹ נָאֶה, כִּי לוֹ יָאֶה

תַּקִּיף בִּמְלוּכָה תּוֹמֵךְ כַּהֲלָכָה תְּמִימָיו יֹאמְרוּ לוֹ
לְךָ וּלְךָ, לְךָ כִּי לְךָ, לְךָ אַף לְךָ, לְךָ יהוה הַמַּמְלָכָה

כִּי לוֹ נָאֶה
כִּי לוֹ יָאֶה

HE IS MAJESTIC

may He build
His house soon,
soon, speedily
in our days.
Build, O God, build, O God,
build Your house soon.

He is chosen,	He is great, unmistakable	He is
He is glorious,	He is venerable,	He is worthy
He is kind,	He is pure,	He is One
He is mighty,	He is learned,	He is King
He is awesome,	He is elevated,	He is strong
He is Savior,	He is righteous,	He is holy
He is compassionate,	He is Almighty,	He is powerful

אַדִּיר הוּא

יִבְנֶה בֵיתוֹ בְּקָרוֹב

בִּמְהֵרָה בִּמְהֵרָה

בְּיָמֵינוּ בְּקָרוֹב

אֵל בְּנֵה אֵל בְּנֵה

בְּנֵה בֵיתְךָ בְּקָרוֹב

בָּחוּר הוּא גָּדוֹל הוּא דָּגוּל הוּא

הָדוּר הוּא וָתִיק הוּא זַכַּאי הוּא

חָסִיד הוּא טָהוֹר הוּא יָחִיד הוּא

כַּבִּיר הוּא לָמוּד הוּא מֶלֶךְ הוּא

נוֹרָא הוּא סַגִּיב הוּא עִזּוּז הוּא

פּוֹדֶה הוּא צַדִּיק הוּא קָדוֹשׁ הוּא

רַחוּם הוּא שַׁדַּי הוּא תַּקִּיף הוּא

may He build
His house soon,
soon, speedily
in our days.
Build, O God, build, O God,

BUILD YOUR HOUSE SOON.

יִבְנֶה בֵּיתוֹ בְּקָרוֹב
בִּמְהֵרָה בִּמְהֵרָה,
בְּיָמֵינוּ בְּקָרוֹב
אֵל בְּנֵה אֵל בְּנֵה

בְּנֵה בֵּיתְךָ בְּקָרוֹב

WHO KNOWS ONE?

Who knows one?
I know one:
our God is One, in heaven and on earth.

Who knows two?
I know two:
two Tablets of the Covenant;
but our God is One, in heaven and on earth.

Who knows three?
I know three:
three fathers,
two Tablets of the Covenant;
but our God is One, in heaven and on earth.

אֶחָד מִי יוֹדֵעַ

אֶחָד אֲנִי יוֹדֵעַ

אֶחָד אֱלֹהֵינוּ שֶׁבַּשָּׁמַיִם וּבָאָרֶץ

שְׁנַיִם מִי יוֹדֵעַ
שְׁנַיִם אֲנִי יוֹדֵעַ
שְׁנֵי לוּחוֹת הַבְּרִית
אֶחָד אֱלֹהֵינוּ שֶׁבַּשָּׁמַיִם וּבָאָרֶץ

שְׁלוֹשָׁה מִי יוֹדֵעַ
שְׁלוֹשָׁה אֲנִי יוֹדֵעַ
שְׁלוֹשָׁה אָבוֹת
שְׁנֵי לוּחוֹת הַבְּרִית
אֶחָד אֱלֹהֵינוּ שֶׁבַּשָּׁמַיִם וּבָאָרֶץ

Who knows four?
I know four:
four mothers, three fathers,
two Tablets of the Covenant;
but our God is One, in heaven and on earth.

Who knows five?
I know five:
five books of the Torah,
four mothers,
three fathers,
two Tablets of the Covenant;
but our God is One, in heaven and on earth.

Who knows six?
I know six:
six divisions of the Mishna,
five books of the Torah,
four mothers, three fathers,
two Tablets of the Covenant;
but our God is One, in heaven and on earth.

אַרְבַּע מִי יוֹדֵעַ
אַרְבַּע אֲנִי יוֹדֵעַ
אַרְבַּע אִמָּהוֹת
שְׁלוֹשָׁה אָבוֹת   שְׁנֵי לוּחוֹת הַבְּרִית
אֶחָד אֱלֹהֵינוּ שֶׁבַּשָּׁמַיִם וּבָאָרֶץ

חֲמִשָּׁה מִי יוֹדֵעַ
חֲמִשָּׁה אֲנִי יוֹדֵעַ
חֲמִשָּׁה חֻמְשֵׁי תוֹרָה
אַרְבַּע אִמָּהוֹת
שְׁלוֹשָׁה אָבוֹת
שְׁנֵי לוּחוֹת הַבְּרִית
אֶחָד אֱלֹהֵינוּ שֶׁבַּשָּׁמַיִם וּבָאָרֶץ

שִׁשָּׁה מִי יוֹדֵעַ
שִׁשָּׁה אֲנִי יוֹדֵעַ
שִׁשָּׁה סִדְרֵי מִשְׁנָה
חֲמִשָּׁה חֻמְשֵׁי תוֹרָה
אַרְבַּע אִמָּהוֹת   שְׁלוֹשָׁה אָבוֹת
שְׁנֵי לוּחוֹת הַבְּרִית
אֶחָד אֱלֹהֵינוּ שֶׁבַּשָּׁמַיִם וּבָאָרֶץ

Who knows seven?
I know seven:
seven days from Sabbath to Sabbath,
six divisions of the Mishna,
five books of the Torah,
four mothers, three fathers,
two Tablets of the Covenant;
but our God is One, in heaven and on earth.

Who knows eight?
I know eight:
eight days to a brit,
seven days from Sabbath to Sabbath,
six divisions of the Mishna, five books of the Torah,
four mothers, three fathers,
two Tablets of the Covenant;
but our God is One, in heaven and on earth.

שִׁבְעָה מִי יוֹדֵעַ
שִׁבְעָה אֲנִי יוֹדֵעַ
שִׁבְעָה יְמֵי שַׁבְּתָא
שִׁשָּׁה סִדְרֵי מִשְׁנָה
חֲמִשָּׁה חֻמְשֵׁי תוֹרָה
אַרְבַּע אִמָּהוֹת שְׁלוֹשָׁה אָבוֹת
שְׁנֵי לוּחוֹת הַבְּרִית
אֶחָד אֱלֹהֵינוּ שֶׁבַּשָּׁמַיִם וּבָאָרֶץ

שְׁמוֹנָה מִי יוֹדֵעַ
שְׁמוֹנָה אֲנִי יוֹדֵעַ
שְׁמוֹנָה יְמֵי מִילָה
שִׁבְעָה יְמֵי שַׁבְּתָא שִׁשָּׁה סִדְרֵי מִשְׁנָה
חֲמִשָּׁה חֻמְשֵׁי תוֹרָה אַרְבַּע אִמָּהוֹת
שְׁלוֹשָׁה אָבוֹת שְׁנֵי לוּחוֹת הַבְּרִית
אֶחָד אֱלֹהֵינוּ שֶׁבַּשָּׁמַיִם וּבָאָרֶץ

Who knows nine?
I know nine:
nine months until birth, eight days to a brit,
seven days from Sabbath to Sabbath,
six divisions of the Mishna, five books of the Torah,
four mothers, three fathers,
two Tablets of the Covenant;
but our God is One, in heaven and on earth.

Who knows ten?
I know ten:
Ten Commandments,
nine months until birth, eight days to a brit,
seven days from Sabbath to Sabbath,
six divisions of the Mishna, five books of the Torah,
four mothers, three fathers,
two Tablets of the Covenant;
but our God is One, in heaven and on earth.

תִּשְׁעָה מִי יוֹדֵעַ
תִּשְׁעָה אֲנִי יוֹדֵעַ
תִּשְׁעָה יַרְחֵי לֵדָה
שְׁמוֹנָה יְמֵי מִילָה   שִׁבְעָה יְמֵי שַׁבְּתָא
שִׁשָּׁה סִדְרֵי מִשְׁנָה   חֲמִשָּׁה חֻמְשֵׁי תוֹרָה
אַרְבַּע אִמָּהוֹת   שְׁלוֹשָׁה אָבוֹת
שְׁנֵי לוּחוֹת הַבְּרִית   אֶחָד אֱלֹהֵינוּ שֶׁבַּשָּׁמַיִם וּבָאָרֶץ

עֲשָׂרָה מִי יוֹדֵעַ
עֲשָׂרָה אֲנִי יוֹדֵעַ
עֲשָׂרָה דִבְּרַיָּא
תִּשְׁעָה יַרְחֵי לֵדָה   שְׁמוֹנָה יְמֵי מִילָה
שִׁבְעָה יְמֵי שַׁבְּתָא   שִׁשָּׁה סִדְרֵי מִשְׁנָה
חֲמִשָּׁה חֻמְשֵׁי תוֹרָה   אַרְבַּע אִמָּהוֹת
שְׁלוֹשָׁה אָבוֹת   שְׁנֵי לוּחוֹת הַבְּרִית
אֶחָד אֱלֹהֵינוּ שֶׁבַּשָּׁמַיִם וּבָאָרֶץ

Who knows eleven?
I know eleven:
eleven stars [in Joseph's dream],
Ten Commandments,
nine months until birth, eight days to a brit,
seven days from Sabbath to Sabbath,
six divisions of the Mishna, five books of the Torah,
four mothers, three fathers,
two Tablets of the Covenant;
but our God is One, in heaven and on earth.

Who knows twelve?
I know twelve:
twelve tribes, eleven stars,
Ten Commandments,
nine months until birth, eight days to a brit,
seven days from Sabbath to Sabbath,
six divisions of the Mishna, five books of the Torah,
four mothers, three fathers,
two Tablets of the Covenant;
but our God is One, in heaven and on earth.

אַחַד עָשָׂר מִי יוֹדֵעַ
אַחַד עָשָׂר אֲנִי יוֹדֵעַ
אַחַד עָשָׂר כּוֹכְבַיָּא
עֲשָׂרָה דִבְּרַיָּא תִּשְׁעָה יַרְחֵי לֵדָה
שְׁמוֹנָה יְמֵי מִילָה שִׁבְעָה יְמֵי שַׁבַּתָּא
שִׁשָּׁה סִדְרֵי מִשְׁנָה חֲמִשָּׁה חֻמְשֵׁי תוֹרָה
אַרְבַּע אִמָּהוֹת שְׁלוֹשָׁה אָבוֹת
שְׁנֵי לוּחוֹת הַבְּרִית
אֶחָד אֱלֹהֵינוּ שֶׁבַּשָּׁמַיִם וּבָאָרֶץ

שְׁנֵים עָשָׂר מִי יוֹדֵעַ
שְׁנֵים עָשָׂר אֲנִי יוֹדֵעַ
שְׁנֵים עָשָׂר שִׁבְטַיָּא
אַחַד עָשָׂר כּוֹכְבַיָּא עֲשָׂרָה דִבְּרַיָּא
תִּשְׁעָה יַרְחֵי לֵדָה שְׁמוֹנָה יְמֵי מִילָה
שִׁבְעָה יְמֵי שַׁבַּתָּא שִׁשָּׁה סִדְרֵי מִשְׁנָה
חֲמִשָּׁה חֻמְשֵׁי תוֹרָה אַרְבַּע אִמָּהוֹת שְׁלוֹשָׁה אָבוֹת
שְׁנֵי לוּחוֹת הַבְּרִית
אֶחָד אֱלֹהֵינוּ שֶׁבַּשָּׁמַיִם וּבָאָרֶץ

Who knows thirteen?
I know thirteen:
thirteen attributes [of God's compassion],
twelve tribes,
eleven stars,
Ten Commandments,
nine months until birth,
eight days to a brit,
seven days from Sabbath to Sabbath,
six divisions of the Mishna,
five books of the Torah,
four mothers,
three fathers,
two Tablets of the Covenant;

שְׁלוֹשָׁה עָשָׂר מִי יוֹדֵעַ
שְׁלוֹשָׁה עָשָׂר אֲנִי יוֹדֵעַ
שְׁלוֹשָׁה עָשָׂר מִדַּיָּא
שְׁנֵים עָשָׂר שִׁבְטַיָּא
אַחַד עָשָׂר כּוֹכְבַיָּא
עֲשָׂרָה דִבְּרַיָּא
תִּשְׁעָה יַרְחֵי לֵדָה
שְׁמוֹנָה יְמֵי מִילָה
שִׁבְעָה יְמֵי שַׁבְּתָא
שִׁשָּׁה סִדְרֵי מִשְׁנָה
חֲמִשָּׁה חֻמְשֵׁי תוֹרָה
אַרְבַּע אִמָּהוֹת
שְׁלוֹשָׁה אָבוֹת
שְׁנֵי לוּחוֹת הַבְּרִית

BUT OUR GOD

IS ONE, IN HEAVEN AND ON EARTH.

אֱלֹהֵינוּ

שֶׁבַּשָּׁמַיִם

וּבָאָרֶץ

ONE LITTLE GOAT

one little goat
my father bought for two zuzim;
one little goat, one little goat.

Along came a cat and ate the goat
my father bought for two zuzim;
one little goat, one little goat.

Then came a dog and bit the cat
who ate the goat
my father bought for two zuzim;
one little goat, one little goat.

Then came a stick and hit the dog
who bit the cat who ate the goat
my father bought for two zuzim;
one little goat, one little goat.

חַד גַּדְיָא חַד גַּדְיָא

דִּזְבַן אַבָּא בִּתְרֵי זוּזֵי
חַד גַּדְיָא חַד גַּדְיָא

וַאֲתָא שׁוּנְרָא וְאָכְלָה לְגַדְיָא
דִּזְבַן אַבָּא בִּתְרֵי זוּזֵי
חַד גַּדְיָא חַד גַּדְיָא

וַאֲתָא כַלְבָּא וְנָשַׁךְ לְשׁוּנְרָא
דְּאָכְלָה לְגַדְיָא
דִּזְבַן אַבָּא בִּתְרֵי זוּזֵי
חַד גַּדְיָא חַד גַּדְיָא

וַאֲתָא חֻטְרָא וְהִכָּה לְכַלְבָּא
דְּנָשַׁךְ לְשׁוּנְרָא דְּאָכְלָה לְגַדְיָא
דִּזְבַן אַבָּא בִּתְרֵי זוּזֵי
חַד גַּדְיָא חַד גַּדְיָא

Then came a fire and burned the stick
that hit the dog who bit the cat
who ate the goat
my father bought for two zuzim;
one little goat, one little goat.

Then came water and put out the fire
that burned the stick that hit the dog
who bit the cat who ate the goat
my father bought for two zuzim;
one little goat, one little goat.

Then came an ox
and drank the water
that put out the fire
that burned the stick
that hit the dog
who bit the cat who ate the goat
my father bought for two zuzim;
one little goat, one little goat.

וַאֲתָא נוּרָא וְשָׂרַף לְחֻטְרָא דְּהִכָּה לְכַלְבָּא
דְּנָשַׁךְ לְשׁוּנְרָא דְּאָכְלָה לְגַדְיָא

דִּזְבַן אַבָּא בִּתְרֵי זוּזֵי
חַד גַּדְיָא חַד גַּדְיָא

וַאֲתָא מַיָּא וְכָבָה לְנוּרָא
דְּשָׂרַף לְחֻטְרָא דְּהִכָּה לְכַלְבָּא
דְּנָשַׁךְ לְשׁוּנְרָא דְּאָכְלָה לְגַדְיָא
דִּזְבַן אַבָּא בִּתְרֵי זוּזֵי
חַד גַּדְיָא חַד גַּדְיָא

וַאֲתָא תוֹרָא וְשָׁתָה לְמַיָּא
דְּכָבָה לְנוּרָא דְּשָׂרַף לְחֻטְרָא
דְּהִכָּה לְכַלְבָּא דְּנָשַׁךְ לְשׁוּנְרָא
דְּאָכְלָה לְגַדְיָא
דִּזְבַן אַבָּא בִּתְרֵי זוּזֵי
חַד גַּדְיָא חַד גַּדְיָא

Then came a slaughterer and slew the ox
who drank the water
that put out the fire
that burned the stick
that hit the dog
who bit the cat
who ate the goat
my father bought for two zuzim;
one little goat, one little goat.

Then came the angel of death
and slew the slaughterer
who slew the ox
who drank the water
that put out the fire
that burned the stick that hit the dog
who bit the cat who ate the goat
my father bought for two zuzim;
one little goat, one little goat.

וַאֲתָא הַשּׁוֹחֵט וְשָׁחַט לְתוֹרָא
דְּשָׁתָא לְמַיָּא
דְּכָבָה לְנוּרָא דְּשָׂרַף לְחֻטְרָא
דְּהִכָּה לְכַלְבָּא
דְּנָשַׁךְ לְשׁוּנְרָא
דְּאָכְלָה לְגַדְיָא
דִּזְבַן אַבָּא בִּתְרֵי זוּזֵי
חַד גַּדְיָא חַד גַּדְיָא

וַאֲתָא מַלְאַךְ הַמָּוֶת
וְשָׁחַט לְשׁוֹחֵט דְּשָׁחַט לְתוֹרָא
דְּשָׁתָא לְמַיָּא דְּכָבָה לְנוּרָא
דְּשָׂרַף לְחֻטְרָא דְּהִכָּה לְכַלְבָּא
דְּנָשַׁךְ לְשׁוּנְרָא דְּאָכְלָה לְגַדְיָא
דִּזְבַן אַבָּא בִּתְרֵי זוּזֵי
חַד גַּדְיָא חַד גַּדְיָא

Then

came the Holy One

and slew the angel of death,
who slew the slaughterer who slew the ox
who drank the water that put out the fire
that burned the stick that hit the dog
who bit the cat who ate the goat
my father bought for two zuzim;
ONE LITTLE GOAT, ONE LITTLE GOAT.

וַאֲתָא

הַקָּדוֹשׁ בָּרוּךְ הוּא

וְשָׁחַט לְמַלְאַךְ הַמָּוֶת
דְּשָׁחַט לְשׁוֹחֵט דְּשָׁחַט לְתוֹרָא
דְּשָׁתָא לְמַיָּא דְּכָבָה לְנוּרָא
דְּשָׂרַף לְחֻטְרָא דְּהִכָּה לְכַלְבָּא
דְּנָשַׁךְ לְשׁוּנְרָא דְּאָכְלָה לְגַדְיָא
דִּזְבַן אַבָּא בִּתְרֵי זוּזֵי
חַד גַּדְיָא חַד גַּדְיָא

The Tales of Rebbe Nahman:

The Tale of the Lost Princess

On the way I told a story, that whoever heard it, had a thought of repentance, and this is the story:

Once there was a king who had six sons and one daughter. The daughter was very dear to him, and he loved her exceedingly and played with her a lot.

One time, while he was together with her on a certain day, he became angry with her and the words "Let the Not-Good take you away" escaped from his mouth.

That night she went to her room, and in the morning, no one knew where she was. Her father was very distraught, and he went here and there looking for her.

The viceroy arose because he saw the king was very distressed, and asked to be given an attendant, a horse, and money for expenses, and he went to search for her. He searched hard for her, for a very long time... he journeyed for a long time, in deserts, fields, and forests, and looked for her for quite a long time. He went in the desert and saw a path from the side. He decided: Since I have been going for such a long time in the wilderness and cannot find her, I will follow this path; maybe I will reach a settled area. He went for a long time.

Later on he saw a castle and many soldiers standing around it.

The castle was very beautiful and well managed and had many soldiers standing around it in fine order. He was afraid of the soldiers lest they not let him enter. He decided, I will go and try, and he left the horse and went to the castle. They let him [enter], and did not stop him at all, so he went from room to room, and they did not stop him. He came to a palace and saw the king sitting there with a crown and many soldiers standing around him. And many were playing instruments for him, and it was very pleasant and beautiful there. And [neither] the king nor any of them asked the viceroy a thing. And he saw delicacies and good foods there, and he went and ate, and went and lay down in a corner to see what would be done there. He saw that the king called for the queen to be brought, and

they went

Song of Songs

An Encounter with our Beloved

According to Jewish history, at midnight on the Seder night, King Shlomo gave Song of Songs to the Jewish people. Song of Songs is a comedy of errors. He knocks on the door, and she doesn't realize she's supposed to come and open up; she runs after him, and he disappears in the marketplaces and streets. Song of Songs is filled with doors, windows, and openings: "My beloved withdrew his hand from the door."[237] "The handles of the latch."[238] "Gazing through the windows."[239] "Open for me, my sister, my love, my dove, my perfection."[240] The whole, entire year, we knock on all the wrong doors, Rabbi Hutner explains. And the whole, entire year, God comes to the wrong windows, as it were, with sacks brimming with life-saving gifts and salvation. But on the Seder night? There are no doors, no windows, no walls. There's no room for mistakes. "The roof breaks off" – the roof flies away! There's no roof. No barriers. No doors, no windows, no latches, no handles. There's no more "Open for me, my beloved." All the impediments that block the love have been removed. The heavens and earth are connected. Everything is united. Tonight, we will have an encounter. It's impossible not to.[241]

to eat, because it is a hard thing to abide by]; therefore choose for yourself a place again, and also stay there a year, as before, and on the last day you will be permitted to eat, just don't sleep and don't drink wine so you don't fall asleep, because the main thing is [not to] sleep. He went and did so.

On the last day, when he was going there, he saw a running spring - its color was red and it smelled of wine. He asked the servant: Have you seen? This is a spring, and there ought to be water in it, but its color is red, and it smells of wine. And he went and tasted from the spring. He immediately fell down and slept many years, for seventy years, and many troops came along, with their trains that followed behind them, and the servant hid himself because of the soldiers. After that came a carriage and covered wagons, and there sat the king's daughter. She stood next to him, went down and sat next to him and recognized him. And she tried very hard to wake him, but he could not be woken. She started to lament over him that he had exerted for so, so many years so, so much great effort and toil in order to take her out, and for one day, when he could have taken her out, he completely lost, and she cried very much about this, because she had great pity on him and herself, for she was here for such a long time and could not go out. Afterward, she took the scarf off her head, and wrote on it with her tears and laid it down next to him, and stood up, and sat in her carriage and rode away. Afterward, he awoke and asked the attendant: Where am I in the world? He [the attendant] told him [the viceroy] the whole story, and that many troops passed through there, and that the carriage was here, and that she [the king's daughter] cried for him and screamed that she has great pity on him and on herself as before. Meanwhile, he glanced and noticed the scarf lying next to him. He asked: Where is this from? He answered him: She wrote on it with her tears. He took it and raised it up to the sun and began to see the letters. He read what was written there, her lamentation and her cries, as mentioned, and that now, she is no longer in the castle as she was before, and he should just search for a golden mountain and a pearl castle. "There you will find me," she wrote.

He left the attendant behind and went alone to seek her. And he went and sought her for many years. He decided that in a settled area there cannot be a golden mountain and a pearl castle, because he was an expert in the world map. "Therefore, I will go to the deserts." He went searching for her in deserts for many years.

Afterward

they went to bring her. And there was a great commotion and a great celebration, and the musicians played and sang vigorously because they were bringing the queen. And they placed a throne for her and seated her next to him. And she was the king's daughter, and he [the viceroy] saw her and recognized her.

Later, the queen glanced and saw someone lying in a corner and she recognized him.

She rose from her throne, went to him, touched him, and asked him: Do you recognize me? And he answered her: Yes, I know you. You're the king's daughter who was lost. He asked her: How is it that you've come here? She answered him: Because of that thing that my father let slip out of his mouth [that "the Not-Good should take you"]. And here, this is the place that is Not-Good. He told her that her father was very distressed, and that he had been searching for many years. And he asked her: How can I take you out? She answered him: You cannot take me out unless you choose for yourself a place and remain there for one year; and the entire year you must yearn for me, to take me out; and whenever you have free time you must only yearn, ask, and hope expectantly to take me out, and you must fast; and on the final day of the year you must fast and you must not sleep for the entire twenty-four-hour period. He went and did so.

And at the end of the year on the final day he fasted and didn't sleep, and he arose and went there [to the king's daughter, to take her out], and he saw a tree, and on this tree grew very beautiful apples, and he really craved them, and he went and ate from them, and as soon as he ate the apple, he fell down and sleep overtook him, and he slept a very long time, and his attendant tried to wake him, but he could not be awakened at all. Later, he awoke from his sleep and asked the attendant: Where am I in the world? He [the attendant] told him [the viceroy] the whole story: You have been sleeping for a very long time. It has already been several years. And I have sustained myself from the fruit. He [the viceroy] agonized very much.

And he went there and found her [the king's daughter] there, and she lamented to him very much: If you had just come on that day, you would have taken me out of here, and because of one day you lost. In truth, not to eat is a very difficult thing, especially on the final day, when the evil inclination becomes very strong [in other words, the king's daughter said to him that now she would make the prohibition more lenient, and he would not be forbidden

> He [this second large man] told him [the viceroy]: Further in the wilderness is my brother; he is appointed over all the winds, and they run throughout the whole world, perhaps they know. He spent many, many years seeking him and again found a large man, as before, who was also carrying a large tree, as before, and also questioned him, as before. He also answered him with the whole story, as before, and he also dissuaded him, as before, and the viceroy implored him likewise. He [the third large man] said to him [the viceroy]: For his sake, he would summon the winds to come and ask them. He summoned them, and all the winds came, and he asked all of them, and not one of them knew of this mountain and castle. He [the third large man] said to him [the viceroy]: Don't you see that you have been told nonsense? And the viceroy began to cry very much and said: I know it surely does exist. Just then, he saw that another wind had arrived. The appointee became angry with him. Why have you so delayed in coming? Didn't I decree that all the winds should come? Why didn't you come with them? He answered him: I was delayed because I had to carry a king's daughter to a golden mountain with a pearl castle. He was overjoyed. The appointee asked the wind: What is precious there? [Meaning, which things are there that are precious and important?] He said to him: Everything there is extremely precious. And the one appointed over the winds said to the viceroy: Since you have been searching for her for such a long time, and you have spent so much effort, and perhaps you will now have a hindrance due to money, therefore I will give you a vessel that when you put your hand into it, you will get money from there. And he summoned the wind to carry him there. The storm wind came and carried him there and brought him to the gate, and standing there were soldiers who did not let him enter the city. He put his hand into the vessel and took out money and bribed them and went into the city, and it was a beautiful city.
>
> And he went to a man of means and rented food and lodging for himself, for he needed to stay there, for one needs to see with wisdom and intellect in order to take her out. And how he took her out – he did not tell. [But] in the end, he took her out.

Song of Songs – the song of the chase, and the escape, and the desperation, "they beat me, they wounded me," but then, "the guards found me,"[242] the night of protection arrived, and he took her out! Welcome home, lost princess. We've been waiting for you for a very long time!

Are You

Afterward, he saw a very large man whose largeness was beyond human dimensions, and he was carrying a large tree, so large that in a settled area such a large tree would not exist, and he [the giant] asked him: Who are you? He answered him: I am a man, and he was amazed and said: I have been in the wilderness for such a long time, and I have never seen a man. He told him the whole story mentioned above and that he was looking for a golden mountain and a pearl castle. He said to him: It certainly does not exist. And he dissuaded him and said to him: They have convinced you with nonsense, because it certainly does not exist. And he started to cry very much [meaning, the viceroy cried very much and said]: It certainly does exist somewhere. But he [the very large man] dissuaded him and said: Certainly, they have convinced you of nonsense. And he [the viceroy] said: Certainly, it exists somewhere.

He [the very large man] said to him: In my opinion, it is nonsense, but because you are insistent, look, I am appointed over all the animals. I will act for your sake and summon all the animals. Since they run all over the world, maybe one of them will know of that mountain and that castle. And he summoned all different sorts of animals, from small to large, and asked them. And they all replied that they had not seen [such a place]. He said to him: See, they have talked nonsense to you; if you want to listen to me, turn back, because certainly you will not find [it], because it does not exist in the world. But he pleaded with him persistently and said: It must surely indeed be. He [the very large man] said to him: Look, I have a brother in the wilderness, and he is in charge of all the birds. Perhaps they will know, since they fly high in the air. Perhaps they have seen this mountain and castle. Go to him, and tell him that I've sent you to him.

He spent many, many years seeking him and again found a very large man, as before, and he also carried a large tree, as before, and also questioned him, as before. And he answered him with the whole story and that his brother had sent him to him, and he too dissuaded him since this [place] certainly does not exist. And he also implored him, and he said to him [the viceroy]: Look, I am appointed over all the birds; I will summon them; perhaps they will know. He summoned all the birds and asked all of them, from small to large. They answered that they do not know of this mountain and castle. He told him: Don't you see it is certainly not here in the world? If you will listen to me, turn back, because it certainly is not here. And he [the viceroy] implored him and said: It certainly is here in the world.

This is the ultimate collapse of barriers that takes place at midnight on the Seder night. You go free – on your own account. Do you realize that this moment is an unparalleled time of favor, and you should ask for something much greater right now? Away with You, my beloved. The lovely prison guard in the white dress has opened the gate for You. Head home. My King, you can return to Your house.

It's incredible. This is freedom. Freedom is the understanding that you have the capacity to set someone else free. Enslavement means being powerless: "I can't help anyone else; I have nothing to give." Suddenly, though, you're a free woman, who sets other slaves free. You're not a freed slave. You've transformed from a freed woman to a woman who sets others free. It's an unbelievable metamorphosis. "Away with You, my beloved, like a gazelle, or a young deer, over perfumed hills. Turn around! My beloved, [be] like a gazelle" – why? Because as it runs for its life, it looks back. I know, God, that when You run home, as it were, You won't forget me. You'll look behind You, and You'll also see me. And You'll remember me. And You'll take me home.

The Or HaḤayim notes that at this exact moment, a heavenly voice bursts forth and declares: "Happy are you, land, whose king is a master."[249]

The land refers to woman. Happy are you, land, whose king is free. It's an incredible statement. The liberation of the kingship is made possible by the simple people. They enable the king to act.

There is no better way to conclude the Seder night. Real freedom means stepping out beyond myself and praying for another. Real freedom means knowing how to move beyond my personal pain. Said differently, real freedom means becoming a nation.

This is the fifth cup of wine, "and I will take you to be My nation."[250] This is the message of the Seder night: You're not alone. You're a nation. You're a mother. "Behold, your King is coming to you, He is victorious and triumphant."[251] He is no less victorious and triumphant than you.

Are You a Free Woman? It's Not Enough...
Be a Woman Who Knows How to Set Others Free

Song of Songs is the climax. It's the grand finale, the incredible conclusion. You find yourself with the protagonist of the story, wandering through the streets and marketplaces.

"The guards found me, those who go around the town, they beat me, they wounded me."[243] Why are you wandering through the streets? They ask you angrily. How could you go out like that?

And you know that now the streets have been transformed into part of the home. The home is the street. It's the night that barriers have fallen. So why are you beating me? Why are you hurting me? Wherever I am, I want a home. Even when you see me wandering through the streets, I'm searching for a home.

And I want to proclaim my own declaration to God: "If You find my beloved, [swear that You will] tell him, tell him I am sick with love."[244] And Rashi explains: "Because of my love for him – I suffered harsh afflictions." I am in so much pain, and I understand that my pain is connected to the love that is greater than me.

Then, tell God something else: "Away with You my beloved, like a gazelle, or a young deer, over perfumed hills."[245]

At the end of the Seder night, something incredible happens. The entire time, you are certain that you are imprisoned, that you are the one who doesn't have a home. And then, at the end of the Seder, when the barriers fall, you realize that the question is really being posed to God: "Tell me, You whom I have loved – here will You pasture? Where will You rest Your flock at noon?"[246] You realize that when He comes home, you will also have a home. That when things have come full circle in a global sense, your small personal story will also come full circle.

And all your prayers take on a new dimension. You say to Him: "Away with You, my beloved." The entire time, I thought it was me who yearned for freedom, that it was me who wanted to run away, but really You were the One who was confined and imprisoned. You need to come again to Mount Moriah – "I shall not enter Jerusalem above [in heaven] until I enter Jerusalem [on earth] below."[247] You are "a King [who] is tangled up among its tresses."[248]

And you say to Him: I dedicate all the pain, all the suffering, all the challenges, that I endured this past year, to You. It's a payoff, a ransom that I'm willing to pay for Your freedom. If this is what it takes to set You free, to restore You to the perfumed hills, then it's worth it. Why – because I'm a suffering martyr? Because I'm a victim? No. Because I understand that when Your suffering is alleviated, my suffering is automatically alleviated too. My story will finally arrive at its happy ending. Master of the world, head home. I'm setting You free.

Our Personal *Avoda:* Song of Songs

As you recite Song of Songs, pray that you won't run away from love.

Pray that you'll be able to skip over those things that seem like mountains.

Pray that we'll open the door for love.

Pray for our sister, that someone should finally make her an offer.

Pray to find peace in His eyes.

שיר השירים

א שִׁיר הַשִּׁירִים אֲשֶׁר לִשְׁלֹמֹה׃ יִשָּׁקֵנִי מִנְּשִׁיקוֹת פִּיהוּ כִּי־טוֹבִים דֹּדֶיךָ מִיָּיִן׃
לְרֵיחַ שְׁמָנֶיךָ טוֹבִים שֶׁמֶן תּוּרַק שְׁמֶךָ עַל־כֵּן עֲלָמוֹת אֲהֵבוּךָ׃ מָשְׁכֵנִי אַחֲרֶיךָ
נָּרוּצָה הֱבִיאַנִי הַמֶּלֶךְ חֲדָרָיו נָגִילָה וְנִשְׂמְחָה בָּךְ נַזְכִּירָה דֹדֶיךָ מִיַּיִן מֵישָׁרִים
אֲהֵבוּךָ׃ שְׁחוֹרָה אֲנִי וְנָאוָה בְּנוֹת יְרוּשָׁלָםִ כְּאָהֳלֵי קֵדָר כִּירִיעוֹת
שְׁלֹמֹה׃ אַל־תִּרְאוּנִי שֶׁאֲנִי שְׁחַרְחֹרֶת שֶׁשֱּׁזָפַתְנִי הַשָּׁמֶשׁ בְּנֵי אִמִּי נִחֲרוּ־בִי
שָׂמֻנִי נֹטֵרָה אֶת־הַכְּרָמִים כַּרְמִי שֶׁלִּי לֹא נָטָרְתִּי׃ הַגִּידָה לִּי שֶׁאָהֲבָה נַפְשִׁי
אֵיכָה תִרְעֶה אֵיכָה תַּרְבִּיץ בַּצָּהֳרָיִם שַׁלָּמָה אֶהְיֶה כְּעֹטְיָה עַל עֶדְרֵי חֲבֵרֶיךָ׃
אִם־לֹא תֵדְעִי לָךְ הַיָּפָה בַּנָּשִׁים צְאִי־לָךְ בְּעִקְבֵי הַצֹּאן וּרְעִי אֶת־גְּדִיֹּתַיִךְ עַל
מִשְׁכְּנוֹת הָרֹעִים׃ לְסֻסָתִי בְּרִכְבֵי פַרְעֹה דִּמִּיתִיךְ רַעְיָתִי׃ נָאווּ
לְחָיַיִךְ בַּתֹּרִים צַוָּארֵךְ בַּחֲרוּזִים׃ תּוֹרֵי זָהָב נַעֲשֶׂה־לָּךְ עִם נְקֻדּוֹת הַכָּסֶף׃
עַד־שֶׁהַמֶּלֶךְ בִּמְסִבּוֹ נִרְדִּי נָתַן רֵיחוֹ׃ צְרוֹר הַמֹּר ׀ דּוֹדִי לִי בֵּין שָׁדַי יָלִין׃
אֶשְׁכֹּל הַכֹּפֶר ׀ דּוֹדִי לִי בְּכַרְמֵי עֵין גֶּדִי׃ הִנָּךְ יָפָה רַעְיָתִי הִנָּךְ יָפָה
עֵינַיִךְ יוֹנִים׃ הִנְּךָ יָפֶה דוֹדִי אַף נָעִים אַף־עַרְשֵׂנוּ רַעֲנָנָה׃ קֹרוֹת בָּתֵּינוּ אֲרָזִים
ב רחיטנו בְּרוֹתִים׃ אֲנִי חֲבַצֶּלֶת הַשָּׁרוֹן שׁוֹשַׁנַּת הָעֲמָקִים׃ כְּשׁוֹשַׁנָּה בֵּין הַחוֹחִים רָהִיטֵנוּ
כֵּן רַעְיָתִי בֵּין הַבָּנוֹת׃ כְּתַפּוּחַ בַּעֲצֵי הַיַּעַר כֵּן דּוֹדִי בֵּין הַבָּנִים בְּצִלּוֹ חִמַּדְתִּי

וְיָשַׁבְתִּי וּפִרְיוֹ מָתוֹק לְחִכִּי: הֱבִיאַנִי אֶל־בֵּית הַיָּיִן וְדִגְלוֹ עָלַי אַהֲבָה: סַמְּכוּנִי
בָּאֲשִׁישׁוֹת רַפְּדוּנִי בַּתַּפּוּחִים כִּי־חוֹלַת אַהֲבָה אָנִי: שְׂמֹאלוֹ תַּחַת לְרֹאשִׁי
וִימִינוֹ תְּחַבְּקֵנִי: הִשְׁבַּעְתִּי אֶתְכֶם בְּנוֹת יְרוּשָׁלִַם בִּצְבָאוֹת אוֹ בְּאַיְלוֹת הַשָּׂדֶה
אִם־תָּעִירוּ | וְאִם־תְּעוֹרְרוּ אֶת־הָאַהֲבָה עַד שֶׁתֶּחְפָּץ: קוֹל דּוֹדִי
הִנֵּה־זֶה בָּא מְדַלֵּג עַל־הֶהָרִים מְקַפֵּץ עַל־הַגְּבָעוֹת: דּוֹמֶה דוֹדִי לִצְבִי אוֹ
לְעֹפֶר הָאַיָּלִים הִנֵּה־זֶה עוֹמֵד אַחַר כָּתְלֵנוּ מַשְׁגִּיחַ מִן־הַחַלֹּנוֹת מֵצִיץ מִן־
הַחֲרַכִּים: עָנָה דוֹדִי וְאָמַר לִי קוּמִי לָךְ רַעְיָתִי יָפָתִי וּלְכִי־לָךְ: כִּי־הִנֵּה הַסְּתָו
עָבָר הַגֶּשֶׁם חָלַף הָלַךְ לוֹ: הַנִּצָּנִים נִרְאוּ בָאָרֶץ עֵת הַזָּמִיר הִגִּיעַ וְקוֹל הַתּוֹר
נִשְׁמַע בְּאַרְצֵנוּ: הַתְּאֵנָה חָנְטָה פַגֶּיהָ וְהַגְּפָנִים | סְמָדַר נָתְנוּ רֵיחַ קוּמִי לְכִי לָךְ
רַעְיָתִי יָפָתִי וּלְכִי־לָךְ: יוֹנָתִי בְּחַגְוֵי הַסֶּלַע בְּסֵתֶר הַמַּדְרֵגָה הַרְאִינִי
אֶת־מַרְאַיִךְ הַשְׁמִיעִנִי אֶת־קוֹלֵךְ כִּי־קוֹלֵךְ עָרֵב וּמַרְאֵיךְ נָאוֶה: אֶחֱזוּ־
לָנוּ שׁוּעָלִים שֻׁעָלִים קְטַנִּים מְחַבְּלִים כְּרָמִים וּכְרָמֵינוּ סְמָדַר: דּוֹדִי לִי וַאֲנִי
לוֹ הָרֹעֶה בַּשּׁוֹשַׁנִּים: עַד שֶׁיָּפוּחַ הַיּוֹם וְנָסוּ הַצְּלָלִים סֹב דְּמֵה־לְךָ דוֹדִי לִצְבִי
אוֹ לְעֹפֶר הָאַיָּלִים עַל־הָרֵי בָתֶר: עַל־מִשְׁכָּבִי בַּלֵּילוֹת בִּקַּשְׁתִּי ג
אֵת שֶׁאָהֲבָה נַפְשִׁי בִּקַּשְׁתִּיו וְלֹא מְצָאתִיו: אָקוּמָה נָּא וַאֲסוֹבְבָה בָעִיר
בַּשְּׁוָקִים וּבָרְחֹבוֹת אֲבַקְשָׁה אֵת שֶׁאָהֲבָה נַפְשִׁי בִּקַּשְׁתִּיו וְלֹא מְצָאתִיו:
מְצָאוּנִי הַשֹּׁמְרִים הַסֹּבְבִים בָּעִיר אֵת שֶׁאָהֲבָה נַפְשִׁי רְאִיתֶם: כִּמְעַט
שֶׁעָבַרְתִּי מֵהֶם עַד שֶׁמָּצָאתִי אֵת שֶׁאָהֲבָה נַפְשִׁי אֲחַזְתִּיו וְלֹא אַרְפֶּנּוּ עַד־
שֶׁהֲבֵיאתִיו אֶל־בֵּית אִמִּי וְאֶל־חֶדֶר הוֹרָתִי: הִשְׁבַּעְתִּי אֶתְכֶם בְּנוֹת יְרוּשָׁלִַם
בִּצְבָאוֹת אוֹ בְּאַיְלוֹת הַשָּׂדֶה אִם־תָּעִירוּ | וְאִם־תְּעוֹרְרוּ אֶת־הָאַהֲבָה עַד
שֶׁתֶּחְפָּץ: מִי זֹאת עֹלָה מִן־הַמִּדְבָּר כְּתִימְרוֹת עָשָׁן מְקֻטֶּרֶת מוֹר
וּלְבוֹנָה מִכֹּל אַבְקַת רוֹכֵל: הִנֵּה מִטָּתוֹ שֶׁלִּשְׁלֹמֹה שִׁשִּׁים גִּבֹּרִים סָבִיב לָהּ
מִגִּבֹּרֵי יִשְׂרָאֵל: כֻּלָּם אֲחֻזֵי חֶרֶב מְלֻמְּדֵי מִלְחָמָה אִישׁ חַרְבּוֹ עַל־יְרֵכוֹ מִפַּחַד
בַּלֵּילוֹת: אַפִּרְיוֹן עָשָׂה לוֹ הַמֶּלֶךְ שְׁלֹמֹה מֵעֲצֵי הַלְּבָנוֹן: עַמּוּדָיו
עָשָׂה כֶסֶף רְפִידָתוֹ זָהָב מֶרְכָּבוֹ אַרְגָּמָן תּוֹכוֹ רָצוּף אַהֲבָה מִבְּנוֹת יְרוּשָׁלִָם:

צְאֶינָה ׀ וּרְאֶינָה בְּנוֹת צִיּוֹן בַּמֶּלֶךְ שְׁלֹמֹה בָּעֲטָרָה שֶׁעִטְּרָה־לּוֹ אִמּוֹ בְּיוֹם
ד חֲתֻנָּתוֹ וּבְיוֹם שִׂמְחַת לִבּוֹ׃ הִנָּךְ יָפָה רַעְיָתִי הִנָּךְ יָפָה עֵינַיִךְ יוֹנִים
מִבַּעַד לְצַמָּתֵךְ שַׂעְרֵךְ כְּעֵדֶר הָעִזִּים שֶׁגָּלְשׁוּ מֵהַר גִּלְעָד׃ שִׁנַּיִךְ כְּעֵדֶר הַקְּצוּבוֹת
שֶׁעָלוּ מִן־הָרַחְצָה שֶׁכֻּלָּם מַתְאִימוֹת וְשַׁכֻּלָה אֵין בָּהֶם׃ כְּחוּט הַשָּׁנִי שִׂפְתוֹתַיִךְ
וּמִדְבָּרֵיךְ נָאוֶה כְּפֶלַח הָרִמּוֹן רַקָּתֵךְ מִבַּעַד לְצַמָּתֵךְ׃ כְּמִגְדַּל דָּוִיד צַוָּארֵךְ בָּנוּי
לְתַלְפִּיּוֹת אֶלֶף הַמָּגֵן תָּלוּי עָלָיו כֹּל שִׁלְטֵי הַגִּבֹּרִים׃ שְׁנֵי שָׁדַיִךְ כִּשְׁנֵי עֳפָרִים
תְּאוֹמֵי צְבִיָּה הָרוֹעִים בַּשּׁוֹשַׁנִּים׃ עַד שֶׁיָּפוּחַ הַיּוֹם וְנָסוּ הַצְּלָלִים אֵלֶךְ לִי אֶל־
הַר הַמּוֹר וְאֶל־גִּבְעַת הַלְּבוֹנָה׃ כֻּלָּךְ יָפָה רַעְיָתִי וּמוּם אֵין בָּךְ׃ אִתִּי
מִלְּבָנוֹן כַּלָּה אִתִּי מִלְּבָנוֹן תָּבוֹאִי תָּשׁוּרִי ׀ מֵרֹאשׁ אֲמָנָה מֵרֹאשׁ שְׂנִיר וְחֶרְמוֹן
מִמְּעֹנוֹת אֲרָיוֹת מֵהַרְרֵי נְמֵרִים׃ לִבַּבְתִּנִי אֲחֹתִי כַלָּה לִבַּבְתִּנִי באחד מֵעֵינַיִךְ בְּאַחַת
בְּאַחַד עֲנָק מִצַּוְּרֹנָיִךְ׃ מַה־יָּפוּ דֹדַיִךְ אֲחֹתִי כַלָּה מַה־טֹּבוּ דֹדַיִךְ מִיַּיִן וְרֵיחַ
שְׁמָנַיִךְ מִכָּל־בְּשָׂמִים׃ נֹפֶת תִּטֹּפְנָה שִׂפְתוֹתַיִךְ כַּלָּה דְּבַשׁ וְחָלָב תַּחַת לְשׁוֹנֵךְ
וְרֵיחַ שַׂלְמֹתַיִךְ כְּרֵיחַ לְבָנוֹן׃ גַּן ׀ נָעוּל אֲחֹתִי כַלָּה גַּל נָעוּל מַעְיָן
חָתוּם׃ שְׁלָחַיִךְ פַּרְדֵּס רִמּוֹנִים עִם פְּרִי מְגָדִים כְּפָרִים עִם־נְרָדִים׃ נֵרְדְּ ׀ וְכַרְכֹּם
קָנֶה וְקִנָּמוֹן עִם כָּל־עֲצֵי לְבוֹנָה מֹר וַאֲהָלוֹת עִם כָּל־רָאשֵׁי בְשָׂמִים׃ מַעְיַן
גַּנִּים בְּאֵר מַיִם חַיִּים וְנֹזְלִים מִן־לְבָנוֹן׃ עוּרִי צָפוֹן וּבוֹאִי תֵימָן הָפִיחִי גַנִּי יִזְּלוּ
ה בְשָׂמָיו יָבֹא דוֹדִי לְגַנּוֹ וְיֹאכַל פְּרִי מְגָדָיו׃ בָּאתִי לְגַנִּי אֲחֹתִי כַלָּה אָרִיתִי מוֹרִי
עִם־בְּשָׂמִי אָכַלְתִּי יַעְרִי עִם־דִּבְשִׁי שָׁתִיתִי יֵינִי עִם־חֲלָבִי אִכְלוּ רֵעִים שְׁתוּ
וְשִׁכְרוּ דּוֹדִים׃ אֲנִי יְשֵׁנָה וְלִבִּי עֵר קוֹל ׀ דּוֹדִי דוֹפֵק פִּתְחִי־לִי אֲחֹתִי
רַעְיָתִי יוֹנָתִי תַמָּתִי שֶׁרֹּאשִׁי נִמְלָא־טָל קְוֻצּוֹתַי רְסִיסֵי לָיְלָה׃ פָּשַׁטְתִּי אֶת־
כֻּתָּנְתִּי אֵיכָכָה אֶלְבָּשֶׁנָּה רָחַצְתִּי אֶת־רַגְלַי אֵיכָכָה אֲטַנְּפֵם׃ דּוֹדִי שָׁלַח יָדוֹ
מִן־הַחוֹר וּמֵעַי הָמוּ עָלָיו׃ קַמְתִּי אֲנִי לִפְתֹּחַ לְדוֹדִי וְיָדַי נָטְפוּ־מוֹר וְאֶצְבְּעֹתַי
מוֹר עֹבֵר עַל כַּפּוֹת הַמַּנְעוּל׃ פָּתַחְתִּי אֲנִי לְדוֹדִי וְדוֹדִי חָמַק עָבָר נַפְשִׁי יָצְאָה
בְדַבְּרוֹ בִּקַּשְׁתִּיהוּ וְלֹא מְצָאתִיהוּ קְרָאתִיו וְלֹא עָנָנִי׃ מְצָאֻנִי הַשֹּׁמְרִים הַסֹּבְבִים
בָּעִיר הִכּוּנִי פְצָעוּנִי נָשְׂאוּ אֶת־רְדִידִי מֵעָלַי שֹׁמְרֵי הַחֹמוֹת׃ הִשְׁבַּעְתִּי אֶתְכֶם

בְּנוֹת יְרוּשָׁלָםִ אִם־תִּמְצְאוּ אֶת־דּוֹדִי מַה־תַּגִּידוּ לוֹ שֶׁחוֹלַת אַהֲבָה אָנִי׃ מַה־
דּוֹדֵךְ מִדּוֹד הַיָּפָה בַּנָּשִׁים מַה־דּוֹדֵךְ מִדּוֹד שֶׁכָּכָה הִשְׁבַּעְתָּנוּ׃ דּוֹדִי צַח וְאָדוֹם
דָּגוּל מֵרְבָבָה׃ רֹאשׁוֹ כֶּתֶם פָּז קְוֻצּוֹתָיו תַּלְתַּלִּים שְׁחֹרוֹת כָּעוֹרֵב׃ עֵינָיו כְּיוֹנִים
עַל־אֲפִיקֵי מָיִם רֹחֲצוֹת בֶּחָלָב יֹשְׁבוֹת עַל־מִלֵּאת׃ לְחָיָו כַּעֲרוּגַת הַבֹּשֶׂם
מִגְדְּלוֹת מֶרְקָחִים שִׂפְתוֹתָיו שׁוֹשַׁנִּים נֹטְפוֹת מוֹר עֹבֵר׃ יָדָיו גְּלִילֵי זָהָב
מְמֻלָּאִים בַּתַּרְשִׁישׁ מֵעָיו עֶשֶׁת שֵׁן מְעֻלֶּפֶת סַפִּירִים׃ שׁוֹקָיו עַמּוּדֵי שֵׁשׁ
מְיֻסָּדִים עַל־אַדְנֵי־פָז מַרְאֵהוּ כַּלְּבָנוֹן בָּחוּר כָּאֲרָזִים׃ חִכּוֹ מַמְתַקִּים וְכֻלּוֹ
ו מַחֲמַדִּים זֶה דוֹדִי וְזֶה רֵעִי בְּנוֹת יְרוּשָׁלָםִ׃ אָנָה הָלַךְ דּוֹדֵךְ הַיָּפָה בַּנָּשִׁים אָנָה
פָּנָה דוֹדֵךְ וּנְבַקְשֶׁנּוּ עִמָּךְ׃ דּוֹדִי יָרַד לְגַנּוֹ לַעֲרֻגוֹת הַבֹּשֶׂם לִרְעוֹת בַּגַּנִּים
וְלִלְקֹט שׁוֹשַׁנִּים׃ אֲנִי לְדוֹדִי וְדוֹדִי לִי הָרֹעֶה בַּשּׁוֹשַׁנִּים׃
יָפָה אַתְּ רַעְיָתִי כְּתִרְצָה נָאוָה כִּירוּשָׁלָםִ אֲיֻמָּה כַּנִּדְגָּלוֹת׃ הָסֵבִּי עֵינַיִךְ מִנֶּגְדִּי
שֶׁהֵם הִרְהִיבֻנִי שַׂעְרֵךְ כְּעֵדֶר הָעִזִּים שֶׁגָּלְשׁוּ מִן־הַגִּלְעָד׃ שִׁנַּיִךְ כְּעֵדֶר הָרְחֵלִים
שֶׁעָלוּ מִן־הָרַחְצָה שֶׁכֻּלָּם מַתְאִימוֹת וְשַׁכֻּלָה אֵין בָּהֶם׃ כְּפֶלַח הָרִמּוֹן רַקָּתֵךְ
מִבַּעַד לְצַמָּתֵךְ׃ שִׁשִּׁים הֵמָּה מְּלָכוֹת וּשְׁמֹנִים פִּילַגְשִׁים וַעֲלָמוֹת אֵין מִסְפָּר׃
אַחַת הִיא יוֹנָתִי תַמָּתִי אַחַת הִיא לְאִמָּהּ בָּרָה הִיא לְיוֹלַדְתָּהּ רָאוּהָ בָנוֹת
וַיְאַשְּׁרוּהָ מְלָכוֹת וּפִילַגְשִׁים וַיְהַלְלוּהָ׃ מִי־זֹאת הַנִּשְׁקָפָה כְּמוֹ־שָׁחַר
יָפָה כַלְּבָנָה בָּרָה כַּחַמָּה אֲיֻמָּה כַּנִּדְגָּלוֹת׃ אֶל־גִּנַּת אֱגוֹז יָרַדְתִּי לִרְאוֹת בְּאִבֵּי
הַנָּחַל לִרְאוֹת הֲפָרְחָה הַגֶּפֶן הֵנֵצוּ הָרִמֹּנִים׃ לֹא יָדַעְתִּי נַפְשִׁי שָׂמַתְנִי מַרְכְּבוֹת
ז עַמִּי נָדִיב׃ שׁוּבִי שׁוּבִי הַשּׁוּלַמִּית שׁוּבִי שׁוּבִי וְנֶחֱזֶה־בָּךְ מַה־תֶּחֱזוּ בַּשּׁוּלַמִּית
כִּמְחֹלַת הַמַּחֲנָיִם׃ מַה־יָּפוּ פְעָמַיִךְ בַּנְּעָלִים בַּת־נָדִיב חַמּוּקֵי יְרֵכַיִךְ כְּמוֹ חֲלָאִים
מַעֲשֵׂה יְדֵי אָמָּן׃ שָׁרְרֵךְ אַגַּן הַסַּהַר אַל־יֶחְסַר הַמָּזֶג בִּטְנֵךְ עֲרֵמַת חִטִּים סוּגָה
בַּשּׁוֹשַׁנִּים׃ שְׁנֵי שָׁדַיִךְ כִּשְׁנֵי עֳפָרִים תָּאֳמֵי צְבִיָּה׃ צַוָּארֵךְ כְּמִגְדַּל הַשֵּׁן עֵינַיִךְ
בְּרֵכוֹת בְּחֶשְׁבּוֹן עַל־שַׁעַר בַּת־רַבִּים אַפֵּךְ כְּמִגְדַּל הַלְּבָנוֹן צוֹפֶה פְּנֵי דַמָּשֶׂק׃
רֹאשֵׁךְ עָלַיִךְ כַּכַּרְמֶל וְדַלַּת רֹאשֵׁךְ כָּאַרְגָּמָן מֶלֶךְ אָסוּר בָּרְהָטִים׃ מַה־יָּפִית
וּמַה־נָּעַמְתְּ אַהֲבָה בַּתַּעֲנוּגִים׃ זֹאת קוֹמָתֵךְ דָּמְתָה לְתָמָר וְשָׁדַיִךְ לְאַשְׁכֹּלוֹת׃

אָמַ֙רְתִּי֙ אֶעֱלֶ֣ה בְתָמָ֔ר אֹחֲזָ֖ה בְּסַנְסִנָּ֑יו וְיִֽהְיוּ־נָ֤א שָׁדַ֙יִךְ֙ כְּאֶשְׁכְּל֣וֹת הַגֶּ֔פֶן
וְרֵ֥יחַ אַפֵּ֖ךְ כַּתַּפּוּחִֽים׃ וְחִכֵּ֕ךְ כְּיֵ֥ין הַטּ֛וֹב הוֹלֵ֥ךְ לְדוֹדִ֖י לְמֵישָׁרִ֑ים דּוֹבֵ֖ב שִׂפְתֵ֥י
יְשֵׁנִֽים׃ אֲנִ֣י לְדוֹדִ֔י וְעָלַ֖י תְּשׁוּקָתֽוֹ׃ לְכָ֤ה דוֹדִי֙ נֵצֵ֣א הַשָּׂדֶ֔ה נָלִ֖ינָה בַּכְּפָרִֽים׃
נַשְׁכִּ֙ימָה֙ לַכְּרָמִ֔ים נִרְאֶ֞ה אִם־פָּֽרְחָ֤ה הַגֶּ֙פֶן֙ פִּתַּ֣ח הַסְּמָדַ֔ר הֵנֵ֖צוּ הָרִמּוֹנִ֑ים שָׁ֛ם
אֶתֵּ֥ן אֶת־דֹּדַ֖י לָֽךְ׃ הַֽדּוּדָאִ֣ים נָֽתְנוּ־רֵ֗יחַ וְעַל־פְּתָחֵ֙ינוּ֙ כָּל־מְגָדִ֔ים חֲדָשִׁ֖ים גַּם־
ח יְשָׁנִ֑ים דּוֹדִ֖י צָפַ֥נְתִּי לָֽךְ׃ מִ֤י יִתֶּנְךָ֙ כְּאָ֣ח לִ֔י יוֹנֵ֖ק שְׁדֵ֣י אִמִּ֑י אֶֽמְצָאֲךָ֤ בַחוּץ֙ אֶשָּׁ֣קְךָ֔
גַּ֖ם לֹא־יָב֥וּזוּ לִֽי׃ אֶנְהָֽגְךָ֗ אֲבִֽיאֲךָ֛ אֶל־בֵּ֥ית אִמִּ֖י תְּלַמְּדֵ֑נִי אַשְׁקְךָ֙ מִיַּ֣יִן הָרֶ֔קַח
מֵעֲסִ֖יס רִמֹּנִֽי׃ שְׂמֹאלוֹ֙ תַּ֣חַת רֹאשִׁ֔י וִימִינ֖וֹ תְּחַבְּקֵֽנִי׃ הִשְׁבַּ֥עְתִּי אֶתְכֶ֖ם בְּנ֣וֹת
יְרוּשָׁלִָ֑ם מַה־תָּעִ֣ירוּ ׀ וּֽמַה־תְּעֹרְר֥וּ אֶת־הָאַהֲבָ֖ה עַ֥ד שֶׁתֶּחְפָּֽץ׃ מִ֣י
זֹ֗את עֹלָה֙ מִן־הַמִּדְבָּ֔ר מִתְרַפֶּ֖קֶת עַל־דּוֹדָ֑הּ תַּ֤חַת הַתַּפּ֙וּחַ֙ עֽוֹרַרְתִּ֔יךָ שָׁ֚מָּה
חִבְּלַ֣תְךָ אִמֶּ֔ךָ שָׁ֖מָּה חִבְּלָ֥ה יְלָדַֽתְךָ׃ שִׂימֵ֨נִי כַֽחוֹתָ֜ם עַל־לִבֶּ֗ךָ כַּֽחוֹתָם֙ עַל־זְרוֹעֶ֔ךָ
כִּֽי־עַזָּ֤ה כַמָּ֙וֶת֙ אַהֲבָ֔ה קָשָׁ֥ה כִשְׁא֖וֹל קִנְאָ֑ה רְשָׁפֶ֕יהָ רִשְׁפֵּ֕י אֵ֖שׁ שַׁלְהֶ֥בֶתְיָֽה׃
מַ֣יִם רַבִּ֗ים לֹ֤א יֽוּכְלוּ֙ לְכַבּ֣וֹת אֶת־הָאַהֲבָ֔ה וּנְהָר֖וֹת לֹ֣א יִשְׁטְפ֑וּהָ אִם־יִתֵּ֨ן
אִ֜ישׁ אֶת־כָּל־ה֤וֹן בֵּיתוֹ֙ בָּאַהֲבָ֔ה בּ֖וֹז יָב֥וּזוּ לֽוֹ׃ אָח֥וֹת לָ֙נוּ֙ קְטַנָּ֔ה
וְשָׁדַ֖יִם אֵ֣ין לָ֑הּ מַֽה־נַּעֲשֶׂה֙ לַאֲחֹתֵ֔נוּ בַּיּ֖וֹם שֶׁיְּדֻבַּר־בָּֽהּ׃ אִם־חוֹמָ֣ה הִ֔יא
נִבְנֶ֥ה עָלֶ֖יהָ טִ֣ירַת כָּ֑סֶף וְאִם־דֶּ֣לֶת הִ֔יא נָצ֥וּר עָלֶ֖יהָ ל֥וּחַ אָֽרֶז׃ אֲנִ֣י חוֹמָ֔ה
וְשָׁדַ֖י כַּמִּגְדָּל֑וֹת אָ֛ז הָיִ֥יתִי בְעֵינָ֖יו כְּמוֹצְאֵ֥ת שָׁלֽוֹם׃ כֶּ֣רֶם הָיָ֤ה לִשְׁלֹמֹה֙ בְּבַ֣עַל
הָמ֔וֹן נָתַ֥ן אֶת־הַכֶּ֖רֶם לַנֹּטְרִ֑ים אִ֛ישׁ יָבִ֥א בְּפִרְי֖וֹ אֶ֥לֶף כָּֽסֶף׃ כַּרְמִ֥י שֶׁלִּ֖י לְפָנָ֑י הָאֶ֤לֶף
לְךָ֙ שְׁלֹמֹ֔ה וּמָאתַ֖יִם לְנֹטְרִ֥ים אֶת־פִּרְיֽוֹ׃ הַיּוֹשֶׁ֣בֶת בַּגַּנִּ֗ים חֲבֵרִ֛ים מַקְשִׁיבִ֥ים
לְקוֹלֵ֖ךְ הַשְׁמִיעִֽנִי׃ בְּרַ֣ח ׀ דּוֹדִ֗י וּֽדְמֵה־לְךָ֤ לִצְבִי֙ א֚וֹ לְעֹ֣פֶר הָֽאַיָּלִ֔ים עַ֖ל הָרֵ֥י
בְשָׂמִֽים׃

Midnight

An Encounter with God

At midnight on the Seder night, as you stand at the entrance of your home, each and every Jewish person achieves the stature of a prophet, according to Rabbi Yaakov Moshe Harlap. God passes through each and every person's home – "Toward midnight I will go forth among the Egyptians."[252] Grab the hemline of God's cloak and don't let go. Ask for everything.

The seven heavens are open. You'll hear yourself asking for things you never knew you wanted, things you never knew you needed. "And each and every person will see how reciting the Haggada made his speech become clear."[253] Your words are clear, coherent, organized. When a prayer comes out of our mouths like this, it's a sign that it's desired and accepted.

The Ḥatam Sofer assures us: "In his prayer, he can request all that he wants."[254] At midnight,[255] offer an enormous prayer for all those things that your heart desires.

Your heartstrings are directed toward the heavens. Use this moment well; it won't return for an entire year.

Now, you'll receive the greatest gift of all.

You, the one who doesn't even know how to ask, and has already forgotten to submit a request.

And even when you do ask, you no longer believe that your request has the capacity to generate an answer – "May the God of Israel grant you what you have asked of Him."[256]

Appendix: The Letter of Rabbi Shimshon of Ostropoli
איגרת רבי שמשון מאוסטרופולי

סוד גדול ונורא, וכתוב שם שכל מי שמעיין בסוד הנפלא והנורא הזה על מכונו, אפילו פעם אחת בשנה, ובפרט בערב פסח, מובטח לו שינצל באותה שנה מכל מכשול וממיתה משונה, ושום אדם לא ימשול בו, וכל אויביו יפלו תחתיו, והוא על במותימו ידרוך, ובכל אשר יפנה יצליח ובכל עסקיו ירויח, עד ביאת הגואל אמן סלה:

שלום לרבני ארץ, גודרי גדר ועומדים בפרץ, יצילם ה׳ מכליון וחרץ, כולם קדושים אשר בארץ, כל חד לפום חורפיה מקשה ומתרץ, אמן סלה, בתכלית הענין מה שכתב האר״י ז״ל בקונטרס שלו הנקרא פלאות רבות בשער הנקרא יציאת מצרים, פרק ג׳ דף מ״ב ע״א וזה לשונו:

״הִנֵּה כְּבָר הוֹדַעְתִּיךָ שֶׁפַּרְעֹה נִלְקָה בְּמִצְרַיִם בְּעֶשֶׂר מַכּוֹת אֵלּוּ עַל יְדֵי שְׁלֹשָׁה אֲלָפִים וּמָאתַיִם וּשְׁמוֹנִים מַלְאֲכֵי חַבָּלָה, הַמְמֻנִּים בִּשְׁלֹשָׁה רְקִיעִים שֶׁל טֻמְאָה, הָאֶחָד נִקְרָא שרע וְהַשֵּׁנִי נִקְרָא תמוך, וְהַשְּׁלִישִׁי נִקְרָא בישהא, וַעֲלֵיהֶם הַשַּׂר הַנִּקְרָא דלפקט, וַעֲלֵיהֶם וְעַל כֻּלָּם הַשַּׂר הַנִּקְרָא תקא, בְּרֵאשִׁית חָסֵר מִן הַשְּׁלִישִׁי עֲשָׂרָה, וְחָסֵר מִן הָרְבִיעִי שִׁשָּׁה, וְחָסֵר מִן הַתְּשִׁיעִי שִׁשָּׁה כַּכָּתוּב, וְהִנֵּה מַה שֶּׁלָּקוּ הַמִּצְרִיִּים בְּמִצְרַיִם עֶשֶׂר מַכּוֹת, וְעַל הַיָּם לָקוּ חֲמִשִּׁים מַכּוֹת, הַשֵּׁם שפ״ו שֶׁבּוֹ אָחַז דָּוִד בֶּן יִשַׁי, וְהַשֵּׁם אָמַר וְהִכָּה. וּמִצַּד הַשֵּׁם תק״ל לָקוּ הַמִּצְרִיִּים בְּמִצְרַיִם אַרְבָּעִים מַכּוֹת, וְעַל הַיָּם לָקוּ מָאתַיִם מַכּוֹת, וְהַשֵּׁם אָמַר וְהִכָּה. וּמִצַּד הַשֵּׁם אשצ״ה לָקוּ הַמִּצְרִיִּים בְּמִצְרַיִם חֲמִשִּׁים מַכּוֹת, וְעַל הַיָּם לָקוּ מָאתַיִם וַחֲמִשִּׁים מַכּוֹת, וּבְמַה שֶּׁהַקָּדוֹשׁ בָּרוּךְ הוּא מַכֶּה, בּוֹ מְרַפֵּא הַגָּלוּת. מַה פָּשְׁעוּ וּמֶה חָטְאוּ, וּמָה הַמַּעַל אֲשֶׁר מָעֲלוּ אֲבוֹתֵינוּ, לִהְיוֹת בְּכוּר הַבַּרְזֶל הַזֶּה, עַד שֶׁגְּאָלָם בְּשֵׁמוֹת אֵלּוּ **דע״ב צד״א כשח״ב**.״ עד כאן לשון האר״י ז״ל:

וְהִנֵּה מוֹרַי וְרַבּוֹתַי קְדוֹשֵׁי יִשְׂרָאֵל, הַדְּבָרִים הָאֵלֶּה פְּלָאִים הֵם, סְתוּמִים וַחֲתוּמִים סָגוּר וְאֵין פּוֹרֵשׁ אוֹתָם. וּכְבָר שְׁאָלוּנִי גְּדוֹלֵי יִשְׂרָאֵל לְבָאֵר לָהֶם דִּבְרֵי הָאֲרִ״י זַ״ל וְלֹא הִגַּדְתִּי. וּמִגֹּדֶל אַהֲבַת מוֹרַי וְרַבּוֹתַי אֲגַלֶּה רָז זֶה שֶׁנִּתְגַּלָּה לִי בַּחֲלוֹם חֶזְיוֹן לַיְלָה, וְעַכְשָׁו אֲגַלֶּה הַדָּבָר בְּרֶמֶז לִפְנֵי כְּבוֹד תּוֹרָתוֹ, וְהוּא רַחוּם יְכַפֵּר:

וְזֹאת הָעִנְיָן:

מַה שֶּׁכָּתַב הָאֲרִ״י זַ״ל שֶׁפַּרְעֹה נִלְקָה בְּמִצְרַיִם עֶשֶׂר מַכּוֹת וְכוּ׳, כַּוָּנָתוֹ כָּךְ: כִּי אָמְרוּ בַּעֲלֵי קַבָּלָה מַעֲשִׂית, שֶׁיֵּשׁ שְׁלֹשָׁה אֲלָפִים וּמָאתַיִם וּשְׁמוֹנִים מַלְאֲכֵי חַבָּלָה הַמְמֻנִּים לְהַכּוֹת אֶת הָרְשָׁעִים וּלְהַעֲנִישָׁם בְּגֵיהִנֹּם וּלְטַהֲרָם מֵעֲוֹנוֹתֵיהֶם. וְעַל

זֶה נֶאֱמַר: "וּלְהַכּוֹת בְּאֶגְרֹף רֶשַׁע", כִּי אֶגְרֹף, רֶמֶז שְׁלֹשָׁה אֲלָפִים מָאתַיִם וּשְׁמוֹנִים, וְעַל יָדָם נִלְקָה גַּם פַּרְעֹה הָרָשָׁע. וְאוֹמֵר אֲנִי הַכּוֹתֵב שֶׁזֶּהוּ סוֹד נִפְלָא כַּאֲשֶׁר הוּא נִכְתָּב בְּמִנְיָן וּבְמִסְפָּר: דָּם. צְפַרְדֵּעַ. כִּנִּם. עָרוֹב. דֶּבֶר. שְׁחִין. בָּרָד. אַרְבֶּה. חֹשֶׁךְ. מַכַּת בְּכֹרוֹת: אֵלּוּ עֶשֶׂר מַכּוֹת כַּאֲשֶׁר כָּתַבְתִּי אוֹת בְּאוֹת, עוֹלִים שְׁלֹשָׁה אֲלָפִים וּמָאתַיִם וּשְׁמוֹנִים מַלְאֲכֵי חַבָּלָה, הַמְמֻנִּים לְטַהֵר אֶת הָרְשָׁעִים, וְהוּא פְּשַׁט נִפְלָא, עַיִן לֹא רָאֲתָה:

וְהִנֵּה הַחֶשְׁבּוֹן מְכֻוָּן כַּאֲשֶׁר נִכְתָּב כִּנִּם חָסֵר יו"ד, גַּם עָרֹב חָסֵר וא"ו. גַּם חֹשֶׁךְ חָסֵר וא"ו. וְאָז הַחֶשְׁבּוֹן מַמָּשׁ, לֹא פָּחוֹת וְלֹא יוֹתֵר מִשְּׁלֹשָׁה אֲלָפִים וּמָאתַיִם וּשְׁמוֹנִים מַלְאֲכֵי חַבָּלָה, שֶׁמַּעֲנִישִׁין אֶת הָרְשָׁעִים.

וְהַיְנוּ מַה שֶּׁכָּתַב הָאֲרִ"י זַ"ל: "כַּכָּתוּב", פֵּרוּשׁ כַּכָּתוּב בְּסֵפֶר תּוֹרָה, וְלֹא כַּאֲשֶׁר כָּתוּב בַּסִּדּוּרִים וּבַעַל הַהַגָּדָה, כִּי שָׁם נִכְתְּבוּ כֻּלָּם מְלֵאִים. אֶלָּא צָרִיךְ לִהְיוֹת חָסֵר כְּמוֹ שֶׁכָּתוּב בְּסֵפֶר תּוֹרָה. וְגַם רַבִּי יְהוּדָה לֹא כָּתַב סִימָנִים כֻּלָּם רַק רָאשֵׁי תֵּיבוֹת, דצ"ך עד"ש באח"ב, כְּמוֹ שֶׁכָּתַב הָרַב יִצְחָק אַבַרְבָּנְאֵל וּכְמוֹ שֶׁכָּתַבְתִּי לְעֵיל:

וְהַיְנוּ מַה שֶּׁכָּתַב הָאֲרִ"י זַ"ל: "בְּרֵאשִׁית חָסֵר מִן הַשְּׁלִישִׁי עֲשָׂרָה", פֵּרוּשׁ: מַכָּה שְׁלִישִׁית שֶׁהִיא כִּנִּם חָסֵר יו"ד. "מִן הָרְבִיעִי שִׁשָּׁה" שֶׁהִיא מַכַּת עָרוֹב גַּם חָסֵר וָא"ו. "וְחָסֵר מִן הַתְּשִׁיעִי שִׁשָּׁה", שֶׁהִיא מַכַּת חֹשֶׁךְ גַּם כֵּן חָסֵר וָא"ו. וּמַה שֶּׁאָמַר "כַּכָּתוּב", רוֹצֶה לוֹמַר שֶׁכֵּן כָּתוּב בְּסֵפֶר תּוֹרָה חָסֵר, כַּנִּזְכַּר לְעֵיל.

וְזֶהוּ סוֹד אֵלּוּ "עֶשֶׂר מַכּוֹת שֶׁהֵבִיא" הַקָּדוֹשׁ בָּרוּךְ הוּא בְּמִצְרַיִם, מְכֻוָּן מַמָּשׁ שְׁלֹשָׁה אֲלָפִים וּמָאתַיִם וּשְׁמוֹנִים מַלְאֲכֵי חַבָּלָה שֶׁהִכּוּ אֶת פַּרְעֹה וְאֶת הַמִּצְרִיִּים בְּמִצְרַיִם, הַמְמֻנִּים בְּאֵלּוּ שְׁלֹשָׁה רְקִיעִים: אֶחָד נִקְרָא **שרע**, וְאֶחָד נִקְרָא **תמוך**, וְאֶחָד נִקְרָא **בישהא**, גַּם בָּזֶה יֵשׁ סוֹד גָּדוֹל וְנִפְלָא, אֵלּוּ שְׁלֹשֶׁת אֲלָפִים וּמָאתַיִם וּשְׁמוֹנִים מַחֲנוֹת שֶׁהִכּוּ אֶת פַּרְעֹה

וְאֶת הַמִּצְרִיִּים בְּמִצְרַיִם כָּאָמוּר, שֶׁמְּמֻנִּים בְּאֵלּוּ שְׁלֹשָׁה רְקִיעִים שֶׁל טֻמְאָה, אָמַר לָנוּ הַכָּתוּב סוֹד נִפְלָא וְנוֹרָא, וְתִקֵּן הַמַּגִּיד כְּמוֹ שֶׁשָּׁנָה אֵלּוּ "עשר מכות שהביא" שֶׁבְּאֵלּוּ שָׁלֹשׁ תֵּיבוֹת נִרְמָזִים הַשְּׁלֹשָׁה רְקִיעִים שֶׁל טֻמְאָה, וּשְׁלֹשֶׁת אֲלָפִים וּמָאתַיִם וּשְׁמוֹנִים מַלְאֲכֵי חַבָּלָה שֶׁהִכּוּ אֶת פַּרְעֹה וְאֶת הַמִּצְרִים בְּמִצְרַיִם, כְּמִנְיַן עֶשֶׂר מַכּוֹת, דְּהַיְנוּ **עשר** אוֹתִיּוֹת **שרע**, **מכות** אוֹתִיּוֹת **תמוך**, **שהביא** אוֹתִיּוֹת **בישהא**, רֶמֶז לְאֵלּוּ שְׁלֹשָׁה רְקִיעִים שֶׁל טֻמְאָה שֶׁבָּהֶם יֵשׁ מְמֻנִּים כְּמִנְיַן שְׁלֹשָׁה אֲלָפִים וּמָאתַיִם וּשְׁמוֹנִים מַלְאֲכֵי חַבָּלָה מַמָּשׁ, כְּמִנְיַן עֶשֶׂר מַכּוֹת דָּם צְפַרְדֵּעַ וְכוּ', וְהֵם שֶׁהִכּוּ אֶת פַּרְעֹה וְאֶת הַמִּצְרִיִּים בְּמִצְרַיִם, כִּי מַלְאֲכֵי חַבָּלָה מְמֻנִּים לְהַכּוֹת אֶת הָרְשָׁעִים לְטַהֲרָם מֵעֲוֹנוֹתֵיהֶם כָּאָמוּר. וְעַל יָדָן הִכָּה אֶת פַּרְעֹה וְאֶת הַמִּצְרִיִּים בְּמִצְרַיִם מִנְיַן עֶשֶׂר מַכּוֹת אֵלּוּ, וְהוּא פֶּלֶא גָּדוֹל:

וּמַה שֶּׁכָּתַב הָאֲרִ"י זַ"ל: "וַעֲלֵיהֶם הַשַּׂר הנקרא **דלפקט**", כַּוָּנָתוֹ הוּא שֶׁשֵּׁם זֶה שָׁרְשׁוֹ יוֹצֵא מִמַּזַּל הַמִּצְרִים, וְהַיְנוּ: שֶׁשְּׁלֹשָׁה רְקִיעִים הֵם: עש"ר מכו"ת שהבי"א וּכְפֵרוּשׁ הַגָּאוֹן, וְנִמְשָׁךְ עַל הַמִּצְרִים שֶׁהוּא שֵׁם דלפקט בָּאוֹתִיּוֹת הַקּוֹדְמוֹת לְאוֹתִיּוֹת

הַמִּצְרִים, והמ"ם אַחֲרוֹנָה הִיא מ"ם הָרִבּוּי וְאֵינָהּ מִן הַשֹּׁרֶשׁ, וְרָמַז לָזֶה הַמַּגִּיד בַּמַּאֲמָר: "אֵלּוּ עֶשֶׂר מַכּוֹת שֶׁהֵבִיא הַקָּדוֹשׁ בָּרוּךְ הוּא עַל הַמִּצְרִים בְּמִצְרַיִם", כְּלוֹמַר הָאוֹתִיּוֹת שֶׁהֵם קוֹדְמוֹת עַל אוֹתִיּוֹת הַמִּצְרִים:

וּמַה שֶּׁכָּתַב הָאֲרִ"י זַ"ל: "וַעֲלֵיהֶם וְעַל כֻּלָּם הַשַּׂר הַנִּקְרָא **תקא**, כַּוָּנָתוֹ, כִּי רָאשֵׁי תֵיבוֹת שֶׁל אֵלּוּ עֶשֶׂר מַכּוֹת, דצ"ך עד"ש באח"ב, בְּגִימַטְרִיָּא תקא, כְּמִנְיַן הַשַּׂר מַמָּשׁ, וּכְמִנְיַן אשר, וְזֶהוּ סוֹד כַּוָּנַת הַכָּתוּב בְּסֵדֶר בֹּא: "וּלְמַעַן תְּסַפֵּר בְּאָזְנֵי בִנְךָ וּבֶן בִּנְךָ אֵת אשר הִתְעַלַּלְתִּי בְּמִצְרַיִם", אשר דַּיְקָא, שֶׁהוּא כְּמִסְפַּר **תקא**, וְכַיּוֹצֵא בּוֹ הַרְבֵּה פְּסוּקִים אֶלֶף, שֶׁמּוֹרִים עַל זֶה לְסוֹד אשר, כְּמִנְיַן רָאשֵׁי תֵיבוֹת שֶׁל עֶשֶׂר מַכּוֹת כְּמוֹ שֶׁבֵּאַרְנוּ, וְיֵשׁ לָנוּ בָּזֶה סוֹדוֹת נִפְלָאִים. וּכְבוֹד אֱלֹהִים הַסְתֵּר דָּבָר:

וּמַה שֶּׁכָּתַב רַבֵּנוּ הָאֲרִ"י זַ"ל: "הַשֵּׁם **שפו** שֶׁבּוֹ אָחַז דָּוִד בֶּן יִשַׁי, וְהַשֵּׁם אָמַר וְהִכָּה אוֹתָם בְּמִצְרַיִם עֶשֶׂר מַכּוֹת, וְעַל הַיָּם לָקוּ חֲמִשִּׁים מַכּוֹת. וְהַשֵּׁם **תקל** אָמַר וְהִכָּה אוֹתָם בְּמִצְרַיִם אַרְבָּעִים מַכּוֹת, וְעַל הַיָּם לָקוּ מָאתַיִם מַכּוֹת. וְהַשֵּׁם **אשצה** אָמַר וְהִכָּה אוֹתָם בְּמִצְרַיִם חֲמִשִּׁים מַכּוֹת, וְעַל הַיָּם לָקוּ מָאתַיִם וַחֲמִשִּׁים מַכּוֹת". כַּוָּנָתוֹ לְסוֹד נִפְלָא וְנוֹרָא, פְּלֻגְתָּא דְּרַבִּי יוֹסֵי הַגָּלִילִי וְרַבִּי אֱלִיעֶזֶר וְרַבִּי עֲקִיבָא הַמֻּזְכָּר בַּהַגָּדָה. רַבִּי יוֹסֵי הַגָּלִילִי אוֹמֵר מִנַּיִן, וְרַבִּי אֱלִיעֶזֶר אוֹמֵר מִנַּיִן, וְרַבִּי עֲקִיבָא אוֹמֵר מִנַּיִן, וְזֶהוּ שֶׁכָּתַב הָאֲרִ"י זַ"ל: וְהַשֵּׁם **שפ"ו** אָמַר וְהִכָּה אוֹתָם בְּמִצְרַיִם עֶשֶׂר מַכּוֹת, וְעַל הַיָּם לָקוּ חֲמִשִּׁים מַכּוֹת, רֶמֶז לְרַבִּי יוֹסֵי הַגָּלִילִי. כִּי **רבִּ"י יוֹסֵ"י הַגָּלִילִ"י** בְּגִימַטְרִיָּא **שפו**, וּמַה שֶּׁכָּתַב שֶׁבּוֹ אָחַז דָּוִד בֶּן יִשַׁי, רָמַז גַּם כֵּן, **דָּוִ"ד בֶּ"ן יִשַׁ"י** גִּימַטְרִיָּא שֵׁם **שפו**, שֶׁבְּאוֹתוֹ הַשֵּׁם דַּוְקָא בָּא דָּוִד בֶּן יִשַׁי. וְרָמַז גַּם כֵּן מַה שֶּׁכָּתַב בְּסֵפֶר סוֹדֵי רָזָא, שֶׁרַבִּי יוֹסֵי הַגָּלִילִי נִצּוֹץ דָּוִד בֶּן יִשַׁי. וְזֶה הַשֵּׁם הִכָּה אוֹתָם. וּמִצַּד הַשֵּׁם **תקל** לָקוּ הַמִּצְרִים בְּמִצְרַיִם אַרְבָּעִים מַכּוֹת, וְעַל הַיָּם לָקוּ מָאתַיִם מַכּוֹת, רָמַז לְסוֹד **רבִּ"י אֱלִיעֶזֶ"ר** בְּגִימַטְרִיָּא **תקל**, וְהַיְנוּ רַבִּי אֱלִיעֶזֶר אוֹמֵר, דַּוְקָא, שֶׁהוּא שֵׁם **תקל**, לָקוּ הַמִּצְרִיִּים בְּמִצְרַיִם אַרְבָּעִים מַכּוֹת, וְעַל הַיָּם לָקוּ מָאתַיִם מַכּוֹת. וּמַה שֶּׁכָּתַב הַשֵּׁם **אשצה** לָקוּ בְּמִצְרַיִם חֲמִשִּׁים מַכּוֹת, וְעַל הַיָּם לָקוּ מָאתַיִם וַחֲמִשִּׁים מַכּוֹת, רָמַז לְסוֹד **רבִּ"י עֲקִיבָ"א**, שֶׁהוּא בְּגִימַטְרִיָּא **אשצ"ה** עִם הַכּוֹלֵל, שֶׁהַשֵּׁם הַזֶּה אָמַר שֶׁיֻּכּוּ הַמִּצְרִיִּים בְּמִצְרַיִם חֲמִשִּׁים מַכּוֹת, וְעַל הַיָּם לָקוּ מָאתַיִם וַחֲמִשִּׁים מַכּוֹת. הֲרֵי מְרֻמָּזִים אֵלּוּ שְׁלֹשָׁה שֵׁמוֹת **שפו תקל אשצה** בְּאֵלּוּ הַשְּׁלֹשָׁה תַּנָּאִים: רַבִּי יוֹסֵי הַגָּלִילִי בְּגִימַטְרִיָּא **שפו**, רַבִּי אֱלִיעֶזֶר בְּגִימַטְרִיָּא **תקל**, רבִּ"י עֲקִיבָ"א בְּגִימַטְרִיָּא **אשצה**, וְהוּא סוֹד נִפְלָא וְנוֹרָא. רָזָא דְרָזִין. סִתְרָא דִּסְתְרִין. הַיְנוּ כַּאֲשֶׁר כָּתַבְתִּי לְמַעֲלַת כְּבוֹד תּוֹרָתוֹ, וְהוּא רַחוּם יְכַפֵּר עָוֹן:

וּמַה שֶּׁכָּתַב רַבֵּנוּ הָאֲרִ"י זַ"ל: "בְּמַה שֶּׁהַקָּדוֹשׁ בָּרוּךְ הוּא מַכֶּה, בּוֹ מְרַפֵּא הַגָּלוּת, מַה פָּשְׁעוּ מֶה חָטְאוּ אֲבוֹתֵינוּ" וְכוּ', כַּוָּנָתוֹ: בְּאֵלּוּ עֶשֶׂר מַכּוֹת שֶׁהֵם דצך עדש באחב, נִרְמָזִים בְּאֵלּוּ אוֹתִיּוֹת סוֹד וְטַעַם יְרִידַת אֲבוֹתֵינוּ לְמִצְרַיִם, כְּמוֹ שֶׁכָּתַבְתִּי לְמַעֲלַת כְּבוֹד תּוֹרָתוֹ. וְהִנֵּה בְּאֵלּוּ הַמַּכּוֹת הִכָּה אוֹתָם, וַיְרַפֵּא אוֹתָנוּ הַקָּדוֹשׁ בָּרוּךְ הוּא וְהִכָּה בָּהֶם מַכָּה רַבָּה אֶצְבַּע אֱלֹהִים הִיא, וּמִן הַמַּכָּה עַצְמָהּ בָּאָה רְפוּאָה לְיִשְׂרָאֵל, שֶׁגְּאָלָם הַקָּדוֹשׁ בָּרוּךְ הוּא, וּכְמוֹ שֶׁכָּתַבְתִּי. וּמַה שֶּׁכָּתַב: "מַה פָּשְׁעוּ" וְכוּ', רוֹצֶה לוֹמַר: בְּאֵלּוּ הַמַּכּוֹת נִרְמַז הַחֵטְא שֶׁל אֲבוֹתֵינוּ שֶׁגָּרַם יְרִידַת מִצְרַיִם. וְיֵשׁ לָנוּ סוֹד נִפְלָא וְנוֹרָא לְתָרֵץ קֻשְׁיָא זוֹ מַה

שֶׁהִקְשׁוּ מַעֲלַת כְּבוֹד תּוֹרָתָם עָלַי, אֲבָל גַּם זֶה נִיחָא כַּאֲשֶׁר כָּתַבְתִּי לְמַעֲלָתָם, נִפְלָאוֹת מִתּוֹרָתוֹ הַקְּדוֹשָׁה וְהַטְּהוֹרָה.

וּמַה שֶּׁכָּתַב הָאֲרִ"י זַ"ל: "שֶׁהַקָּדוֹשׁ בָּרוּךְ הוּא גָּאַל אוֹתָנוּ בְּשֵׁמוֹת אֵלּוּ **דעב צדא כשחב**", כַּוָּנָתוֹ כִּי הָאוֹתִיּוֹת רִאשׁוֹנוֹת שֶׁל דצך עדש באחב הֵם **דע"ב**, וְהָאוֹתִיּוֹת שְׁנִיּוֹת הֵם **צד"א**, וְהָאוֹתִיּוֹת הָאַחֲרוֹנוֹת הֵם **כשח"ב**, וְנִרְמָזִים בְּאֵלּוּ הַשְּׁלֹשָׁה שְׁמוֹת הָרְפוּאָה שֶׁרִפָּא הַקָּדוֹשׁ בָּרוּךְ הוּא לְיִשְׂרָאֵל, שֶׁגָּאַל אוֹתָנוּ בָּהֶם, הֲרֵי בְּאוֹתָן הַמַּכּוֹת שֶׁהֻכּוּ בָּהֶם הַמִּצְרִיִּים, נִרְמָזִים הַגְּאֻלָּה וְהָרְפוּאָה לְיִשְׂרָאֵל. וִיהֵא רַעֲוָא לִפְנֵי הַקָּדוֹשׁ בָּרוּךְ הוּא שֶׁיַּרְאֵנוּ בִּיאַת מְשִׁיחֵנוּ בִּמְהֵרָה בְיָמֵינוּ, עִם הַמַּלְאָכִים הַשַּׁיָּכִים לַגְּאֻלָּה, וִיקֻיַּם בָּנוּ מִקְרָא שֶׁכָּתוּב: כִּימֵי צֵאתְךָ מֵאֶרֶץ מִצְרָיִם אַרְאֶנּוּ נִפְלָאוֹת, אָמֵן נֶצַח סֶלָה:

Endnotes

1 Deut. 6:20.

2 Mishna Pesaḥim 10:8.

3 Ex. 2:24.

4 *Derekh HaMelekh Toldot*, from the Piaseczno Haggada – Pesaḥ Haggada based on the teachings of the Rebbe of Piaseczno, ed. Amotz Schapira (Dani Sefarim, 2022).

5 Rabbi Elhanan Nir, *Hayom Atem Yotzim – Iyunei Daat VeLev LeḤag HaḤerut ULekhol HaShana* (Yediot Books, 2022).

6 "Shagar" is an acronym for the rabbi's full name, Shimshon Gershon Rosenberg.

7 Rabbi Shagar, *Leha'ir et HaPetaḥim – Derashot UMaamarim LeYemei Ḥanukka*, Institute of Rabbi Shagar's Writings (2014).

8 Pesaḥ Haggada, *Maggid*.

9 Zelda Schneerson Mishkovsky (1914–1984), known as "Zelda," was born in Russia and moved to Jerusalem at the age of twelve with her family. She worked as a schoolteacher and went on to become one of Israel's most renowned poets.

10 Shayna Zelda Schneurson-Mishkovsky, "Kaasher Berakhti al HaNerot," in *Shirei Zelda* (Kibbutz HaMeuḥad, 1985), 100. © All rights reserved to author and Acum.

11 Rabbi Elḥanan Nir, *Hayom Atem Yotzim – Iyunei Daat VeLev LeḤag HaḤerut ULekhol HaShana*.

12 Leah Goldberg, "MiShirei Eretz Ahuvati," Poem A ("Mekhora Sheli"), in *Shirim*, vol. 2 (Po'alim Press, 1973), 199–200. © All rights reserved to Hakkibutz Hame'uchad Publishers – Po'alim Press.

13 Paraphrase of Song of Songs 3:1–2: "Upon my bed at night I sought the one I love; I sought him, I did not find him. I shall rise, I shall go all around the town – through the streets, across the squares – searching for the one I love. I searched for him but did not find him."

14 Song. 5:3.

15 I Sam. 20:29.

16 Haim Nahman Bialik, *Kumi Tzi'i*.

17 Prov. 24:4.

18 Song. 7:6.

19 Ibid. 1:4.

20 Rabbi Shagar, *Zeman shel Ḥerut, Derashot LeḤag HaPesaḥ* (Dabri Shir).

21 Rabbi Elḥanan Nir, *Hayom Atem Yotzim – Iyunei Daat VeLev LeḤag HaḤerut ULekhol HaShana.*

22 Pesaḥ Haggada, the son who does not know how to ask.

23 A New Guy Came to the Neighborhood [Hebrew], composer, author, and musical arranger, Alon Ularchik.

24 Yehuda Gizbar, *Sippur: Haggada* (Yediot Books, 2022).

25 Zohar HaKadosh on *Parashat Emor*.

26 Ex. 3:9.

27 Ezek. 16:8.

28 Ex. 13:7.

29 Ibid. 2:24–25.

30 Song. 5:2: "I am asleep; my heart is awake – my beloved's voice, he is knocking – 'Open for me, my sister, my love, my dove, my perfection, for my head is covered with dew, my locks with drops of the night,'" and Ibn Ezra explains: "'For my head is covered with dew, my locks with drops of the night': from the tears of *Knesset Yisrael*."

31 Rabbi Yisrael of Salant.

32 Prov. 20:27.

33 Rabbi Shimshon David Pincus, cited in the introduction to his Pesaḥ Haggada, *Tiferet Shimshon*.

34 Ps. 136:4.

35 Rabbi Ben Tziyon Mutzafi, *Pesaḥ BeTziyon*.

36 Ibid., 78.

37 Song. 3:1.

38 Ibid.

39 Rabbi Mutzafi, *Pesaḥ BeTziyon*, "Biur *Ḥametz*," 153.

40 Berakhot 17a.

41 Rabbi Hayim David Azulai (Ḥida), *Avodat HaKodesh*.

42 A liturgical poem recited on *Shabbat HaGadol*.

43 Ps. 23:5.

44 Rabbi Shalom *Rokeach*, the Sar Shalom of Belz, in his commentary on the Pesaḥ Haggada.

45 Berakhot 3a.

46 Mal. 3:23.

47 Ibid., v. 24.

48 Bava Metzia 84a.

49 Song. 4:3 and Berakhot 57a.

50 The liturgical poem "And so – it happened at midnight," in the Pesaḥ Haggada.

51 Translated from "*Bo,*" Rita. Melody, Rami Kleinstein, lyrics, Miri Feigenbaum © all rights reserved to author and Acum.

52 Rabbi Nir, *Hayom Atem Yotzim* (Yediot Books, 2022).

53 Rabbi Mutzafi, *Pesaḥ BeTziyon*, 221.

54 Different communities have different customs about how to arrange the items on the Seder plate.

55 Rabbi Mutzafi, *Pesaḥ BeTziyon*.

56 Song. 6:4.

57 Ex. 3:22.

58 Gen. 27:27.

59 Rabbi Mutzafi, *Pesaḥ BeTziyon*.

60 Ibid., p. 182, sect. 11. This idea is based on the Ben Ish Ḥai's discussion of *Parashat Vayera*.

61 Rabbi Kalonymus Kalman Schapira of Piaseczno, *Ḥovot HaTalmidim*.

62 Shelah HaKadosh on Pesaḥ.

63 Rabbi Elimelekh Biderman, *Be'er HaḤayim*, Pesaḥ Haggada.

64 The prayer *Vezakeinu Legadel*, recited at candle lighting on Friday night.

65 Rabbi Mutzafi, *Pesaḥ BeTziyon.*

66 Ps. 139:12, and *Or HaḤayim* on Ex. 12:30.

67 Ps. 41:5: "I prayed, 'O Lord, show me mercy; heal me, for I have sinned against You.'"

68 Rabbi Joseph B. Soloveitchik, Pesaḥ Haggada – *Masoret HaRav*, ed. Rabbi Menachem Genack.

69 Rabbi Elimelekh Biderman, *Haggada shel Pesaḥ– Be'er HaḤayim* (Be'er HaEmuna Institute, Nisan 5774).

70 Song. 1:7.

71 Ibid. 5:5.

72 Mishna Pesaḥim 10:4.

73 Rabbi Biderman, *Haggada shel Pesaḥ – Be'er HaḤayim.*

74 Rabbi Alexander Ziskind, *Yesod VeShoresh HaAvoda*, sect. 9, ch. 6.

75 Ps. 118:5.

76 Rabbi Biderman, *Haggada shel Pesaḥ – Be'er HaḤayim* 163.

77 Paraphrase of Rashi on Lev. 9:7: "'Come near to the altar' – for Aharon was embarrassed and afraid to go near [the altar]; Moshe said to him, 'Why are you embarrassed? For this purpose you have been chosen.'"

78 Yoma 38b: "One reign does not overlap with another even a hairbreadth."

79 Rabbi Shlomo Wolbe, *Daat Shlomo – Maamarei Geula, Purim-Pesaḥ.*

80 *Haggadat Ishei Yisrael*, 278. The Gematria value is inclusive, which adds 1.

81 Rashi on Ex. 12:13.

82 Berakhot 7a.

83 The liturgical poem *Areset Sefateinu*, in the Rosh HaShana service: "And may You accept with mercy and with favor the order of our shofar verses."

84 Kiddush text recited on the festivals.

85 Rabbi Joseph B. Soloveitchik, Pesaḥ Haggada – *Masoret HaRav.*

86 *Pirkei DeRabbi Eliezer* 32:14: "The nightfall of the festival day of Pesaḥ came, and Yitzḥak called unto Esav his elder son, and said, 'My son, tonight the whole entire world recites praise; on this night the treasuries of dew are opened; make me savory meat while I am still alive, and I will bless you.' The Holy Spirit rejoined, saying to him: 'Do not eat of a stingy man's food' (Prov. 23:6). He went to fetch it and was delayed there. Rivka said to Yaakov, 'My son, on this night the treasuries of dew will be opened, and on this night the angels utter a song; on this night in the future your children will be redeemed from slavery, on this night in the future they will recite a song; make savory meat for your father, that he may bless you while he lives.'" See also Ḥizkuni on Gen. 27:4.

87 Rabbi Mutzafi, *Pesaḥ BeTziyon*, ch. 15.

88 "Leaning while in a sitting position or half-lying position was customary in palaces and symbolized the status of comfort and honor. One should recline when he drinks the four cups [of wine], eats matza and *korekh*."

89 Ex. 13:18.

90 Ibid., v. 17.

91 Rabbi Nahman of Breslov, *Likkutei Maharan*, *Tinyana* 48.

92 Ex. 12:42.

93 Rabbi Hayim Navon, "Ḥinukh Beiti," *Motzash Magazine*, *Makor Rishon*, April 15, 2022.

94 Rema on *Oraḥ Ḥayim* 472:4: "The Raavya holds that nowadays there is no obligation to recline because it is not common in our land to recline the rest of the year. Rather, one may sit as per usual. The women rely on this and do not recline."

95 Pesaḥim 108a.

96 Rabbi Moshe Feinstein, *Iggerot Moshe, Oraḥ Ḥayim* 5:20.

97 *Siḥot Rabbi Shimshon David Pincus al Hamo'adim*, "Pesaḥ-Sefirat HaOmer – Shavuot."

98 Gen. 40:11–13.

99 Ibid., v. 23.

100 Ibid. 41:14.

101 Rabbi Moshe Shapira, *Laila KaYom Ya'ir: She'arim el HaSeder shel Pesaḥ*, compiled and edited by his student, Rabbi Avraham Baum.

102 Sota 2a.

103 Pesaḥim 118a.

104 Song. 5:6.

105 Ex. 19:3 and Exodus Rabba, sect. 28.

106 Exodus Rabba, sect. 28.

107 Song. 1:7.

108 Gen. 3:16.

109 Kiddushin 49b.

110 Rabbi Yitzchak Hutner, *Paḥad Yitzḥak,* Pesaḥ.

111 Rabbi Hayim Navon, "Ḥinukh Beiti," *Motzash Magazine*, *Makor Rishon*, April 15, 2022.

112 Deut. 12:5: "Rather only at the place that the Lord your God will choose from among all your tribes to place His Name shall you seek out His Presence and come there."

113 Ramban on Deut. 12:5: "The meaning of 'shall you seek out His Presence' is that you are to come from distant countries and ask 'Where is the road leading to the House of God?' and a man will say to his fellow 'Come, let us go up to the mountain of the Lord to the House of the God of Yaakov' (Is. 2:3) like the words 'They shall inquire for Zion, in that direction their faces shall turn' (Jer. 50:5)."

114 Rabbi Nahman of Breslov, Book of Stories, "The Lost Princess."

115 *Haggadat Mesorat HaRav*, Pesaḥ Haggada, with the explanations of Rabbi Joseph Ber HaLevi Soloveitchik (Hebrew), Koren Publishers, 25.

116 From the text of the Haggada: "Anyone who does not say these three things on Pesaḥ has not fulfilled his obligation and these are they: Pesaḥ, matza, and *maror*."

117 Ex. 2:23: "And the children of Israel groaned under the burden of work and they cried out, and their plea rose to God from amid the work."

118 Exodus Rabba, sect. 5, 5:18.

119 Ex. 12:31.

120 Irit Linor, Facebook, April 15, 2022.

121 Ex. 12:4: "If the household is too small for a lamb let it share one with a neighbor who dwells nearby in proportion to the number of persons you shall contribute for the lamb according to what each household will eat."

122 Rabbi Wolbe, *Daat Shlomo – Maamarei Geula, Purim-Pesaḥ.*

123 Rabbi Shagar, *Zeman shel Ḥerut*, *Derashot LeḤag HaPesaḥ,* "Lev Avot al Banim," ed. Eitan Abramovitz, Institute of Rabbi Shagar's Writings, 122.

124 Avoda Zara 3a–b.

125 Maharal, *Gevurot Hashem*.

126 I Sam. 1:17.

127 Rabbi Nahman of Breslov, *Likkutei Maharan, Torat Hashem*.

128 Tosefta Pesaḥim 10:12.

129 Gen. 42:11.

130 Pesaḥ Haggada: "The Torah relates to four types of sons – one who is wise, one who is wicked, one with a simple nature, and one who does not know how to ask."

131 Rabbi Jonathan Sacks, *Pesaḥ al Shum Ma*, Pesaḥ Haggada (Maggid Books).

132 According to the Midrash Rabba on *Parashat Shemot*.

133 Rabbi Hayim Ephraim Zeitchik, commentary on the Pesaḥ Haggada.

134 Makkot 24a; Sanhedrin 101a.

135 Y. Pe'ah 1:1.

136 Taanit 7a.

137 Ex. 12:11: "This is how you shall eat it: your loins girded, your sandals on your feet, and your staff in your hand; and you shall eat it hurriedly: it is a Paschal sacrifice for the Lord."

138 Rabbi Avraham Stav, "HaPotential shel Ziyuf," *Motzash Magazine*, *Makor Rishon*, April 15, 2022.

139 *Kuntres Leil HaSeder – Siḥot Maran Rosh HaYeshiva, Rabbeinu HaGaon Rabbi Shmuel Markowitz*, 6th ed., April 2016, based on students' notes.

140 Rabbi Mutzafi, *Pesaḥ BeTziyon*.

141 From the prayer book, second blessing in the *Amida*.

142 Rabbi Mutzafi, *Pesaḥ BeTziyon*.

143 *Haftara* for *Shabbat HaGadol,* Mal. 3:23–24.

144 *Likkutei Maharan, Tinyana* 48.

145 Ibid., 78.

146 Rabbi Wolbe, *Daat Shlomo – Maamarei Geula, Purim-Pesaḥ*.

147 ibid.

148 Rabbi Nahman of Breslov, Book of Stories, "The Rabbi's Son."

149 Deut. 21:18, 20.

150 Paraphrase of Ruth 3:12: "But, while it is true I am a redeeming kinsman, there is another redeemer closer than I."

151 Ps. 69:19 and the liturgical poem "Lekha Dodi" composed by Rabbi Shlomo HaLevi Alkabetz.

152 Berakhot 7a.

153 Rabbi Nahman of Breslov, Book of Stories, "The Exchanged Children."

154 Ps. 12:8.

155 Deut. 6:20; Pesaḥ Haggada, *Maggid*.

156 Mishna Pesaḥim 10:4.

157 Ps. 139:12.

158 Num. 23:19.

159 Berakhot 26b.

160 Gen. 27:22.

161 Rabbi Nahman of Breslov, Book of Stories, "A Matter of Trust."

162 Rabbi Shlomo Ibn Gabirol, *Keter Malkhut*: "If You will seek out my sin, I will run from You toward You. And I'll hide from Your wrath in Your protection."

163 Ezek. 16:6–7.

164 Deut. 26:5.

165 Ex. 12:11: "This is how you shall eat it: your loins girded, your sandals on your feet, and your staff in your hand; and you shall eat it hurriedly: it is a Paschal sacrifice for the Lord."

166 Ibid. 3:7: "And the Lord said: I have marked well the plight of My people in Egypt and have heeded their outcry because of their taskmasters; yes, I am mindful of their sufferings."

167 Rabbi Joseph B. Soloveitchik, Pesaḥ Haggada – *Masoret HaRav*.

168 Ezek. 16:7 and Rashi's explanation on that verse. Is. 26:4: "Trust in the Lord forever and ever, for in God the Lord you have an everlasting Rock."

169 Ex. 2:23.

170 Genesis Rabba 8:5: "Rabbi Simon said: When the Holy One, blessed be He, came to create Adam, the ministering angels divided into various factions and various groups. Some of them said: 'Let him not be created,' and some of them said: 'Let him be created."

171 Ex. 15:26; this is also cited in the prayer of Rabbi Shimshon of Ostropoli in the Pesaḥ Haggada.

172 Yehuda Gizbar, *Sippur*, *Haggada* (Yediot Books, 2022).

173 Rabbi Nahman of Breslov, Book of Stories, "The Treasure Beneath the Bridge."

174 *Zohar HeḤadash*, *Midrash Rut*, 213.

175 A paraphrase of Genesis Rabba 63:5.

176 Gen. 35:8: "Devora, Rivka's nursemaid died." Genesis Rabba 81:5 maintains that this verse actually refers to Rivka's death.

177 Zohar HaKadosh, vol. 2, 183b: "Mikhla Demiheimanuta." The *Edot HaMizraḥ* Pesaḥ Haggada states: "On you we eat matza, which is healing, to be elevated to the secret of faith. This is the bread through which Israel became wise in the supernal wisdom of the Torah and ascended to its paths."

178 Ps. 37:3: "Trust in the Lord and do good, abide in the land and feed [your] faith."

179 Rabbi Mutzafi, *Pesaḥ BeTziyon*.

180 Genesis Rabba 5:4: "Rabbi Berekhya said: The lower waters separated from the upper only with weeping [*bekhiya*]. As it is written: 'He dams the depths of [*mibekhi*] the rivers' (Job 28:11)."

181 Ps. 137:1.

182 Lam. 2:19.

183 Ex. 12:18.

184 Deut. 16:3.

185 Zohar HaKadosh, *Parashat Bo*, sect. 167.

186 Pesaḥim 115b; see also Pesaḥim 36a.

187 Rabbi Hutner, *Paḥad Yitzḥak*, Pesaḥ.

188 Jer. 2:2.

189 Berakhot 40a.

190 Rabbi Shneur Zalman of Liadi (the Alter Rebbe), Tanya 284:73.

191 Rabbi Mutzafi, *Pesaḥ BeTziyon*.

192 Rabbi Wolbe, *Daat Shlomo*, *Maamarei Geula* – Purim-Pesaḥ.

193 Ex. 12:32.

194 Rabbi Wolbe, *Daat Shlomo – Maamarei Geula, Purim-Pesaḥ*.

195 Ari HaKadosh, *Shaar HaKavanot*.

196 Gen. 30:1.

197 Ibid., v. 15.

198 Yoma 38b.

199 Rabbi Wolbe, *Daat Shlomo – Maamarei Geula, Purim-Pesaḥ.*

200 Ari HaKadosh, *Shaar HaKavanot, Maror Korekh*, pg. 83c. Cited in *Pesaḥ BeTziyon*. Also cited in the *Peri Etz Ḥayim*, *Shaar Hag HaMatzot*, ch. 7.

201 Rabbi Mutzafi, *Pesaḥ BeTziyon*, ch. 17, p. 374.

202 Berakhot 60a: "The Sages taught: There was an incident involving Hillel the Elder, who was coming on the road when he heard a scream in the city. He said: I am certain that [the scream] is not [coming] from my house. And of him, the verse says: 'He shall not be afraid of evil tidings; his heart is steadfast, trusting in the Lord.'"

203 Sanhedrin 103b: "Rabbi Yoḥanan says in the name of Rabbi Yosei ben Kisma: Great is eating, as it distanced two clans from the Jewish people, as it is stated: '[An Ammonite or a Moabite shall not enter into the assembly of the Lord…] because they met you not with bread and with water' (Deut. 23:5). And Rabbi Yoḥanan himself says: [Food] distances the near, and draws near the distant."

204 *Ḥayei Maharan*, 260.

205 Gen. 27:4.

206 Ibid., v. 5.

207 Ibid.

208 Ibid., vv. 28–29.

209 Ibid., v. 31.

210 Ibid., v. 36.

211 Ibid., v. 35.

212 Ibid., v. 37.

213 Berakhot 26b.

214 From the text of the Haggada.

215 Original citation appears in Jer. 10:25. *Pirkei DeRabbi Eliezer*, ch. 31, and the text of the Pesaḥ Haggada.

216 Ari HaKadosh, *Shaar HaKavanot*.

217 Prov. 27:21.

218 Pesaḥim 85b.

219 Ps. 9:15.

220 Midrash, "Panim Aḥerim," sect. 6, in *Sifrei DeAggadata*, Esther.

221 II Kings 19:35.

222 *Midrash Tehillim* 1:20, 15:5; *Yalkut Reuveni*, *Beshalaḥ*, sects. 82, 89. Zohar HaKadosh, sect. 2, 170:2.

223 Genesis Rabba 8:5.

224 Dan. 8:12.

225 Ex. 8:18: "But on that day I will set apart the region of Goshen, where My people dwell, so that no swarms of insects shall be there, that you may know that I the Lord am in the midst of the land."

226 Ibid. 4:22.

227 Ezek. 16:6.

228 A paraphrase of Mal. 3:24: "He shall reconcile parents with children and children with their parents."

229 Ps. 2:4.

230 Ps. 22:4.

231 Rabbi Hutner, *Paḥad Yitzḥak*, Pesaḥ.

232 Rabbi Mutzafi, *Pesaḥ BeTziyon*.

233 Pesaḥim 85b.

234 Rabbi Mutzafi, *Pesaḥ BeTziyon*.

235 Ibid.

236 Ibid.

237 Song. 5:4.

238 Ibid. 5:5.

239 Ibid. 2:9.

240 Ibid. 5:2.

241 Rabbi Hutner, *Paḥad Yitzḥak*, Pesaḥ.

242 Song. 5:7.

243 Ibid.

244 Ibid., v. 8.

245 Ibid. 8:14.

246 Ibid. 1:7.

247 Taanit 5a.

248 Song. 7:6.

249 Eccl. 10:17.

250 Ex. 6:7: "And I will take you to be My people, and I will be your God. And you shall know that I, the Lord, am your God who freed you from the labors of the Egyptians."

251 Zech. 9:9: "Rejoice greatly, fair Zion. Raise a shout, fair Jerusalem. Behold, your king is coming to you, he is victorious and triumphant, yet humble, riding on a donkey, on a yearling, purebred."

252 Ex. 11:4.

253 Rabbi Yaakov Moshe Ḥarlap, Pesaḥ Haggada – *Am Mei Marom*, Yeshivat Beit Zevul Publishing House.

254 Ḥatam Sofer, Pesaḥ Haggada.

255 Usually, midnight on Seder night is between 12:38 a.m. and 12:48 a.m. in Israel (daylight saving time).

256 I Sam. 1:17.

The author would like to express gratitude to Matthew Miller and Yehoshua Miller of Koren Publishers Jerusalem, as well as to the Koren staff: Caryn Meltz, Rabbi Reuven Ziegler, Taly Hahn, Ashirah Firszt, Ita Olesker, Gila Chitiz, Efrat Gross, and Debbie Ismailoff.